LIGHTING THE WAY

LIGHTING THE WAY

An Anthology of Short Plays About the Climate Crisis

EDITED BY **CHANTAL BILODEAU**
AND **THOMAS PETERSON**

Published by the Centre for Sustainable Practice in the Arts and The Arctic Cycle
www.sustainablepractice.org | www.thearcticcycle.org

First Edition

Cover design and typesetting by Miblart

Printed in the United States of America

ISBN 978-0-578-73427-9
ISBN 978-0-578-73428-6 (ebook)

Enormous thanks for that, especially at the beginning of this panel when we're taking up this question of art. That was just a magnificent moment, and there have been a series of them, so many thanks to the Climate Change Theatre Action project for this work.

– Bill McKibben, journalist, activist, founder of 350.org,
speaking at Festival Albertine: The Climate Moment, New York City

Many of us students were inspired by today's movements for action against the world's biggest threat: climate change. The general education seminar "Climate Change Theatre Action," organized and lead by Prof. Dr. Ilka Saal and Dr. Verena Laschinger, presented a perfect opportunity for us to become active on this issue: Go out there, spread the word, and break peoples' habits by bringing the fight for climate justice right in front of their eyes!

– Julius Keinath, student, University of Erfurt, Germany

It was exciting to bring together scientists and artists working to achieve a common goal – we value these connections and conversations, and are grateful to CCTA for providing a vehicle through which to foster these relationships within our community.

– Cassie Greer, Artistic Director, Bag&Baggage Productions, Hillsboro, Oregon

CCTA: Lighting the Way was a successful intergenerational event where audiences were riled up and inspired by the art, and then given the opportunity to connect with local environmental groups in search of volunteers for their projects. Two thousand dollars was raised for local tree-planting initiatives.

– Emily Pearlman, Artistic Director, Mi Casa Theatre, Almonte, Ontario, Canada

We had such a beautiful mix of ages and abilities present. There was a high school group, mums, dads, a professional drama group, people with special powers (or disabilities, depending on how you look at it) and a group from Extinction Rebellion. I think the positive connectedness rippled out to all the people attending. The message about climate change can be presented in so many ways and had so many sides and angles to it. For me, using theatre as a tool to communicate this message was really powerful and gentle at the same time.

– Mirjam De Oude, Educator, Te Manawa Museum, Palmerston North,
New Zealand

CONTENTS

ACKNOWLEDGMENTS

This book is the product of the work of an astonishing number of extraordinary people: writers, organizers, designers, editors, researchers, artists, and activists, among many others. First and foremost, we want to express our deepest gratitude to the playwrights featured in these pages, whose words made Climate Change Theatre Action 2019 possible. Their portraits of climate heroes of all stripes and species show us how we might light the way to a just future. We thank them for their poetry and for their belief that we might change this world for the better, one play at a time. In the fall of 2019, they inspired more than 26,000 people around the world with their words; with the publication of this anthology, their work may reach many thousands more.

Many heartfelt thanks go to our brilliant and tireless friend and collaborator Julia Levine, who helped shape this project from genesis to fruition, and directed the performances that opened and closed the CCTA 2019 season. We also want to thank our friend and organizing partner Ian Garrett of York University, who helped us bring this anthology from idea to reality.

We are grateful for researcher and PhD candidate Brooke Wood, who chose Climate Change Theatre Action 2019 as the subject of her dissertation. Her research on the impact of CCTA events on audience attitudes will be invaluable in maximizing the emotional resonance and political efficacy of the initiative going forward. We thank her for sharing her preliminary findings in this anthology. CCTA 2019 was also enriched by the remarkable work of Triga Creative, the Toronto-based design collaborative that created a month-long "Eco-Design Charette" in collaboration with Ian Garrett, developing design concepts for each of the CCTA plays as a means of exploring the practice of ecoscenography. We thank Alexandra Lord, Michelle Tracey and Shannon Lea Doyle for sharing their experiences and insights with us. We also thank Keith Barker of Native Earth Performing Arts and Charissa Menefee of Iowa State University for their reflections on organizing CCTA events.

Our thanks go to the designers at Miblart for transforming our unwieldy word document into the book you now hold. In addition, we are extremely grateful for the support of the Centre for Sustainable Practice in the Arts in the publishing of this book.

We also want to acknowledge the contributions of the many friends and supporters who donated to our crowdfunding campaign in late 2018: your generosity made CCTA 2019 possible – without your donations, we could not have commissioned the plays that make up this anthology. You saw the value of communal storytelling in building a movement that responds to the climate crisis and demands a just transition. We thank you.

Last but not least, we cannot overstate the importance of the more than 3,000 CCTA organizers and artists who participated in the 200-plus events that made up this project. You proved to us that these plays could do just what we hoped they might: build communities of resistance and resilience, inspire climate action, and plant seeds of hope. We are forever grateful for your trust and humbled by your multitude: we can all draw strength from the knowledge that there were people in every U.S. state and on every inhabited continent who were willing to come on this adventure with us.

INTRODUCTION

Chantal Bilodeau

This anthology is a leap of faith. It is one attempt to address the climate crisis, one item on a long list of efforts by scientists, engineers, academics, politicians, activists, writers, thinkers, dreamers, communities large and small, and, increasingly, artists. It is a tool for reflecting and grieving, for learning and growing, and for dreaming and acting. It was conceived to bring us together around a complex and polarizing issue, and to give us the strength to not only ask for, but also *enact* significant change.

The stories we tell each other matter – often more than we realize. Whether made-up or true, they are a reflection of our beliefs and values, of the many unspoken rules that shape culture and our understanding of reality. We grow up hearing them informally from our parents and families. They are further refined through formal education, conversations with friends and strangers, and our awareness of the moment and place in which we live. Ultimately, they are affirmed through personal experience. They are such an integral part of our identity that when challenged, we will fight to the death to protect their integrity. Our stories are, quite literally, who we understand ourselves to be. And yet, they are constructed – an act of imagination.[1]

We don't have to look very far to see the power of stories in action. In a court of law, although the facts are the same for everyone, the side most skilled at weaving those facts together – in essence, the side with the most compelling story – wins. In politics, narratives determine policy: whether we care about biodiversity loss, extractive practices, or environmental justice is a function of the story we tell ourselves about how important these things are and who should be responsible for them. In our personal lives, stories bind us together as families and communities – so much so that the first thing we do when we meet each other is to ask for a story: How are you?

---

[1] For more on how stories influence who we are, see *The Patterning Instinct: A Cultural History of Humanity's Search for Meaning* by Jeremy Lent, Prometheus, 2017.

The importance of narrative is why artists are well-positioned to contribute to the climate change conversation. Through their craft, artists can create stories that tackle huge, seemingly intractable problems and break them down into smaller, more relatable components; stories that weave the facts of climate change into meaningful narratives to help us understand what it all means; stories that present alternatives to the dominant discourse and dysfunctional status quo; and stories that start to imagine what a better future, not just for the privileged few, but for everyone, could look like.

In industrialized countries, the mainstream environmental movement has for too long been dominated by white male voices and experts. It is not uncommon for the lived experiences of frontline, racialized, and low-income communities, and the lived experiences of women, to be considered less important or less valuable than white male expert opinions, or to be ignored all together. While we decidedly must heed the advice of scientists – as we are painfully learning through the many failures to control the COVID-19 pandemic in the U.S. – there is also a need for subjective experiences, for hearing about the struggles of human beings no matter where they fall on the economic scale or color spectrum, for the messiness of emotions, and for every other unquantifiable thing that makes us human.

American poet Lucille Clifton famously said: "We cannot create what we can't imagine." Research has shown that imagining an act can activate and strengthen regions of the brain involved in its real-life execution.[2] In addition to validating our experiences and giving voice to those whose experiences are not recognized, we have the power to shape our reality, to use our most unique human feature – our imagination – to dream up stories that can bring into existence what we want to actualize.

The global climate crisis is, well, global. Which means we all have a role to play in reversing it. We all have skills and networks of influence that can be called upon. That's why a few years ago, Climate Change Theatre Action (CCTA), the project that is the impetus for this anthology, was born. As artists, we were not going to just stand to the side and watch the crisis unfold. There was something we could do.

---

[2]   University of Colorado at Boulder. "Your brain on imagination: It's a lot like reality, study shows." *ScienceDaily*. December 10, 2018. www.sciencedaily.com/releases/2018/12/181210144943.htm

What is Climate Change Theatre Action?

Inaugurated in 2015 and hosted biennially, CCTA is a worldwide series of readings and performances of short plays about climate change, presented to coincide with the United Nations Conferences of the Parties – the annual meetings where world leaders gather to discuss strategies to reduce global carbon emissions. It is spearheaded by The Arctic Cycle, in partnership with the Centre for Sustainable Practice in the Arts. A New York-based organization, The Arctic Cycle uses theatre to foster dialogue about our global climate crisis, create an empowering vision of the future, and inspire people to take action. The Centre for Sustainable Practice in the Arts is a Toronto-based think tank for sustainability in the arts and culture.

We typically commission fifty playwrights (although this year we ended up with only 49), representing at least a dozen countries, to write a five-minute play about an aspect of the climate crisis. We then make this collection of plays available to anyone interested in presenting an event in their community during a three-month window in the fall. Events may range from readings to fully-produced performances, and from podcasts to film adaptations. Event organizers can design their event to reflect their own aesthetic and community, and include additional material by local artists.

To emphasize the "Action" part of Climate Change Theatre Action, we also encourage organizers to think about an action – educational, social, or political – that can be incorporated into their event. These actions may involve the scientific community, local environmental organizations, or political or direct action. In the past, organizers have hosted panel conversations with climate scientists, pledged to reduce consumption or adopt plant-based diets, and written letters to legislators to demand policy change.

The five-minute format of the CCTA plays is not accidental. We want the plays to be as user-friendly as possible so they can be presented in a variety of contexts and fit in a wide range of budgets, including no budget at all. The short format means that the plays require few resources to perform, can be presented individually as part of larger events – like conferences or festivals – or grouped together in any number to create an evening of theatre. They can also be studied in classes, shared at family gatherings, read in podcasts or at marches – the possibilities are endless.

Lighting the Way

CCTA 2019 took place from September 15 to December 21, 2019. Earlier in the year, we reached out to playwrights, keeping an eye on gender and racial representation to make sure that our group was well balanced.[3] Once we had the playwrights assembled, we offered the following prompt:

> This year, we want to give center stage to the unsung climate warriors and climate heroes who are *lighting the way* towards a just and sustainable future. These may be individuals or communities fighting for justice or inventing new technologies; they may be animals, plants, or spirits imparting wisdom; or it may be a part of yourself you didn't know was there. Feel free to be literal – or not – and to travel forward or backward in time.

The prompt was intended as a starting point for the research and writing process, with each writer free to interpret it in their own way. But it also hinted at a route we prefer that the narratives avoid, which is the apocalyptic narrative. For one thing, as my friends Lanxing Fu and Jeremy Pickard, co-directors of eco-theatre group Superhero Clubhouse, often remind us: the apocalypse is a privileged narrative. It assumes that the terrifying future that is imagined, with food shortages and power failures and wars over resources, doesn't already exist. It suggests that this is the worst thing that could happen to society while completely disregarding the fact that many communities already live under those conditions.

Furthermore, as I mentioned earlier, the brain can be activated to actualize what we imagine, so if we only imagine the worst, the worst is what we're going to create. Writers often cite the desire to scare people into action – to make so vivid the consequences of our shortcomings and inaction that audiences will be compelled to act differently. And yet, it seems like the opposite may be true. In a recent paper examining the impact on readers of Paolo Bacigalupi's dystopic cli-fi novel *The Water Knife*, Matthew Schneider-Mayerson found that:

---

[3]   For more on how gender parity and racial diversity plays out in CCTA, see my article "What I Learned About Gender Parity and Racial Diversity from Running a Global Participatory Initiative" on Artists & Climate Change, April 18, 2019. https:// artistsandclimatechange.com/2019/04/18/what-i-learned-about-gender-parity-and-racial-diversity-from-running-a-global-participatory-initiative/

A vivid depiction of desperate climate migrants engaged in a self-interested and violent struggle for survival can backfire, since even liberal readers might not empathize with climate migrants, but fear them. This is a real risk, and it's one that authors and other cultural producers should take seriously. It's possible that narratives like *The Water Knife* might not motivate progressive environmental politics, as authors and critics often hope, but support climate barbarism – callously allowing the less fortunate to suffer – or even ecofascism.[4]

There should still be room for these apocalyptic narratives in the climate conversation, but they certainly shouldn't dominate our imaginary landscape as much as they currently do. Between scientific predictions, extreme weather events and their coverage in mainstream media, blockbuster movies, and artists' dystopian depictions of the climate crisis, we are surrounded by narratives of failure. Our CCTA prompt was intended to encourage the playwrights to look beyond the apocalypse and bring to the surface the stories that are not being told.

How to Use This Book

The goal of this anthology is to make the 49 plays included here available to as many people as possible. While the official CCTA 2019 season is over, there are no restrictions on using the plays in private or in classroom settings. However, if plays are presented in a public space in front of an audience, we ask that permission from the playwrights be secured first. Most playwrights are easily contacted online, but if you need help reaching anyone, you can email info@thearcticcycle.org and we will assist you.

For ideas on how to use the plays and to see what organizers have done in previous years, visit the Events page on the Climate Change Theatre Action website.[5] Venues have ranged from private backyards to National Forests, and from theatres to libraries and churches. Some events were

[4] Brady, Amy. "An Interview with Author and Scholar Matthew Schneider-Mayerson." *Artists & Climate Change*, August 6, 2020. https://artistsandclimatechange.com/2020/08/06/an-interview-with-author-and-scholar-matthew-schneider-mayerson/

[5] http://www.climatechangetheatreaction.com/

fully produced and presented on the main stage of universities, others were intimate readings for family and friends. What they all had in common, however, was a desire to bring people together around an important issue to have a conversation.

In addition to the plays, the first section of this book includes a series of essays by members of our greater CCTA family, providing insights on various aspects of the project. Organizer, writer, director, and my co-editor Thomas Peterson, who was part of the organization of CCTA 2019, shares statistics and writes about the reach and impact of the project on communities near and far. Theatre artist and producer Julia Levine, a member of The Arctic Cycle's core team since 2017, who directed or produced kick-off events for both CCTA 2017 and 2019, reflects on her experience working on the 2019 event in New York City. Keith Barker, Artistic Director of the Indigenous theatre company Native Earth in Canada, writes about his thought process on deciding to get involved with CCTA. Charissa Menefee, Associate Professor in the Department of Music and Theatre at Iowa State University, shows what is possible when bringing CCTA into educational settings. And Toronto-based Triga Creative, comprised of Shannon Lea Doyle, Alexandra Lord, and Michelle Tracey, describes their month-long CCTA Eco-Design Charrette and their goal to create seed design concepts for all 49 plays.

Last but not least, to formalize our observations and identify additional ways to increase our impact, Brooke Wood, PhD candidate in Fine Arts at Texas Tech University, designed a formal research study that will determine if artworks focused on climate change have a discernible impact on people's perceptions of climate change and their motivations to take action. While at the time of assembling this book, Brooke was still analyzing the data she collected, she contributed an article about her preliminary findings.

Going Forward

Local communities are often isolated in their environmental struggles, even when the problems are systemic and widespread, such as sea level rise or pollution from fossil fuel extraction. My hope is that through stories from and about various parts of the world, this book can help unite people who share a common experience, an essential feature in driving action at the scale required to address the climate crisis. For example, a play about deforestation in India might resonate with a community in Brazil, or a story about Indigenous land rights in New Zealand might have echoes in Canada.

I also hope that the 49 CCTA plays included here can help people find common ground across political and ideological boundaries, and across disciplines. In the past, they have provided a means for stakeholders with very different perspectives to come together and build trust. Past presenters have commented on their ability to bring together people from disparate ends of the political spectrum to discuss charged issues, or to build bridges between different departments at their institutions.

Finally, it is my sincere hope that this anthology will encourage more people to think and talk about the climate crisis in ways that are thought-provoking and empowering instead of demoralizing and paralyzing. May this book inspire students to find out more and get involved, professors to consider new ways of teaching about the climate crisis, and artists to lend their voices to this most pressing and dire of issues. May it contribute to showing the role that the arts and storytelling can play in shifting our culture toward greater resilience and justice, and, ultimately, toward sustainable living.

PART 1:

THOUGHTS ON CLIMATE CHANGE THEATRE ACTION

CCTA 2019 BY THE NUMBERS
This Is How We Respond to the Burning World

Thomas Peterson

From mid-September 2019 to mid-February 2020, I was greeted daily by emails, winging their way to me from all over the world, describing performances of short plays about the climate crisis. Somewhere between one and 700 people attended each of these performances, which occurred not just in theatres, but also at universities, in elementary schools, parks, community centers, churches, and public squares, and even on kayaks. The plays were performed in cities, from Manila to Nairobi to London; in towns like Lamoni, Iowa, and Duino, Italy; and outdoors in places like Lair o' the Bear Park in Colorado, Biscayne Bay in Florida, and busy streets in Wellington, New Zealand. These were the performance events that made up the 2019 edition of Climate Change Theatre Action. A complete archive of these performances is available at climatechangetheatreaction.com under "Events."

The emails sometimes told of disappointments – a smaller audience than expected, a last-minute venue change, park rangers interrupting at inopportune moments – but they also celebrated successes – a sold-out run, demand for a reprise in the spring (sadly, few of these actually occurred, necessarily postponed by the COVID-19 pandemic), requests from local government to bring the plays to schools throughout the city, an invitation to perform at the European Parliament. I learned that audiences often laughed together, shared fears and anxieties about the climate emergency at hand, and then left the performance feeling hopeful, joyful, even motivated. That's no small feat. It is difficult – difficult, but vitally important – to spend sustained time thinking about global heating without despairing. I've been trying to hold on to that hope and that motivation.

The 49 short plays making up our 2019 collection were written in a range of forms and on a range of issues: global and local, massive and minute, practical and existential. They included folktales retold for an age of mass extinction, absurd farces on climate denialism and political ineptitude, tragicomedies navigating anxieties about individual and societal environmental impacts. It was thrilling to see the impact of these plays as feedback rolled into my inbox.

Once I'd received all the emails, I tallied up the numbers, diligently reported by the organizers and artists who participated in CCTA. Between September 15 and December 21, 2019, community-oriented theatre actions took place in 229 locations around the world (a 60 percent increase from the 2017 edition of the initiative), including all 50 U.S. states, 29 countries, and every inhabited continent. The events incorporated 1,067 productions of the plays, meaning that on average, each event presented roughly five of the 49 plays. Each play was presented an average of 22 times globally during the three-month period.

As most CCTA plays are written in English, performances were heavily concentrated in countries in which English is widely spoken. In future years, we will endeavor to put resources towards translation in order to expand the initiative outside the anglophone world. For now, the project is relatively U.S.-centric: around 60 percent of CCTA 2019 events occurred in the United States (144), while Canada, Germany, and New Zealand held the largest numbers of events outside the U.S., with 18, 10, and 9 respectively. Within the United States, the states of Massachusetts and New York led the way with 18 events each, followed by Florida and California, with 11 each. Special recognition goes to the remarkable Jan Maher, who organized a dozen events in the town of Greenfield, Massachusetts, involving 373 community members.

The playwrights came from 15 different nation states, as well as seven Indigenous cultures. Fifty-three percent of the playwrights identified as women or non-binary, and 55 percent identified as people of color. While the playwrights' demographics reflect the racial and gender diversity of the United States, where the initiative is based and where the majority of the events still occur, we have work to do in ensuring that playwrights for coming iterations of the initiative are more representative of the global community that CCTA aims to serve. This will mean increasing the representation of playwrights of color, particularly those from Asia, Africa, and Latin America.

CCTA 2019 was presented at 78 universities around the world, meaning that roughly a third of all CCTA events occurred at institutions of higher learning. This number, added to the primary and secondary schools that hosted events, indicates the continued significance of educational institutions in supporting engagement with the climate crisis through the arts.

In total, the performances that made up CCTA 2019 were created by 3,046 artists, organizers, and activists, reaching 12,613 live audience members and another 10,415 and counting via radio, podcast, and livestream. The initiative therefore directly impacted more than 26,000 people, more than double the number who engaged with CCTA 2017. On average, each event had a live audience of 58 people.

While many individual events are small, the aggregated impact of CCTA is significant, reaching as many people as several weeks of a Broadway show, or a month or more of shows at a major off-Broadway or regional theatre, at only a fraction of the cost. This low-cost, high-impact model of theatrical production may become all the more important now that COVID-19's devastating consequences for the theatre are an unavoidable reality. Small, inexpensive, sustainable, and locally-tailored performances that actively engage with the issues facing a given community may play a major role in the future of the dramatic arts. The rapid and continued growth of Climate Change Theatre Action with each edition of the initiative demonstrates that this is a model that can succeed at scale.

But the numbers don't communicate the myriad ways in which this initiative makes an impact. The numbers do not tell of the performance in Lebanon postponed due to ongoing protests against political corruption and economic inequality, nevertheless rescheduled for a few weeks later; or about finding solace in the plays during a horrific wildfire season in Australia; or about a performance in a town in West Virginia with high rates of climate denial receiving coverage from a local TV station. The numbers don't tell you about "engrossed" audiences at an event in Mumbai produced by the National Center for the Performing Arts, or about an event in Calgary, Alberta, the "oil capital" of Canada, that offered an opportunity for locals, used to being shamed for expressing concern about climate, to support each other in taking action. Nor do the statistics tell you about Professor Alyssa Schmidt's students at the Boston Conservatory at Berklee, who "proved to themselves that theatre can be a change agent in sustainable practice and living, as well as a home for those extreme feelings such as deep grief or abiding joy."

The emails I received in the fall and winter of 2019, like the interviews and survey responses gathered by Brooke Wood in her study of American CCTA audiences, offered evidence of communal perseverance and hope. These sentiments were palpable both to Brooke, attending the performances in person, and to me, reading the organizers' reflections. Together, they provide incontrovertible proof that small groups of people around the world are meeting and listening and planning for a future together on this rapidly changing planet. This is how we respond to the burning world. We unite, gathering for a few hours in our beloved localities to share joy and inspire action. With each Climate Change Theatre Action feedback email, this message becomes a little clearer.

LAUNCHING CCTA 2019
Setting the Stage for a Better Planet

Julia Levine

For the past two iterations of CCTA (2017 and 2019), I have helped to produce the launch event. This kick-off cabaret performance helps set the tone for that year's global climate theatre action. It has been important to me that these events be collaborative, joyful, and center around local action. For the core organizers of CCTA, this means engaging residents of New York City, a hub of the theatre industry, where we are based. We have some of the most wonderful actors and theatre practitioners in our midst – which makes assembling the team a treat. I used each meeting and rehearsal to embody the collaborative and engaging spirit of CCTA, bringing people from all walks of life together to generate something new and special.

In building the afternoon for the CCTA 2019 kick-off event, CCTA co-founder Chantal Bilodeau and I teamed up with poet and founder of Poetic People Power, Tara Bracco. Tara brought her years of experience producing shows and panels that combine poetry and activism. We also called upon Giovanni Ortega, writer, performer, assistant professor of Theatre and Dance at Pomona College, and one of our regulars, who has been involved with CCTA in various capacities since its inception in 2015. Gio traveled to New York from California and acted as our incredible host, keeping the audience engaged between acts and the afternoon moving along. Joining up midway through rehearsals after coming back from a year studying in Paris, Thomas Peterson took on the role of stage manager. We were a well-oiled operation!

When it came to casting, I started with a pool of diverse actors I had worked with in the past. Adam Basco-Mahieddine, Lizzy Lincoln, Caiti Lattimer, Shetal Shah, and Brandon C. Smith flexed their acting muscles through the selected plays: *A Letter from the Ocean* by Caridad Svich, *Laila Pines for the Wolf* by Hassan Abdulzzarak, *The Story of the Bountiful Window and the Last Rope* by Vinicius Jatobá, *The Donation* by Jordan Hall, and *It Starts With Me* by Chantal Bilodeau. We chose these plays with a diversity of geographies and styles in mind. We represented four countries, paid attention to gender representation, and made sure we had a mix of comedy and drama. Rounding out our cast were musician Jane Bruce and poet Bogar Alonso.

In addition to the collection of plays we provide, we encourage CCTA event organizers to include work from local artists – which we modeled. We commissioned Tara Bracco to write the song *Rise*, performed by Jane, and we included performances of spoken-word poetry by Shetal and Bogar, of Poetic People Power. They each performed original environmental justice pieces, titled *The Sweet Life* and *Wasserman Wars with the Wind*, respectively. Bringing together this group of artists was a joy and made for a varied, holistic kick-off event, which we titled: "Setting the Stage for a Better Planet." We arrived at this title because we wanted to convey a positive, solutions-oriented outlook, and also as a way to look toward the forthcoming thirteen weeks of global climate action through theatre.

Staying true to the action component of CCTA, we assembled an all-female panel of experts to discuss local climate issues. Our panelists, climate scientist Kate Marvel, policy expert Katherine Walsh, and Climate Museum founder Miranda Massie, along with environmental journalist Janet Babin as a moderator, discussed the climate emergency, what needs to happen in New York, and why art matters. Kate advocated for climate courage and against nihilistic climate narratives; Katherine championed the need for local climate policies and announced her run for State Assembly; and Miranda expressed the need for creative and diverse climate stories. We chose to place the panel in the middle of our event, to break up the performances, which worked well, and the audience was very engaged. As a continuation of our actions, during intermission, the cast offered audiences a chance to draw an action from a jar – things as simple as showering less to actions as substantial as offsetting air travel.

The kick-off event took place on a beautiful afternoon in September at Caveat in Manhattan's Lower East Side. A downtown cabaret space, Caveat specializes in performance events tackling scientific topics – so not only was the space a fit, we also fit into the venue's mission. Add to that livestreaming capability and we were able to reach a global audience beyond the sold-out house of 125 or so people.

As the house lights lowered, the sound of youth activist Greta Thunberg's voice, on The 1975's titular track, echoed through the space. Greta would be arriving in New York less than a week after our event for the September 20th Global Climate Strike, so the track felt like an apt opener. We closed out the evening with Chantal's 2019 rallying call, *It Starts With Me*. With the audience on their feet and the cast leading the call-and-response, the room lit up with just the type of energy we want to actualize with CCTA: people gathering with courage and joy around creative solutions to our world's greatest problem.

A NOTE FROM KEITH BARKER, ARTISTIC DIRECTOR OF NATIVE EARTH

A year ago, I was introduced to Climate Change Theatre Action through a symposium at the Banff Centre and the National Arts Centre's Climate Change Cycle. The co-organizers of CCTA, Ian Garrett and Chantal Bilodeau, were guest speakers, along with other climate change scientists, activists, and artists.

During the symposium weekend, one of the speakers, Sonali McDermid, Assistant Professor of Environmental Studies from New York University said, "as scientists it is our responsibility to share the facts with the public, but as artists it is your responsibility to inspire people with compelling storytelling." This resonated with me. A focus on inspiring, provoking, and questioning our ideas around climate change was far more appealing to me as an artist than educating people. I work in the theatre, after all, and not the classroom.

When I found out that four Indigenous artists from Canada, many of whom Native Earth had worked with before, were contributors to the 2019 Climate Change Theatre Action play series, I wanted to know more. Upon my return to Toronto, the team at Native Earth read the plays. We decided to showcase the climate change work at our Weesageechak Begins to Dance Festival. We hired director Clayton Windatt to explore the plays with actors. We opened four nights of the festival with a play from the series. Post-show conversations revolved around climate activism, relationships and responsibility to the land, and how we tell these stories in the art we make.

In truth, this small action was in line with a lot of the work Indigenous artists are already creating. It reinvigorated our commitment to these narratives. Personally, the experience inspired me to look past my own despondency about the emergency that is climate change and start making necessary changes in my life and my practice, while re-considering my responsibility to future generations.

All my relations,

Keith Barker

THEATRE AS ACTION IS THEATRE IN ACTION
CCTA On Campus and Off

Charissa Menefee

Performing outdoors is risky. No matter how much planning is in place, you know you are not in control. You are at the mercy of the temperature, the weather, passersby, insects, dogs, children, sirens, car horns, and so on. Presenting in October in Iowa means constant weather watching; it could be a hot sunny day or it could snow. Most likely, though, wind and rain will threaten. For our outdoor production of Climate Change Theatre Action in 2017, Iowa State University's cast and crew lucked into a sunny couple of hours after one rainstorm and before the next.

In 2019, we wisely planned a rain location, hoping we'd have no need of it. Instead, we had a powerful performance on the porch of the university library in Ames, Iowa, with a dramatic backdrop of plummeting temperatures followed by howling wind and pouring rain. There was no escaping the concept – and reality – of climate and weather extremes as the audience huddled and shivered together under the building's overhang and the actors adapted, moment to moment, adjusting volume, blocking, and entrances as needed to communicate their urgent and essential message.

Even indoors, theatre actions are risky. The audience is asked to accept a different definition of theatre – not as a building or even in a building, not as a formal event that requires expensive tickets and dressing up, not as an experience that allows you to lean back in your comfy chair, passively witnessing, letting it harmlessly wash over you. You have to watch where your feet are, listen carefully, notice the person next to you, be prepared for what's next. You may be invited to answer questions, sing, dance, or interact with the performers or other audience members. Observing from a safe distance means you'll miss something important.

Theatre as action is theatre in action. This kind of performance could be described as disruptive – as in disrupting the performers' and audiences' expectations – but we could also call it eruptive, couldn't we? Our intention is to let the performance, the dialogue, the education, the sense-making, and the understanding catch us all off-guard and transform the landscape, with the performers, crew, and producers as touched and changed as the audience. The late Ursula K. Le Guin wrote, after a return visit to Mount St. Helens, "It was amazing to come back twenty-five years later to the same places and find them utterly changed, the mountain remaking herself in her own way and time, not only with the upwelling magma in her crater, but in all the great and small lives on her slopes." Theatre as action may bring the immediate response of applause, but the true measurement of its success is in what follows, which may ripple out over many years and many lives.

Service learning, community engagement, outreach, raising awareness: how do colleges and universities take these concepts beyond buzzwords and turn them into real educational experiences for students? How can institutions leverage their resources, talent pool, ambition, and good will into positive action for environmental justice?

Iowa State's 2017 CCTA event, co-produced by director Vivian M. Cook and myself, was substantial and effective, but scrappy, with a next-to-nothing budget and a reliance on bartering and partnering for resources. The 2019 version would open the university's theatre season as a full-scale production. We did not want to lose the ethos and intentionality of the earlier event, which featured free public performances and partnerships with campus and community organizations. The new production team, led by Vivian, decided that our theatre action would actually be a collection of actions, with multiple means of engaging audiences, partners, and participants. Performance would not be the only action, but excellent performances were needed to draw audiences. Our event could happen inside a theatre, but it also had to happen in other spaces, such as outdoors and at the public library, where people who don't usually attend plays could feel comfortable and welcome. It had to be free, so that income would not hinder accessibility. It had to involve multiple stakeholders and partners. Production decisions should be grounded in the ethos of eco-theatre, with sustainability and green design as foundational principles, and all production elements would also function as actions: directing, dramaturgy, performance, writing, design, and technology.

Before auditions were held, the director analyzed the available plays, considering thematic and stylistic connections, as well as educational value, flexible casting options, and potential for promoting useful dialogue. She created a shortlist, in consultation with other team members, but the final curation happened after choosing the ensemble. The 2019 list was also narrowed by the gender equity focus of ISU Theatre's HERoic season. The performances included plays from this volume, such as *The Butterfly That Persisted*, *A Letter from the Ocean*, *Tres Marias: Categories* and *Luz, Breathing Space*, and *Drip*, as well as plays from the 2015 and 2017 collections and songs and poems written by local artists.

Open auditions were held on campus in both 2017 and 2019, and calls for actors and crew members were shared in the community as well. The 2017 ensemble included undergraduate students pursuing majors not only in the arts, but in the sciences, communication, education, and engineering, as well as graduate students, international exchange students, recent alumni, and Ames community members. Because the 2019 production was part of the ISU Theatre season, the ensemble featured a greater number of performing arts majors, but still included students from other departments, community members, and university alumni. Many participants specifically cited interests in climate science, activism, and/or social change as the reason they auditioned.

To produce CCTA 2019, ISU Theatre partnered with the MFA Program in Creative Writing & Environment, The EcoTheatre Lab, Ames Public Library, Parks University Library, the Center for Excellence in the Arts & Humanities, the Office of Sustainability, and Humanities Iowa. The array of actions included a juried environmental visual arts exhibit, a call for music and poetry from local artists, a dramaturgy display (including information about the climate platforms of political candidates), a symposium discussion with climate science experts and activists, a youth matinee, a study guide spotlighting youth climate activism, a performance at a town hall climate strike, the extension of the set design into the lobby and into the audience seats, and a sustainability resource fair during the intermission at all performances.

Sustainability resource fair participants signed audience members up for solar panels, to vote, and to participate in local environmental and sustainability organizations. They demonstrated composting, small animal rehabilitation, sustainable agriculture principles, and carbon footprint assessment. They introduced audience members to literary journals, natural resources management, the farmers' union, and local ecological initiatives and classes. The actions continued past the two production weekends, as CCTA participated in campus sustainability fairs and the Des Moines Climate Crisis Parade, and also committed to future participation in the City of Ames' Eco-Fair and Iowa State's SciNite.

Of course, in a college or university setting, one of the primary purposes of a project like this is the education of the cast and crew. We extended this goal by asking the actors to be in action, even off-stage, by joining audience members during intermission and leading small groups in post-show discussions. In addition, students had the opportunity to share their experiences during the community symposium roundtable, in a conversation with the production's humanities scholar, and in a performing arts seminar class, where one student said that CCTA "is about the future, not about the past like a lot of other plays, so it feels like with this show and this season we are launching ourselves, ISU Theatre, and our community into the future."

The success of the project as an academic endeavor depends on a committed team that embraces the theatre action as essential communication and as a gift to their communities. This is a critical part of educating not just future artists, but future citizens who will contribute to the ecologies and economies of their communities, who will have learned a new measure of success, one that values investment in imagining a hopeful future and taking active steps to create it.

Who's to say whether a CCTA audience member is most affected by one of the plays or songs, a series of photographs, an analysis of their own carbon footprint, an acting ensemble portraying a hurricane at the downtown climate strike, or an opportunity to join a local community-supported agriculture (CSA) cooperative? Or watching ice slowly melt on stage, hearing a student's enthusiasm about the worms in his composting bin, or sitting next to a theatre seat that is covered in trash and caution tape? Or maybe all of these things.

The next step, the next action, is up to that audience member, that witness.

What will you do? Now that you know?

A COLLECTIVE EXPLORATION OF ECOSCENOGRAPHY
Reflections on Triga Creative's CCTA Eco-Design Charrette

Triga Creative

After the 2019 Global Climate Strike we, Triga Creative, were inspired to take on a leadership role in our local sustainability movement through the mentorship of Ian Garrett of the Centre for Sustainable Practice in the Arts. Comprised of Shannon Lea Doyle, Alexandra Lord, and Michelle Tracey, Triga formed in 2018 as a collective of Toronto-based designers who share the goal of developing new working models for theatre design and live performance. In addition, we committed to providing our creative community of independent designers with resources – a physical studio space, intergenerational mentorship opportunities, and values-based artistic exchange – in order to increase the sustainability of their lives and careers in a precarious and competitive industry.

After feeling the enthusiasm of the Global Climate Strike, we wanted to learn more about ecoscenography as a conceptual approach to dramaturgy and as a practical framework to design for theatre and performance. We saw that Triga was well-placed to provide our community with access to the resources and knowledge we, as individual designers, were seeking, and hoped our collective could encourage greater creative ecological thinking among our peers.

We found just such an opportunity when Ian introduced us to the 49 short plays commissioned by Climate Change Theatre Action in early 2019. Ian suggested CCTA as a platform for reaching the international community of playwrights and other theatre artists involved in this project. We leapt at the idea. The CCTA short plays focus on aspects of the climate crisis, providing a unique opportunity to explore ecoscenographic practices and to share this exploration with an established network of artists. We dreamt of bringing designers together to read, discuss, and develop design concepts for all 49 plays. We imagined that through rapid design seeding, we could expand the manner in which a community of designers imagines ecoscenography and its power to change the world.

To understand ecoscenography, we refer to the writing of Australia-based ecological designer Tanja Beer, who coined the term. She writes, in an article titled "What Is Ecoscenography?" on the website ecoscenography.com:[6]

> Being "ecological" means integrating an awareness that no decision stands on its own: every choice is intertwined with social, environmental, economic and political consequences that are far reaching and capable of having long term effects. Ecoscenography demonstrates that those consequences need not be negative; that the choices that ecoscenographers make can just as easily achieve positive social, political and environmental outcomes, and that this can inspire new modes of artistic practice and engagement.

From this vision, we developed the Eco-Design Charrette concept: a gathering of designers, including leading professionals, to teach local designers about sustainable artistic practices and ecoscenography, and to begin putting these principles into practice right away. We wanted to create a welcoming open-studio space that allowed for experimentation, contemplation, research, and discovery of the multifaceted definitions of these concepts. We approached artists with several bold questions: Is combating climate change a priority for you? Would you like to practice ecoscenography? Would you like to connect with like-minded creatives, who hold sustainability as a central value of their creative process?

The word "charrette" is common in the field of architecture. It refers to a collaborative design process within a constrained time frame, or a final push to complete a project. We came to understand the word's meaning as an intensive period of design thinking and solution generation. A charrette can also be defined as a gathering of people to collectively solve a problem. Not wanting to tie ourselves to the expectation of entertainment that the word "festival" carries, and committed to highlighting the collective and participatory nature of the project we were undertaking (which "workshop series" doesn't always communicate), we landed on the word "charrette."

---

6   Beer, Tanja. "What is Ecoscenography?" Ecoscenography.com.
     https://ecoscenography.com/what-is-ecoscenography/

Our Eco-Design Charrette was centered around the creation of seed concepts for each of the 49 CCTA plays, and provided each participant with knowledge and inspiration to design with ecological consciousness. Over a span of three weeks, each participating designer was invited to create initial scenographic gestures for between one and four CCTA plays. Designers gathered to work alongside one another, while Triga provided them with studio space, meals, tools and equipment, and flexible scheduling.

We programmed the Charrette as a radical working model: participants were asked to focus on their artistic work while prioritizing their health and other personal commitments. Although the concepts of work-life balance, five-day workweek, and overtime pay are *de rigueur*, or at least paid lip service, in many professional contexts, they have been notably absent in our freelance careers in a big Canadian theatre city. To address this in our own small way, we made sure the schedule for the Charrette was flexible, and work only took place between 10:00 am and 6:00 pm, Monday through Friday, acknowledging that while designers often work long hours, we did not want to perpetuate that professional standard. We made sure there was time to eat well, engage with the local community, and take part in yoga classes provided onsite. We emphasized the interconnectedness between personal sustainability – health, inspiration, and work-life balance – and the ability to work towards the greater sustainability of our art form.

To complement the studio-based work of the Charrette, Triga curated a series of ecoscenography workshops and panel conversations, in collaboration with Ian, to develop both the hard skills and the conceptual frameworks that inform and support an ecoscenographic practice. Aisha Bentham helped foster conversation with an improvisational food-preparation performance, which drew on her own values and her connection to her ancestors. Astrid Janson shared her experience designing for large-scale theatres and box sets, and proposed a radical shift in how we design for repertory theatre. Donyale Werle upended typical design systems and shared hands-on techniques for building sustainable models. Hunter Cardinal spoke to the complicated nature of land acknowledgements and offered a way forward. Ian introduced approaches to design for immersive landscapes. Joel Ong and Mick Larusso used scientific observation techniques combined with theatrical tools to grow a microbial stage and show the interconnectedness of microscopic living organisms. Mohebat Ahmadi introduced concepts of ecodramaturgy and presented her original and provocative take on producing theatre in the Anthropocene. Mona Kastell and Andrea Carr were cyber-present from their homes in the United Kingdom and shared their ecoscenographic designs and personal design manifestos. Sage Paul led a reflection on how participants' personal values can shape and ground their business as well as their designs. Shawn Kerwin brought the everyday concerns of the contemporary artist into a conceptual and metaphorical space, allowing for play and the proposition of innovative solutions. Yulia Shtern engaged the cohort in conversation about the modern recycling system and shared her own practice of upcycled art creation. Anne-Catherine Lebeau and Devon Hardy spoke about the circulation of material resources between cultural organizations and the dissemination of best environmental production practices. Each workshop or conversation expanded the multifaceted definition of ecoscenography.

We took time each day to read the CCTA plays aloud and brainstorm ecoscenographic ideas. Each play offered a unique artistic perspective on the wide-ranging implications of climate change and sparked discussion and collaboration. The plays also provided the impetus we needed to begin rapidly generating designs – which took the shape of rough ideas, models, and sketches – from an ecodramaturgical perspective. We were curious how, without pressure or too many restraints, intuitive artistic gestures would echo the thinking of the workshops and panel conversations. We asked artists to *begin* their process, not to have the whole concept figured out. The emphasis was on provocation, and on considering the context of a performance in order to determine a design direction that stands in relation to that context's ecology. Approaches to developing design seed concepts ranged from explorations of innovative technology, renewable energy forms, and sustainable materials, to upcycling local waste streams, public education, and community building.

In group discussions, we often found ourselves asking questions about context. How could an exceptional design for each short play cause the work to have an exceptional impact? How could we demand the greatest possible engagement from audiences? We reflected on the fact that our challenge as theatre makers is to harness the unique power of the live artistic experience to encourage change. We were consistently surprised and delighted by our cohort and by how a values-centered ecoscenographic approach sparked passionate, creative proposals.

Alexandra Lord and Julia Nelle's design seed concept for *Vanilla Ice Cream* by Mexican playwright Monica Hoth, translated by Georgina Escobar, is a great example of an ecoscenographic approach that directly employs upcycling and includes an educational component. *Vanilla Ice Cream* features a woman sorting waste at a collection facility, contemplating the effectiveness of individual actions towards the collective good, as well as government-led societal or industrial change. Discussion of this text led to a site-specific, generative, set design concept, which would utilize waste material from the local waste stream. This concept was designed as a school tour with an accompanying educational program on effective recycling and composting.

Another play, *A Dog Loves Mango* by Georgina Escobar, references mango leather, which prompted Katrina Carrier and Michelle Tracey to investigate fruit-based "leather," as well as other sustainable, organic textiles, as a base for potential costume design. This curiosity about alternative material use in costuming inspired continuing conversation between designers while working on many of the other plays.

Astrid Janson's workshop proposed a design challenge: sharing scenic elements between multiple productions. Designers collaborated on set design seed concepts that could serve two to three CCTA plays. This prompted us to question the ecosystem of our local theatre community. How, with greater interdependence, can we manage resources to maximize creative use of materials and minimize waste? How can our creative influence as designers improve the sustainability of an entire company simply by deepening our collaboration with one another?

We engaged in discussion about responsible use of materials, and were deeply inspired by cradle-to-cradle thinking. As a cohort, we referred to the Hannover Principles – a set of design principles developed by architect William McDonough and chemist Michael Braungart that seek to move design towards a circular model. Acknowledging that designers work in a material art form and that we have influence over the materials we engage with, we asked ourselves how we can respect our interdependence with the natural world by planning for the full life-cycle of our work. How, in our own small ways, can we influence a shift towards circular design and a circular economy?

We looked at our work as a microcosm for what is possible on a larger scale. Ecoscenography, as a way of thinking, can be applied far beyond theatre. If we look at theatre as a rehearsal for real life, every production becomes an opportunity to investigate or inspire societal change. Theatre can broaden our philosophical understanding of climate change and increase/support our ability to affect it.

The Charrette introduced and demonstrated practical skills we can use in our design practices to have a significant impact on production processes. All of the designers learned "green" model-making techniques, utilizing only organic, recycled, or recyclable materials. We learned to turn our daily "waste" into scavenged art materials, to be inspired by the quality of found materials, and to see the artistic potential in what we already have on hand.

Some of the most rewarding outcomes of our time together were the many connections made between like-minded designers and theatre makers: participants discovered an international and intergenerational community of fellow ecoscenographers. We realized that there is a huge range of work being done in relation to sustainable design, but little of this work is publicized in our local performance and theatre communities. There is an interest and a desire for sustainability consultation from theatre leaders but, at the same time, a hesitation to integrate ecoscenography into mainstream theatre-making processes and programming. We hope to continue to increase the visibility and feasibility of sustainable design, and to help our artistic peers who are not designers understand the value of this process.

The Eco-Design Charette was hopefully the start of something bigger. We are hungry for art that deeply considers its context and materials, and renews our relationship to the natural world. Through future charrettes, Triga hopes to produce ecoscenographic work for the public, lifting the seed concepts not only "off the page" but "out of the model box." We would love to program more time and space for dedicated research and exploration, for testing sustainable materials and technologies. Finally, we continue to long for stronger relationships between ecoscenographic design mentors and mentees. It is clear to us that there is a desire in our community to increase the integration of sustainability into both our day-to-day lives and our artistic processes, to sustain not just the planet but each individual artist navigating an industry in which healthy, sustainable careers are too rare. We are thrilled to be developing the values-based connections needed to respond to this collective desire through facilitating experiences like the Eco-Design Charrette in collaboration with Climate Change Theatre Action.

HOPE IN ACTION
Studying the Impacts of Climate Change Theatre Action 2019

Brooke Wood

"Well, about two weeks ago I was ready to abandon this project entirely... but I'm beginning to believe that this event will actually happen!" So said Elaine when I reached out about attending her Climate Change Theatre Action event in the fall of 2019. This was my first glimpse of the tenacity, hopefulness, and passion I would find among Elaine and her fellow CCTA organizers. She admitted she wasn't sure how many people would show up, noting that it could be hard to get people in her small, northeastern community to attend events of any type, and that much of the community was not particularly open-minded about climate change. "But," she said, "I feel passionate about this, so I decided to just try to make a statement in every way that I can." In the end, approximately sixty people came to the performance, some noting that it was a novel experience for them. Many attendees were pleased to see this group of citizens acting, in more ways than one, to spark change.

* * *

I live in Alaska, a state that is warming twice as fast as the rest of the country, so climate change is often on my mind.[7] This reality, combined with a job working for an environmental nonprofit and my search for a research topic for my doctoral dissertation in early 2019, led me to Climate Change Theatre Action. I knew I wanted to combine my background in the fine arts with my knowledge of conservation efforts in Alaska. As I began reading and learning more about climate change, I also learned about the challenges scientists often face in communicating both the data and the urgency of this global crisis. I set out to see if and how the arts could help address these challenges.

---

[7] Di Liberto, Tom. *High temperatures smash all-time records in Alaska in early July 2019.* Climate.gov, July 16, 2019. https://www.climate.gov/news-features/event-tracker/high-temperatures-smash-all-time-records-alaska-early-july-2019

When I met Chantal Bilodeau, co-founder of CCTA, and learned about the initiative, I decided it would be the perfect project to study. Over these next few pages, I will review the research process and early findings of the CCTA study. Names of all research participants have been changed, except that of the CCTA co-founder. Federal law regarding Human Research Protection requires all studies involving human subjects be approved by an Institutional Review Board. To protect the identity of research participants, the Institutional Review Board requires that individual identifiers be removed. These include names and any geographic identifier smaller than a state name. The CCTA co-founder's name is used with her permission and, given that this article is published in the anthology she co-edited, it would be impossible to conceal her identity.

Structure of the Study

I proposed two research questions:
1. Do perceptions of climate change alter when exposed to artworks addressing this issue?
2. Do any altered perceptions result in motivations to take action?

In order to answer these questions, I designed a mixed-methods study featuring a series of interviews with audience members and a post-event survey component. Given the scale of CCTA, which, in 2019, took place in more than two dozen countries, this study was limited to events based in the United States. However, to reach the widest possible audience, an online version of the survey was made available to organizers of all 135 U.S. CCTA events.

For audience interviews, I traveled to five events in distinct parts of the country. Research participants were asked to engage in a series of four interviews: 1) immediately before they experienced the event; 2) immediately after the event; 3) two weeks following the event; and 4) four weeks following the event. The series of interviews was designed to determine if climate change perceptions altered and if participants elected to take action regarding climate change.

Further, there was an effort to understand the longevity of any impact of the event on the participants. The online survey instrument was only available to audiences following the event. Its questions were designed to address changes in perceptions about climate change and intentions to take action for the first time or to initiate new actions, adding to those already part of a respondent's regular routine.

Traveling to events across the country offered an education about theatre action, the passion of community members for ensuring a healthy place to live, and the flexibility in the structure of CCTA, which allowed event organizers to design an event most appropriate for their own community. For my research, I defined five broad regions of the country – Northeast, Southeast, Midwest, West, and Alaska. In addition, I attended the CCTA kick-off event in New York City, held on September 15, 2019. While multiple states make up four of the five regions defined for the study, I attended events in Iowa (Midwest), Pennsylvania (Northeast), North Carolina (Southeast), and California (West).

The five regional events studied varied in size and design. Locations ranged from rural to metropolitan and the format from theatrical, script-in-hand readings to fully staged productions. Audience size spanned from approximately 20 to 200. Three events, including the kick-off event, incorporated both original and popular music. Most included a panel or post-show dramaturgical discussion, and two featured original visual artworks, which were displayed throughout the performance space.

All organizers showed thoughtfulness in curating their event to best resonate with their particular community, in meeting audiences where they were on the issue, and in urging them beyond that point to a more motivated and enlightened state of mind. In interviews, organizers' most commonly stated goals included raising awareness, building community, starting conversations, and inspiring action. These goals reflect one of the CCTA founders' primary missions: to "promote storytelling as an entry point into a difficult and often emotionally charged conversation."[8] Early analysis of audience interviews reflects some success in achieving these goals.

From the five events, 26 people agreed to participate in interviews. Fourteen of the participants completed the full four-interview series. They were asked

[8] Bilodeau, Chantal (ed.). *Where Is the Hope? An Anthology of Short Climate Change Plays.* The Center for Sustainable Practice in the Arts, 2018.

questions in the following categories: their own perceptions about climate change, the actions they believe are important regarding climate change, and the actions, if any, that they are personally taking regarding climate change. Participants were also asked to describe their feelings and share anything they learned during the event, share if they decided to take any new action regarding climate change following the event, and to compare the CCTA event they attended to other forms of climate change communication they had previously experienced. Three hundred nine CCTA event attendees from across the U.S. returned post-event surveys.

Study Results

The majority of interviewees believe the issue of climate change is "very important" and are "somewhat worried" to "very worried" about the effects of climate change on their lives. They held these perspectives prior to attending a CCTA event. The Yale Program on Climate Change Communication's "Six Americas Super Short Survey" was used to define CCTA audiences' perceptions about the issue.[9] Using only four questions, this survey is designed to sort respondents into one of six groups: alarmed, concerned, cautious, disengaged, doubtful, and dismissive. Overwhelmingly, CCTA audiences sorted into the alarmed category: 87 percent fit this description. The remaining twelve percent sorted into the concerned category.

Themes from Interview Responses

Common themes emerging from participants' post-event interviews include: the use of humor by the playwrights, community, personal relevance of the issue, hope, and action. These responses reflect a correlation to organizer goals, particularly those of building community, raising awareness, and inspiring action.

Participants appreciated the use of humor to treat a topic that is often considered hopeless and dark. One participant pointed out that using humor

---

[9]   Cryst, Breanne; Marlon, Jennifer; Wang, Xinran; van der Linden, Sander; Maibach, Edward; Roser-Renouf, Connie; and Leiserowitz, Anthony. Six Americas super short survey (SASSY!), 2018. Retrieved from: http://climatecommunication.yale.edu/visualizations-data/sassy/

can "keep people engaged, otherwise it's not really a fun topic." Another said, "it's much easier to take when you can smile a little bit while you're facing it." Some interviewees did note that the humor was often dark, but most found the use of levity a positive entry point into the subject. The use of humor bears consideration when framing climate change messaging for audiences with varying interest in and knowledge of the topic, particularly for those not especially invested in the issue.

One of the most significant themes to emerge in interviews, both with audience members and with event organizers, is that of community. For most, the theme of community was expressed as an increased awareness of like-minded neighbors. For event organizers, partnering with non-arts organizations resulted in knowledge sharing, increased resources and capacity, and greater opportunities to make change. For audience members, this sense of community was often reflected in a feeling of comfort at seeing and interacting with more people than they expected from their town, indicating a more widespread concern for the issue. One audience member said she was inspired to see that people in her community had "publicly stepped up." Another explained that "just knowing that all these people are doing these things, it is energizing for me. It keeps me wanting to do more things that I can."

It is worth mentioning that there was often an awareness among study participants that the majority, if not all, of the audience was likely to be sympathetic to the cause of climate change action. All event organizers expected this to be the case, one observing that her audience would largely be, "those people who know something about climate change." Audience members recognized this fact as well, with one noting that the "audience was probably the converted" and some using the well-known phrase, "preaching to the choir." A few interviewees suggested that the name of the event could be a barrier to entry. Despite reservations that an audience sympathetic to the cause was not who needed to hear the message, participants already concerned about the issue reportedly left hopeful and motivated. New conversations about climate change were begun, ideas for action were considered, and new actions were taken. Some event organizers established new partnerships with local organizations, increasing their ability to reach more of their communities.

Interview participants found that the plays offered relatable characters and dealt with personally relevant subject matter. One participant explained this as a valuable way to communicate climate change by connecting "it back to real human experiences." One audience member pointed out that "we're watching real humans," and said, "it's just very hard to not hear someone when they're standing in front of you." Another explained that "this event ... puts a very personal aspect to climate change; they are real people ... you can relate to those people through this type of event, through this type of play." Another interview participant described the effect: "These plays, because they were so tightly woven into people's lives in terms of their applicability, it really allowed people to relate to them." Because climate change is such a vast issue, it can often seem impersonal. Converting it to a scale that is human and relatable seemed to emerge as a significant element of successful climate change messaging.

A chief goal of CCTA is to change the mainstream negative, disaster-based climate narrative to one of hope. All interviews with event organizers reflected this goal, and many interview participants indicated they left their event with hope. One participant drew that feeling from those producing the event, saying, "All of the energy and the dedication of people that are volunteering to be here and do all this, that is very hopeful and inspiring." Another found hope by recognizing there was a larger group of concerned people in her community than she previously realized, saying "When I come together with people that I didn't even necessarily know were like-minded and we can all talk about something like this... I feel more hopeful that things can move forward."

New action on climate change by event attendees is a fundamental goal of CCTA. Several interview participants did report a new climate-friendly action. For some, it came in the form of talking about their experience at CCTA and the issue of climate change with people in their lives. Some participants had talked about climate change before attending events and now were increasing that frequency; others began engaging in discussion with relations and acquaintances for the first time. Someone bought recycling bins for their home, someone started incorporating resale shopping into their buying habits, and another has started looking more closely at the ingredients of personal hygiene products and selecting those with fewer or no harsh chemicals.

Forty-three percent of survey respondents indicated their intentions to take action following the event were "very high" and 34 percent were "high".

It is unclear if these would be new actions or continued actions, given that 85 percent of survey respondents indicated they already took some personal action regarding climate change. Survey respondents were also asked to identify one or more of seven actions they would take following the event, including an "other" option and an "all of the above" option. Twenty-four percent indicated they would "vote for candidates with a plan to mitigate climate change," 22 percent would "change my personal habits," and 20 percent would "talk to my family and friends about climate change."

Summary

At the time of this publication, there is still much detailed data analysis to undertake in the research process. I hope to learn more about the longevity of impact from these events upon attendees. Are there elements of an event that remain with participants over the long-term? What feelings and ideas change over time? Is it possible to determine at what point after a CCTA experience the impetus for action occurs? Further, can anything learned about lasting impact of an artistic experience be used to support the inclusion of the arts in the climate change movement or other social causes? It is hoped that by identifying what resonated with audiences and what did not, the findings from this study could be used by future CCTA organizers to curate effective events.

Humor and making climate change personally relevant emerged as resonant themes among interview participants. Positive reactions to these two themes indicate a recommendation for their use in framing effective climate change messaging. As I continue the analysis process, I hope to see additional recommendations emerge, resulting in a list of framing options to be considered when developing climate change messaging for various audiences.

I have also begun to consider methodologies and designs for potential future studies. For instance, is there a way to design a more succinct methodology that could be applied to pop-up styled events, in public locations, to determine if those events draw an audience with more diverse perspectives on climate change? Would it be possible to do a comparison study among events using the CCTA title and those opting to not use the title?

There is much to learn from the rich data collected; still, this early look at results reflects optimism that CCTA is meeting its goal of action. People all over the country acted by presenting an event in their local communities. They provided hope, laughter, and connection. Audience members left with heightened awareness about specific impacts of climate change, with greater determination to engage friends, family, and others in conversation about the issue, and some even adopted a climate friendly action as part of their daily lives.

*   *   *

We sat on the floor of the theatre lobby, house lights low and sunlight growing dim outside. The theatre was hushed – a faint buzz of creativity and connection still in the air. It was the end of a long weekend with three CCTA events back to back and now there was finally time for me to interview Scarlett and Melissa about their experience as event organizers. All three of our minds were full, reflecting on what we had learned that weekend and what we hoped had been, and still would be, accomplished. Melissa described our hope as a "ripple effect," saying that is

> what happens if you reach one person a little bit, or maybe their mind is opened at least this amount to start reading a little bit more about it [climate change] or understand it or have some different kinds of questions. Those aren't things we can measure, not really, but they are things where we can try to make a difference even if you can't measure that difference. So if someone comes in and says, "I don't believe in climate change," they see our show, maybe they have some questions that they didn't have before and maybe that makes a difference in some small way.

Producing CCTA is an enormous undertaking, but organizers' hope rested in small things: one new question, one new conversation, one new action. They all believe that the small actions of individuals can collectively create great change.

For the 2019 iteration of CCTA, playwrights were asked to write about their climate heroes, "those who are lighting the way towards a just and sustainable future." I had no idea that in the course of this research I would meet my own climate heroines and heroes, but that is exactly what happened. As a qualitative researcher, my role is to observe, to take notes on what I see, to listen carefully to the study's participants, and to consider whether research questions are answered and if other questions are generated. In CCTA, I had much to observe – the production of an event, actors' presentations, energy of the space, and audience reaction to and engagement with productions. However, time and again at events I found myself to be both a passive and an active observer. That is the power of CCTA: the power of live theatre, of storytelling, and well-executed craft. Drawn into that experience, I learned from the plays and discussions, and was pushed to consider things differently, often in similar ways to the study's participants. At each event, I laughed and cried along with the audience. I was welcomed as part of the community by organizers and actors.

Meeting Chantal and learning about Climate Change Theatre Action has been a significant and meaningful experience in my life. I learned and benefited from CCTA events in similar ways to the audience members whom I interviewed. I learned who my climate heroines and heroes are. They are the dedicated and passionate citizens of communities all over the country who strive each day to turn the tide of climate change, one action and one person at a time. We do not often hear about these climate heroes, but I was fortunate to meet them and see them in action, pursuing change creatively through the arts. To all the CCTA participants, keep being heroes. Your work changes lives.

PART 2:

THE PLAYS

LAILA PINES FOR THE WOLF

Hassan Abdulrazzak

This play was inspired by an article entitled "Climate Change Is Burning a Wolf Pack's Last Bridge to Survival" by Taylor Hill.[10] This year's theme, Lighting the Way, encouraged the inclusion of animals that might be inspirational in the fight for a sustainable future, so I thought it would be appropriate to tell the story of Little Red Riding Hood from the perspective of the maligned Wolf who is struggling to survive because of climate change. In Arabic culture the story of Little Red Riding Hood is known as Laila and the Wolf, or *Laila wa al theeb*.

CHARACTERS:
WOLF
LAILA
GRANDMA
MOTHER
(GRANDMA and MOTHER can be played by the same actor if necessary)
/ indicates an overlap

SCENE ONE

WOLF: This is how the story goes…

MOTHER: Laila, your grandmother isn't well. I want you to take this cake and bottle of wine to her. Oh and Laila, don't step off the path. And leave things in the forest as you find them.

LAILA: Yes, mother. I'll do everything right, don't worry.

WOLF: But Laila was a liar. She not only veered off the path, she began to pluck the flowers and plants of the forest as she always did. This is where I enter the story. *(to LAILA)* Good morning Little Red Riding Hood.

10   Hill, Taylor. "Climate Change Is Burning a Wolf Pack's Last Bridge to Survival." *TakePart.* March 16, 2015. http://www.takepart.com/article/2015/03/12/there-are-9-wolves-left-island-and-climate-change-burning-bridge-their-survival

LAILA: Don't call me that, wolf. I hate it when you call me that. My name is Laila.

WOLF: Good morning Laila. And where are you going so early in the morning?

LAILA: To Granny's house.

WOLF: And what's in that basket of yours?

LAILA drinks from the bottle of wine.

LAILA: Granny is ill. My stupid mother thought she could cure her with cake.

WOLF: And what's in that bottle you're drinking?

LAILA: Pretty awesome Malbec. Wasted on the old hag if you ask me. Want a sip?

WOLF: I wouldn't mind a drop.

WOLF drinks. He's thirsty.

WOLF: I live on the island over there. It's where I was born. I crossed what was left of the frozen water that connects the island to the mainland here. Let me tell you, it's getting harder and harder to cross because of climate / (change).

LAILA: Is this a sob story? Cause I really don't have time for a sob story.

WOLF: I don't suppose you could spare some of that cake.

LAILA: Not a chance.

WOLF: Are you heading to your grandmother's house? I could walk with you.

LAILA: Not before I pick some more flowers.

WOLF: For your grandma. How thoughtful.

LAILA: Hell no, they're for me.

WOLF, *to the audience*: And so I leave Laila as she sets about clearing more of the forest and I go to her grandma's house. I knock on the door.

GRANDMA: Who's there?

WOLF: A weary traveler. *(to the audience)* Grandma opens the door. She's got a gun! *(to GRANDMA)* I didn't mean to scare you. I was just wondering if you've got any scraps I could eat. It's getting harder and harder to get here from my island. I'm famished.

GRANDMA: I got nothing for a scrawny-assed wolf. Except this bullet.

WOLF, *to the audience*: She fires the gun which is old and rusty. The recoil knocks her off her feet. Her head smashes against the bed frame. She is dead as a doornail. I'm panicking, even though I had nothing to do with her death. Any minute Laila will be here. I don't want her to be traumatized by the sight of her grandma's cracked head. I try to hide grandma under the bed; she's too big. In the cupboard; it's full of clothes and piles and piles and piles of plastic bags. I've got to hide her corpse before Laila gets here. What do I do? There's only one thing for it – and this is where things get a little weird. I eat grandma and put on her clothes.

LAILA: Hello Grandma.

WOLF: Hello Laila.

LAILA: Why was the door open?

WOLF: It must've been the wind.

LAILA: Oh Grandma what big ears you've got.

WOLF: All the better to hear you with.

LAILA: What big eyes you've got.

WOLF: All the better to see you with.

LAILA: What big hands you've got.

WOLF: All the better to hug you with.

LAILA: And, oh, Grandma, what a great grim ghastly mouth you've got.

WOLF: All the better to kiss you with.

LAILA: You're not my grandma! You're the big bad wolf!

WOLF, *to the audience*: And that's when she takes out her .44 Magnum and blows my brains out.

SCENE TWO

MOTHER: Laila, your grandmother isn't well. Take this cake and bottle of wine to her.

LAILA: Yes, mother.

WOLF: Good morning Laila. And where are you going so early in the morning?

LAILA: To Granny's house.

WOLF: And what's in that bottle you're drinking?

LAILA: Want a sip?

WOLF: Yes please.

LAILA: Forget it.

WOLF: I'm famished. It's getting hotter every year which means when the water freezes, it forms a much thinner ice sheet than in the past.

It makes crossing from the island to the mainland tricky. You have to watch your step. It's exhaust/(ing).

LAILA: Boring! I'm off to pick flowers.

WOLF: You've got to stop destroying the forest. That's what's causing the ice to melt.

LAILA: Let me tell you, I make some serious cha-ching out of these flowers.

WOLF: Then at least give me a piece of the cake. Please!

LAILA: Get lost.

WOLF, *to the audience*: I go to her grandma's house.

GRANDMA: Who's there?

WOLF: A weary traveler. *(to the audience)* Grandma opens the door. Before she has the chance to point her gun at me, I drop dead from hunger.

LAILA: Grandma!

GRANDMA: Hello darling. Did you bring me cake and wine?

LAILA: Did you kill the wolf?!

GRANDMA: I didn't touch him, I swear. He just dropped dead.

LAILA: What are we going to do now? He's supposed to eat you and then I kill him and then the cycle starts again.

GRANDMA: Well he's dead anyway. Maybe if we wait a little.

LAILA: It doesn't work like that. He has to be alive when I shoot him in the head. Then everything goes back to the start. Damn it! Damn it! Damn it!. This means I'm stuck here forever.

GRANDMA: Shoot me.

LAILA: What?

GRANDMA: Shoot me and free yourself.

LAILA: I can't shoot you. You're my grandma.

GRANDMA: You call me "old hag" behind my back. You think I don't know that.

LAILA: I call you that cause I love you, you stupid old thing.

GRANDMA: Shoot me.

LAILA: No.

GRANDMA: Shoot me.

LAILA: No.

GRANDMA: It's the only way to save yourself, Laila.

WOLF: And that's when Laila takes out her .44 Magnum and blows grandma's brains out.

SCENE THREE

MOTHER: Laila, your grandmother isn't well. You've got to go and kill her.

LAILA: Yes, mother.

WOLF, *to the audience*: Laila plucks the flowers as usual. But this time I don't show up because the water between the island and the mainland never froze. So she stays stuck in the forest, which is no longer a forest, just a clearing. She plucks and plucks until there is nothing left.

LAILA, *to the audience*: The last thing I hear is a cry from the island. It's the wolf.

HASSAN ABDULRAZZAK is an award-winning playwright of Iraqi origin, born in Prague and living in London. His plays include *The Special Relationship* (Soho Theatre, 2020), *And Here I Am* (Arcola Theatre, 2017 and UK tour; Europe, Middle East, and Africa tour, 2018-2019), *Love, Bombs and Apples* (Arcola Theatre, 2016 and UK tour; Golden Thread, San Francisco, 2018 followed by a second UK tour; Kennedy Centre, Washington D.C., 2019), *The Prophet* (Gate Theatre, 2012), and *Baghdad Wedding* (Soho Theatre, 2007; BBC Radio 3, 2008; Belvoir St Theatre, Sydney, 2009; Akvarious Productions, Delhi and Mumbai, 2010).

THE ROOKERY:
A Play for Steller Sea Lions

Elaine Ávila

Eighty percent of the Steller sea lion population has disappeared, leaving fewer than 75,000 in the wild.[11] For this play, I interviewed Dr. Andrew Trites at the University of British Columbia, who gave me special access to the Marine Mammal Research Unit. The trainers there told me the story of a sea lion's dramatic 12-hour disappearance. Humans who care about sea lions are an inspiration, but so are the sea lions themselves.

Special thanks to Dr. Andrew Trites, Marine Mammal Research Unit, University of British Columbia and the Vancouver Aquarium; Dr. David Zandlviet, Environmental Education, Simon Fraser University; trainers Nigel Waller, Brianna Cairns, and Juno Avila-Clark; and sea lions Sitka, Hazy, Boni, and Yasha.

For whatever we lose (like a you or a me)
it's always ourselves we find in the sea
– e.e. cummings

SETTING:
A rock, not far from the Open Water Research Laboratory in Port Moody, British Columbia, Canada.

CHARACTERS:
SITKA, a Steller sea lion, trained to do research, female, 17
BRUNHILDA, a wild Steller sea lion, female, 17

Based on true events, inspired by Boni's twelve-hour disappearance.

---

[11] For more, see the Vancouver Aquarium website: https://www.vanaqua.org/education/aquafacts/steller-sea-lions

SITKA swims up. BRUNHILDA looks down on her from the perch on her rock. They begin barking at each other.

SITKA: But seriously. (*more barking*) Is there room? (*more barking*) On that rock, or not?!

BRUNHILDA, *bellows, but decides to scoot over to make room*: You're not from here, are you?

SITKA, *looks wistful, smells the air*: I am.

BRUNHILDA: Your accent is so... weird!

SITKA: I was raised by humans.

BRUNHILDA begins barking.

SITKA: What is it?

BRUNHILDA: Humans?!

SITKA doesn't understand, shrugs, bobs her head.

BRUNHILDA: Do you see this scar? See it? Those mofos came up, wearing fleece, in this boat, and shot me, and I fell into the water like I was dead, and they dragged me over to their boat with these metal hoop things, they used a knife to cut this awful thing off my neck, stapled my flippers with these tags, then stuck me with this sharp thing and suddenly I was full of energy and swam off. But not soon enough! I had to listen to them crying! They said they'd saved me! Crazy mofos!

SITKA: They did save you.

BRUNHILDA: What's wrong with you?

SITKA: They did.

BRUNHILDA: I don't see how.

SITKA: That thing around your neck could have killed you. It's called a common plastic packing strap. They're always talking about them at the research center. Whole teams go out to save sea lions from those straps. You swam into one. You were about to die a horrible miserable slow death. But they cut it off of you. See? That gun was a tranquilizer gun, it's not to kill you –

BRUNHILDA: Honey, humans have been trying to kill us for millennia. They shoot us with bullets, stab us in the head with spears – what's wrong with you?

SITKA: No. It can't be true.

BRUNHILDA: Don't they tell histories at your rookery?

SITKA: My what?

BRUNHILDA, *groans*: Rookery. *(groans)* Breeding colony.

SITKA: Breeding... colony?

BRUNHILDA, *groans*: Wait a second. Who made them – what you call them – common –

SITKA: Common plastic straps?

BRUNHILDA: Yeah. What are they?

SITKA: They use them for packing things... tying... things.

BRUNHILDA: Yeah, well, who made them? Who dumped them into the sea so I could swim into one and die a horrible miserable slow death?

SITKA: Humans.

BRUNHILDA: I rest my flipper. They are crazy, crazy mofos. They nearly kill me so they can save me?

SITKA: They're not all the same.

BRUNHILDA: They look the same. Why do you think they're so great?

SITKA: They're cute. They all have different personalities. I brought them up a sea star, and this human, he bared his teeth like this – so cute –

BRUNHILDA, *groans*: Like what?

SITKA: Like this. They call it a "smile."

BRUNHILDA: Euww. Looks horrible.

SITKA: It's cute.

BRUNHILDA: Why do you do all that for them? Bring them sea stars?

SITKA: It's part of my training. It's a pleasure. We're close. They feed me.

BRUNHILDA: They feed you?

SITKA: I don't have to go looking for anything.

BRUNHILDA: Huh. That'd be nice. You never have to hunt?

SITKA: Never.

BRUNHILDA: Never have to go hungry?

SITKA: Never.

BRUNHILDA: That'd be nice. *(groans)* I can't imagine never having to worry about where my next meal – ooo – did you see that? Fish?

> BRUNHILDA *jumps in the water, grabs a fish, comes back, swallows it whole.*

SITKA: You shouldn't eat so much of that.

BRUNHILDA: What?

SITKA: Pollock. It's junk food.

BRUNHILDA: It's fish.

SITKA: It fills you up too fast. Some of the scientists have discovered that's why we're 80 percent extinct.

BRUNHILDA, *eating*: Huh?

SITKA: Didn't you notice? There's less of us.

BRUNHILDA: I did, kind of – I heard – some of the rookeries are – super dull these days – no barking, low attendance, the parties are crap. And the ladies, the ladies at the molting salon –

SITKA: Molting salon?

BRUNHILDA: I know, I know, it's only once a year, but some of us like to look stylish even when our hair falls out in clumps. I know, I know, it grows back in even more beautiful, but still. The molting ladies said they've been nursing for years. OMG, years. Used to wean those pups in a season. Now it's years. Pollock you say. Huh. How do you know this?

SITKA: I'm a research sea lion. I'm part of trying to save us. They study my breathing and my diet and my diving.

BRUNHILDA: Well. Nice for you. I guess.

SITKA: It is. Nice. You should see my trainers. They're so cute.

BRUNHILDA: Why are you out here then?

SITKA: I don't know. Something in me. It's... wild.

BRUNHILDA: Something in you is sick of those mofos. You know I'm right. Why don't you stay? Don't go back.

Pause. SITKA sucks on her fin.

OMG. What are you doing?

SITKA: Suckling my fin.

BRUNHILDA: Why?

SITKA: I find it comforting.

BRUNHILDA: I've never seen any sea lion do that.

SITKA: I know. They wrote about me in a journal.

BRUNHILDA: Why do you do that?

SITKA: I didn't nurse. They fed me with tubes –

BRUNHILDA, *gasps, bobs head*: You're in estrus!

SITKA: What? Yes, I'm feeling – a bit –

BRUNHILDA: Which harem are you going to join this year?

SITKA: Which what?

BRUNHILDA: You know, at the rookery. Which dude are you going to hook up with? Bob throws the best parties but Stan is the best in bed. Alfred is the sweetest. He smells the best. And his whisker foreplay – forget about it.

SITKA: I don't – I've never –

BRUNHILDA: Never what?

SITKA: I'm kind of a nun for research. I've never had s-e-x.

BRUNHILDA: You've been around humans too long. We're not uptight like that. We don't have to spell. We just say. How old are you?

SITKA: Seventeen.

BRUNHILDA: Jeezus. So am I. You should have been breeding for years. You should be a great great great – oh, I don't know, I can't keep track – grandmother by now.

SITKA, *changes the subject*: How many pups do you have?

BRUNHILDA: There's Suzy and Stevie and Sally and – not sure. Lost track. Sammy's been suckling for years.

SITKA: What's it like?

BRUNHILDA: What? Sex?

SITKA: The rookery.

BRUNHILDA: Kind of crazy but great. Loud. Party. You should come.

SITKA: I'm not sure I – whoa, I'm hungry.

BRUNHILDA: Well get yourself some fish. There's plenty. Ooo. I think I see an octopus. You have dibs. Go for it.

SITKA: I don't – how do you –

BRUNHILDA: Didn't your mama teach you to hunt? You know, the glory of the hunt. Noshing on fish, how to smash a seal...

SITKA: I told you. I was raised by humans.

BRUNHILDA: Whoa. You sure give up a lot for science.

SITKA: I got to go.

BRUNHILDA: Stay, stay.

SITKA: I miss them. I can't help them figure out how to save us if I stay.

BRUNHILDA: Oh, they'll find another one of us.

SITKA: It took them years to raise me up – I'm – no offense – I'm kind of – under-stimulated – you don't interact with me all that much.

BRUNHILDA: Whoa. Aren't you the princess. But – wait – before you swim off –

SITKA: Yes?

BRUNHILDA: You know you can always come back. I'll show you around.

SITKA: Thanks.

BRUNHILDA: Are you sure? The humans may be cute, but they are, you have to admit –

SITKA: I'm sure.

BRUNHILDA: I'll miss you. Thanks for all that research stuff you do.

SITKA: You're welcome.

SITKA swims off, BRUNHILDA bellows.

ELAINE ÁVILA is an American and Canadian playwright, a co-founder of Climate Change Theatre Action, and a Fulbright Scholar to the Azores, Portugal for 2019. Her plays tell untold stories of women, workers, the Portuguese, and climate change. Favorite Best New Play Awards: Disquiet International Literary Program in Lisbon, Victoria Critics Circle, Panama City's Festival de los Cocos. She is distinguished as a *descendentes notáveis* (Notable Descendant) for her theatre work by the Government of the Azores, Portugal.

IT STARTS WITH ME

Chantal Bilodeau

This play is inspired by Greta Thunberg, Katharine Hayhoe, Wangari Maathai, Alexandria Villaseñor, Naomi Klein, Rebecca Solnit, Sheila Watt-Cloutier, Alexandria Ocasio-Cortez, Christiana Figueres, and countless more women who are fighting for us all.[12]

Think of this play as a battle cry. The goal is to channel as much power and energy as possible and to fill the room with it. Use as many female actors as you need – of all ages, sizes, and colors – and build to a crescendo.

NOTE:

I have indicated whether one or several actors are speaking. Feel free to distribute the lines in the manner that best suits your ensemble.

~~~~~~~

A woman stands center stage. Other women/girls enter or are revealed as they say their lines.

SINGLE VOICE: It starts with me
   A woman
   A sister
   A mother

SINGLE VOICE: It starts with me
   A girl
   A niece
   A daughter

MULTIPLE VOICES: It starts with me

---

[12] Statistics from WECAN (Women's Earth and Climate Action Network) on the power of women in climate solutions and the climate iniquities faced by women: https://www.wecaninternational.org/why-women

SINGLE VOICE: A student

SINGLE VOICE: A scientist

SINGLE VOICE: An Elder

MULTIPLE VOICES: Me

SINGLE VOICE: A politician

SINGLE VOICE: An environmentalist

SINGLE VOICE: A writer

MULTIPLE VOICES: It starts with me

SINGLE VOICE: Because I may be young
But I can stand in front of world leaders
And demand that they do their job

SINGLE VOICE: Because I may be poor
But I can fight to address female wellbeing and ecological health

Together

SINGLE VOICE: Because I may be marginalized
But I can draw upon Indigenous traditional knowledge
And heal the Earth

SINGLE VOICE: Because I may be inexperienced

SINGLE VOICE: Ambitious

SINGLE VOICE: Angry

SINGLE VOICE: Religious

SINGLE VOICE: And I may be just me

SINGLE VOICE: But I've had enough of the patriarchy
    To call it what it is – and dismantle it

SINGLE VOICE: I've had enough of politicians' dysfunction
    To run for office – and win

SINGLE VOICE: I've had enough of capitalism

SINGLE VOICE: Greed

SINGLE VOICE: White supremacy

SINGLE VOICE: Denialism

SINGLE VOICE: To ignore those invested in the status quo – and take
    matters in my own hands

Start building.

MULTIPLE VOICES: It starts with me!

SINGLE VOICE: Because I'm 14 times more likely to die in a natural disaster
    Than a man!

SINGLE VOICE: Because I'm four times more likely to be a climate refugee
    Than a man!

SINGLE VOICE: Because after a natural disaster, I'm 300 times more
    likely to be abused
    By a man!

SINGLE VOICE: Because I'm vulnerable to toxins and pollutants!

MULTIPLES VOICES: Always!

SINGLE VOICE: To human trafficking!

MULTIPLES VOICES: Always!

SINGLE VOICE: To poverty, hunger, and death!

MULTIPLES VOICES: Always!

Keep building.

MULTIPLE VOICES: It starts with me!

SINGLE VOICE: Because I'm willing to make sacrifices to reduce emissions

MULTIPLE VOICES: Yes!

SINGLE VOICE: Because I'm responsible for half of global food production

MULTIPLE VOICES: Yes!

SINGLE VOICE: Because I'm inclined to ratify international environmental agreements

MULTIPLE VOICES: Yes!

SINGLE VOICE: Because I will no longer be abused!

MULTIPLE VOICES: No!

SINGLE VOICE: I will no longer be silenced!

MULTIPLE VOICES: No!

SINGLE VOICE: I will no longer be belittled, dismissed, discounted!

MULTIPLE VOICES: No!

You're almost there. Go all out. Channel all the emotions — all the hope, rage, fear, disappointment — you have about being a woman in this world.

SINGLE VOICE: It starts with me! *(stomp loudly on the word "me")*

MULTIPLE VOICES: It starts with me! *(stomp)*

SINGLE VOICE: It starts with me! *(stomp)*

MULTIPLE VOICES: It starts with me! *(stomp)*

> *Repeat these two lines for as long as it takes to get most women and girls in the audience to join the chorus. Use whatever means it takes — gesture to them, walk up to them, plant actors in the audience, etc. Once you have them on board, repeat one or two more times and then move on to —*

SINGLE VOICE: Me! *(stomp)*

MULTIPLE VOICES: Me! *(stomp)*

SINGLE VOICE: Me! *(stomp)*

MULTIPLE VOICES: Me! *(stomp)*

SINGLE VOICE: Me! *(stomp)*

MULTIPLE VOICES: Me! *(stomp)*

> *Silence. Hold. After a beat —*

SINGLE VOICE, *softly*: It starts with me
Because without me there is no salvation for anyone
Or the planet

> *Actors should hug each other. Make it okay for the audience to do the same. If appropriate, hug the women and girls in the audience.*

CHANTAL BILODEAU is a Montreal-born, New York-based playwright and translator whose work focuses on the intersection of science, policy, art, and climate change. She is the Artistic Director of The Arctic Cycle, the founder of the online platform Artists & Climate Change, and a co-founder of Climate Change Theatre Action. She is currently working on a series of eight plays that look at the social and environmental changes taking place in the eight Arctic states.

DRIP

Yolanda Bonnell

I feel that people aren't thinking enough about their personal relationship with the living, breathing land they are on. Many humans have become power hungry and want to control everything. This includes the land. Ownership. We need to have ownership over all sorts of things. This is what drives the engine of capitalism. Instead, I believe we must revolutionize our land-body-spirit relationship. We are sick because the land is sick and vice versa. What do we need to do to heal ourselves and, in turn, heal the land?

Drip was created on the land of Tkarón:to where the original caretakers include the Mississaugas of Credit River as well as other Anishinaabe peoples, the Haudenosaunee – Six Nations Confederacy, and the Wendat.

Somewhere on the North Dakota prairie a Lakota woman had a dream that a black snake was coming to devour our people.

> – Tom Goldtooth, Executive Director, Indigenous Environmental Network

When the Eagle of the North flies with the Condor of the South, the spirit of the land she will re-awaken.

> – Inca prophecy

SETTING:
Four beings live in the cracks and chasms of an ice-covered mountain. There is dirt covering the floor of the chasm.

VESSELS:
EZRA
SEENA
WICKONAY
NEEBAH
THIMB

NOTES:

Characters are gender and ethnically non-specific, with the intention of ensuring that they are portrayed by (or given in preference to) Indigenous, Black, and other peoples of color, particularly women, queer, non-binary, and trans folks.

It is important to recognize and understand the history of the land that you are standing, living, working, resting on. Please open with an acknowledgement of the land this work is being performed on and your relationship to it.

This piece is meant to be physical and should include movement scores. Body exhaustion in relationship to land exhaustion.

~~~~~~~~~~~~~~~~~

In the darkness we hear hissing
It begins as one but turns into more
And more

Light bleeds in
Five beings are intertwined together in the dirt

Breath

EZRA: A Lakota end of time prophecy says that

ALL: From the North
A black snake will come.

They begin to unravel from each other
Their bodies become snakes and they slither towards the edge,
where the chasm meets the witnesses

WICKONAY: It will cross our lands, slowly killing all it touches

THIMB: And in its passing

NEEBAH: The water will become poison

They sustain a sssssssss

Water drips on them from above
They look up
They take a deep breath

Darkness

The sound of ice groaning
Cracking
Moving
Waking up

Sunlight peaks through

EZRA plays with a piece of ice
They hold it out
They take in the witnesses
More light bleeds in as they speak
They smile and speak the following with general lightness
almost as if they're doing a TED Talk
They continue to play with the ice

EZRA: Frostbite occurs when skin and the underlying tissues freeze or – in extreme cases – die. Fingers
Toes
Earlobes
Cheeks
And the tip of the nose are most susceptible because the body prioritizes keeping your core and head warm at the cost of everything else. That means blood flow to extremities tends to be redirected when the body is exposed to extreme cold. Less blood flow means the skin freezes faster.

Beat
They take in the witnesses

EZRA: I read that on BusinessInsider.com

Breath

The body

They examine their body

It sacrifices parts of itself
Literal parts of itself to stay alive in its core
To keep its heart beating

Fingers

Light hits WICKONAY
They are a tree falling
The sound of a tree falling

Toes

Light hits THIMB
They are earth excavated
The sound of earth being excavated

Earlobes

Light hits NEEBAH
They are a hurricane
The sound of a hurricane

Cheeks

Light hits SEENA
They are twisted plastic in an animal's stomach
The sound of an animal crying

And the tip of the nose

Light hits all bodies
They are poisoned water
The sound of a tap turning on

Boiling water
Boiling
They are all boiling

I wonder how long it takes to get to the core

EZRA hands the remaining chunk of ice to a witness willing
to take it; if no one is willing, they place it in the dirt
The five come together, humming chorally
Water drips on them from above
They stop
They look up
Then back out

SEENA: Take a stab at me

WICKONAY: With a sharp, sharp spoon

ALL: Dig out my eyes

NEEBAH: Plant them in the clouds

WICKONAY: Somewhere in between

ALL: Somewhere in between

SEENA: The melting

ALL: All of the melting

THIMB: Dig

ALL: Dig in my skin

EZRA: Scraping metal

THIMB: Pounding

WICKONAY: Compounding

NEEBAH: And compounding

SEENA: And

> *SEENA separates from the group, runs to one side, grabs*
> *a water barrel*
> *Runs to the other side of the stage, fills it with water*
> *Runs it back to the other side of the stage*
> *Pours it into a pot*
> *"Boils it"*
> *The water disappears*
> *They repeat and continue to repeat*

NEEBAH: Temperature

ALL: Mercury

NEEBAH & THIMB: Temperature

ALL: Mercury

SEENA: The water is sick

ALL: The water is —

> *THIMB puts their hand to the ground*

THIMB: When I was very little, my Mom had a garden in the backyard
    I was so surprised to see food come from the ground
    I didn't know you had to plant seeds
    I thought food just... grew there
    Carrots and peas and lettuce
    She used to sing to it
    And I guess I thought
    I guess I thought that
    That's what made the food grow

They lie down in the earth
They sing

You are my sunshine
My only sunshine
You make me happy
When skies are grey

NEEBAH joins in

THIMB & NEEBAH: You'll never know dear
How much I love you
Please don't take my sunshine away

The two continue to hum, lying in the earth

WICKONAY: An open letter to our land and water defenders

EZRA: You are the future

WICKONAY: You are our warriors

EZRA: I look at you and think

EZRA & WICKONAY: I wish I had that much fight in me

WICKONAY: Your ability to never back down
To never stop fighting

EZRA: To put yourself on the front lines

WICKONAY: To drum until your hands are sore

EZRA: To sing until your throats are dry

WICKONAY: You are the future

EZRA: If we even have a future...

WICKONAY: We acknowledge you and respect you

SEENA, *as they're running back and forth*: Bath water
    Brush your teeth
    Wake up
    Coffee
    Make pasta
    Brush your teeth
    Shower
    Feed the baby
    Make sure the baby –

ALL: Doesn't drink the water!

> *SEENA stops and falls to the ground*
> *The others begin to cover her in dirt, singing*

ALL: The other night dear
    As I lay sleeping
    I dreamt I held you in my arms
    When I awoke dear
    I was mistaken
    And I hung my head and I cried

> *Water drips on them from above*
> *Then more*
> *Then a dump of water falls on all of them*
> *They lie in the mud*

> *The sun begins to peak through from above*

> *SEENA begins to grow from the dirt*
> *They each begin to grow*
> *And grow*
> *And grow*
> *And grow*

YOLANDA BONNELL (she/her) is a Queer Two-Spirit Anishinaabe-Ojibwe and South Asian, European mixed performer, playwright, multidisciplinary artist, and creator. Originally from Fort William First Nation in Thunder Bay, Ontario (Superior Robinson Treaty territory), her arts practice is now based in Tkarón:to (Canada). In 2016, Yolanda and Michif (Métis) artist Cole Alvis began *manidoons collective*, a circle of artists creating Indigenous performance. In February 2020, Yolanda's four-time Dora nominated solo show *bug* was remounted at Theatre Passe Muraille. She was also a part of Factory Theatre's *The Foundry*, a creation program for new career writers, where her play, *Scanner* continues to be developed towards production.

ICE FLOW

Philip Braithwaite

This play was inspired by "Ice Watch," a project by artist Olafur Eliasson in which huge blocks of ice were taken from Greenland, where climate change has melted them off the ice sheet. They were floating in the water, and were hauled to London to melt on the South Bank. Eliasson says the blocks "are individual, they are like beings, they whisper to you. If you put your ear to them, you can hear the air bubbles. And that air is fresh and clean – it has half the CO_2 of the air outside."

NOTES:
A sufficiently "icy" look might be to have the actors in white puffer jackets. You can cut out one of the icebergs for brevity if needed. This is meant to be performed at quite a pace.

~~~~~~~~~~~~~~~~~

> *Three ICEBERGS speak to us. They are in different parts of the performance space. They interact with the audience. The audience represents the crowd looking at them as art installations.*
>
> *The ICEBERGS should probably be sitting down, as icebergs are inert, but feel free to take some creative license. Perhaps they're already starting to float?*

ICEBERG 1: I only ask that you might forgive me.

ICEBERG 2: What do you mean, I'm dying? I've never felt so alive!

ICEBERG 3: It's rude, that's what it is!
   If I could get a hold of the bastard who put me here...

ICEBERG 1: The problem is, I don't know... what I've done.

ICEBERG 2: For centuries I've been stuck, just sitting there, joined up.
I meant nothing, to anyone.
Now I'm important.

ICEBERG 3: I'm known for being someone who doesn't take anyone's shit.
I'm known as someone who gets on with things, gets things done.

ICEBERG 1: I spent many years... centuries... not hurting anyone. Not
doing anything.
Perhaps it was that? That I should've been doing more? Helping
more?
Perhaps this is my penance?

ICEBERG 3: I was cemented to my family.
On what you call the ice sheet.
I held sway over them. I disciplined them.
I was strict, yes, but I was fair.
No one crossed me.
No one messed with me.

ICEBERG 2: You get pleasure from seeing me!
How can you get pleasure from something that's dying?

Pause.

Trouble is, I'm starting to think...

ICEBERG 1: There's clean air still inside me.
I can feel it as it flows through me.
But the outside – it's something else.
It doesn't sing, it cries. It weeps.

Beat.

It chokes me.

ICEBERG 2: I think about what I'm doing here. And why.

ICEBERG 3: I've been hearing a lot of talk, too much talk, about how this might've been down to a weakness in leadership. People, some people, have been putting it about.

That's what you call it.

I don't know who started that rumor, but that's all it is – a rumor.

ICEBERG 1: What is the... *(struggles for word)* ice sheet?

That's what you keep calling it: the ice sheet.

I was there. Now I'm in *(again struggling)* South Bank.

That's what you call it.

You say, "Look, this iceberg is all the way from the ice sheet... from Greenland."

So I am from Ice Sheet Greenland. And now I am in South Bank.

And I am iceberg.

ICEBERG 1: I am getting warmer.

ICEBERG 3, *allowing a note of sorrow to creep in*: I... I was separated from them. My family.

They did not push me off!

ICEBERG 2: You bring your children and they put their ears on me. Listening. For something.

Something that I used to be.

Oh well, it seems to make them happy.

ICEBERG 1: So you push your fingers into me, down my spine, stick your tongues at me, making me flow and run.

I don't mind.

> *Pause.*

I mind... a little bit.

ICEBERG 2: My master won't let me die.

I've come a long way. My master, he took me on a long journey.

He's a good man, my master.

ICEBERG 3: I was dislodged, we'll say. I fell off the sheet.
Into the water.

ICEBERG 2: He'll come for me. He'll be back for me. I know he will.
But if you see him, could you...?
He won't let me die here. He won't let me melt away. I know he's too
good for that.
He took me away from my home; took me from my family, but I know
he did it for a good reason.
He took me thousands of miles on a boat. I haven't travelled much.
That's the first time I've travelled in...
I've not travelled much.
But my master, he must know what he's doing. He must've put me here
for a reason.
He rescued me.
I was floating when my master, he fished me up.
I used to belong to my siblings. We were one.
But my master, he'll save me.

ICEBERG 3: It was no one's fault, but the sooner I can talk to someone...
The sooner things can return to normal and I can instill a bit of discipline...

ICEBERG 1: I am an installation.
That's what you say. You say, "We're here to see the installation."
If I could talk to someone, plead with someone... to help me?
Perhaps I could offer some way, some means of paying my debt?
Otherwise...

ICEBERG 2: My master, he's an artist. That means...
He does art.

ICEBERG 1: South Bank will swallow me.

ICEBERG 2: And his art is me.
Is that right?
You should know, you've come here to see me.
Me, shrinking. Me, dwindling. That's what his art does. It shows me,
naked.

Pants down.

It's a little embarrassing, to be honest.

Pause.

I am... a little...

When I get a chance to think, that's when... when I feel scared.

ICEBERG 3: You – or you – yes, you over there!

Why are you touching me?

Why are you licking me? It's disgusting!

Anyway, you! Tell whoever put me here to come and talk to me. We'll have a frank and firm discussion.

ICEBERG 2: I'm sorry. I know I should have more faith. But sometimes I worry...

If you see him, my master, could you just remind him?

That I'm here?

ICEBERG 1: Back in the glaciers, back home, hunters and harpoons, the forest of white. Now the towers across the river, watching me with judgement in their million glass eyes, looming over me and aiming their sun rays and smoke at me so that I'll flow into somewhere, into the river of South Bank, into memories, and I'll be traces of water and I'll be yesterday and I'll be a full stop and I'll be gone.

ICEBERG 3, *softening*: I just... I worry, you see.

My family, they're not much good without me. They need my firm hand.

ICEBERG 2: It's alright.

I'm not dying. I'm having fun.

ICEBERG 3: Without me they get... they tend to get lazy, disorganized.

I... miss them. That is, they need me.

ICEBERG 1: I'll be an example. Of what happens. When they let the sun and the sky take away more of my family and we all melt into some South Bank somewhere.

So many South Banks.
Killing us.

ICEBERG 2, *less sure*: I'm having fun.

PHILIP BRAITHWAITE is a playwright and lecturer. His plays have been produced in New Zealand, Australia, the UK, and the U.S. He is originally from New Zealand, but he is now living, writing and teaching in the UK.

STEAMY SESSION IN A SINGAPORE SPA

Damon Chua

This play was inspired by *BIOSPHERE BBQ*, a 2019 work by artist and environmental activist Justin Brice Guariglia, featuring text by Timothy Morton.[13]

SETTING:
Split stage. On one side, a lectern for EXPERIMENT GUIDE. On the other, a small cement bench for SPA USER.

CHARACTERS:
EXPERIMENT GUIDE, an older man
SPA USER, a younger man

NOTE:
The tone should be kept light and comedic until the last moments of the play.

~~~~~~~~~~~~~~~~~~~~~

Lights up on EXPERIMENT GUIDE. He is smartly dressed. He stands at the lectern and addresses the audience.

EXPERIMENT GUIDE: To carry out the experiment, you'll need… a man.

Lights up on SPA USER. He is naked except for a towel wrapped around his waist.

EXPERIMENT GUIDE: Towel is optional. And you'll need a steam room. A typical one found in any spa.

SPA USER mimes touching all four walls.

EXPERIMENT GUIDE: Plus steam, created by heat.

---

[13]   Guariglia, Justin Brice. *Biosphere BBQ*, 2019, text, neon sign. https://www.guariglia.com/biosphere-bbq

Steam billows around SPA USER.

EXPERIMENT GUIDE: That's it. Then, we wait.

SPA USER: Wait?

EXPERIMENT GUIDE: Yes.

SPA USER: For?

EXPERIMENT GUIDE smiles a cryptic smile.

EXPERIMENT GUIDE: When I was a young man – foolish, willful – I used to go on long runs. In the blistering heat. In the middle of nowhere. Once, I got lost. Almost died of heat stroke. Luckily, someone found me. Just in time.

A beat, then, to SPA USER.

How are we doing?

SPA USER, *starting to perspire*: It's sweltering in here.

EXPERIMENT GUIDE: Tell us where you are.

SPA USER: Uh, in a steam room.

EXPERIMENT GUIDE: Which is where?

SPA USER: In a spa.

EXPERIMENT GUIDE: Which is...

SPA USER: Inside a gym.

EXPERIMENT GUIDE: And that is...

SPA USER, *not sure where this is going*: ...

EXPERIMENT GUIDE *gives up*: You're in Singapore, right? Singapore?

SPA USER: Yes.

EXPERIMENT GUIDE: What's the temperature there?

SPA USER: In the steam room?

EXPERIMENT GUIDE: Singapore!

SPA USER: Hot.

EXPERIMENT GUIDE, *to audience*: Mean temperature of 27°C or 80°F. Doesn't sound too bad. Except it's heating up, twice as fast as the rest of the world. By year 2100, we'll see a daily max of 37°C. Which is, as you may realize, our body temperature.   *98°F*

SPA USER: What we need is AC.

EXPERIMENT GUIDE: If the grid is working. If energy prices stay low. If you can get there in time. Heat stroke kills within minutes. Remember those poor little babies left unattended in cars on a hot day? B-B-Q.

SPA USER: Someone should invent a low cost AC. Solar-powered. Portable.

EXPERIMENT GUIDE: AC condensers give off heat. Adding to the rising temperatures. In urban areas, because of hard surfaces, the effect is multiplied.

   Beat.

   (to SPA USER) Did I say the steam room has no doors?

SPA USER: Uh, what?

EXPERIMENT GUIDE: No doors.

SPA USER: How do I get out?

EXPERIMENT GUIDE: You don't.

SPA USER: But –

EXPERIMENT GUIDE: Don't worry. It won't take long. (*to audience*) When ambient temperature remains above 40°C or 104°F, with high humidity, the body is no longer able to sweat. No sweating means no cooling. No cooling means our internal organs heat up. Start to fail. Muscle cells are wrecked, spilling their contents into the bloodstream, overloading the kidneys. Proteins in the spleen start to cook. The blood-brain barrier that keeps pathogens out of the brain becomes permeable, allowing toxins to invade.

> *Referring to SPA USER.*

As you will see.

SPA USER: Uh, funny.

EXPERIMENT GUIDE *aside, to the audience*: Not pretty.

SPA USER: How long do I have to stay in here?

EXPERIMENT GUIDE: Thought I was clear.

> *SPA USER doesn't quite get it. Dripping with sweat, he tries to locate the steam room's exit.*

SPA USER, *as he does so*: Must be here somewhere.

EXPERIMENT GUIDE: As I said –

SPA USER, *with sudden insight*: Wait. This is one of those "Escape Rooms," right? Follow a series of clues and you're outta here?

EXPERIMENT GUIDE: Uh, no.

SPA USER: Gimme the first clue.

> *When there's no response.*

C'mon!

EXPERIMENT GUIDE, *to audience*: It's done in the interest of science. For the faint of heart, you may want to avert your eyes now. Ready?

> *EXPERIMENT GUIDE claps his hands twice. More heat. More billows of steam.*

SPA USER: What's happening?

> *EXPERIMENT GUIDE doesn't say anything. Reality begins to sink in for SPA USER.*

SPA USER: Wait a minute ...

> *Beat.*

This is ...
(to audience) Help! SOMEONE!

> *Panicking, SPA USER rushes about to find an exit. In vain.*

EXPERIMENT GUIDE, *to audience*: Don't try this at home. Unless home happens to be an equatorial country like Singapore, where it's super humid. Then you don't even need to try. You're there.

> *EXPERIMENT GUIDE claps twice.*

> *Blackout.*

DAMON CHUA is a New York-based playwright. He was a member of The Public Theater's Emerging Writers Group 2014-15 and is a current member of Ma-Yi Theater's Writers Lab. Off-Broadway plays include *Film Chinois*, *Incident at Hidden Temple* and *The Emperor's Nightingale*. He is published by Samuel French, Smith & Kraus, and Plays for Young Audiences. Damon also writes poetry and short stories.

APPEALING

Paula Cizmar

I often come across images that are staggeringly beautiful in the abstract, but when I take a closer look I realize, in reality, ohmygod, that's a devastated watershed or this is a ruined section of forest. Isn't it weird that in order to light the way, in order to get people to really look at what is going on, we have to remember that humans like things that are shiny and pretty?

SETTING:
The photo department of an environmental media outlet – print, TV, or electronic.

TIME:
The present.

CHARACTERS:
JANA, female, any age, any ethnicity. She is thoughtful, empathetic, focused, ambitious.
J, any gender, any age, any ethnicity. J appreciates a great image, isn't without scruples, but has a job to do.

NOTE:
Please try to cast like the real world, which is open and tangled and diverse and mixed and all the more wonderful because of people of all types.

/ indicates an overlap

~~~~~~~~~~~~~~~~~~~~~~~~~~~~~

> *JANA is carefully studying photo after photo, facing the audience as if the photos are on the fourth wall. Each photo is beautiful in its own way. J enters and studies the photos along with her.*

J: The colors.

JANA: Yes. The colors.

J: Wow. So saturated. Intense. Unreal almost. And the light. And the composition.

JANA: Oh yeah. This one in particular.

J: Stunning composition. These are great photos.

JANA: But. But should I really be trying to make something attractive? You know? Should I really be trying to appeal to the viewer's eye/

J: /That was the assignment/

JANA: /when in fact, these are photos of a great tragedy? Great devastation? Should I? I mean, why am I trying to make what's ugly beautiful? Why do I take these pictures? You know? Should I? What should I do?

J: I don't know. But the colors —

JANA: Yes. The colors.

> *If we haven't seen the actual images yet, and if we are going to see them, we see them now – projected over the stage, or on all the walls, or on a huge screen. JANA and J study them. We see that they are all photos of ocean water – filled with debris. The color of the water is bright aquamarine, or sea glass green, or deep marine purple. In the water are colorful soda cans, sections of plastic six-pack tabs, plastic bags, coffee cups. One of the photos is a vast trash pile the size of a small island – all floating in open ocean. The photos are striking.*

J: Spectacular. They could be in a gallery.

JANA: It's crazy. You're asking me to make art out of an environmental calamity.

J: Well, not me. I'm not.

JANA: Your boss is. Our boss.

J: We have to illustrate the story somehow. We can't just tell it. In words.

JANA: Words aren't enough.

J: No.

JANA: No one listens to words.

J: Not anymore.

JANA: So we need images.

J: To attract the eye.

JANA: So that someone engages. And cares.

J: Yeah.

JANA: But do they?

J: Well, that's our job. Get them to care –

JANA: But will they?

J: Again. Our job –

JANA: Yeah yeah yeah. I know. I KNOW. I know.

J: Got a better idea?

JANA: Oh don't. Stop. Just. Don't push me. Don't push me.

J: Look. Take a break. Why don't you? Go. Do something else for a while.

JANA: For how long? An hour? A day? A month? The clock is ticking faster and faster and every day there's some new disaster, some new evidence of some new consequences, some new devastation, and no, I don't think we can afford to wait one more minute before –

J: The story isn't scheduled until the end of the week! You can afford an hour. Just. Don't get so wound up –

JANA: Somebody has to –

J: One thing at a time. Take a break. Take your mind off things. Go look at something else.

JANA: Something beautiful.

J: Yeah.

JANA: Something that isn't all gunked up with human nonsense and human interference and human evil.

J: Something like that.

JANA: What's left, really? What's left that hasn't been destroyed by human intervention?

J: Well. Deep wilderness.

JANA: It's just a matter of time. If there's a pure stream, it's in danger of pollution from industrial waste upstream or the debris from a drilling operation. If there's a remote gorgeous mountain meadow, it's in danger of pollution from drifting smog. If there's a broad expanse of ocean, it's in danger of this this this this this crap, this this refuse, this mountain of plastic bags and cans and straws and bottles floating into a great big graveyard of trash rubbish crap ruining the habitat for god knows how many species for god knows how many thousands of miles.

J: Well there's still a little bit of something left. Go for a hike. Well. Okay. Not around here. But. I don't know. There's some wilderness nearby somewhere. Or. We must have some photos of deep wilderness somewhere in some library or. Somewhere.

JANA: Don't tell me you're going to try to put a happy face on this and I should just calm down.

J: No.

Beat.

I could hire someone else.

JANA: Yeah. You could. Why don't you?

J: Same problem. The job is the job.

JANA: And the job is some weird juxtaposition: make something horrific attractive.

J: Illustrate something horrible with something compelling.

JANA: I mean, to really do this justice, I should find the ugliest of shots. Photos of a baby dolphin with a plastic Coke can ring around its snout. Photos of baby ducks pecking at a Styrofoam cup. Photos of a dead otter, washed up on the beach with a plastic bag wrapped around its neck –

J: Okay, stop –

JANA: To really do this job right, I should find the most repulsive, the most disgusting, the most revolting images so that people will get the idea.

J: That won't give them the idea –

JANA: It will. They'll be confronted with the truth –

J: But then they will just look away.

JANA: Haven't they already?

> *J is silent. It's true. No one cares. JANA looks sadly at more of the images. Finally J tries again.*

J: But. We don't want to give up. Do we?

> *JANA takes this in. She shakes her head. She takes a breath.*

JANA: Okay. So. Let's do this. What colors are the most appealing? What will best attract someone to the story? What will draw the eye in?

> *JANA and J study more of the photos.*

> *Lights fade.*

PAULA CIZMAR is a Los Angeles-based award-winning playwright and librettist whose work has been produced all over the world. Theatres presenting her work include Cal Rep, Portland Stage Company, the Women's Project (NYC), Jungle Theatre, and Playwrights Arena. Her work, even in the musical/opera world, is devoted to combining art with social justice issues. She is a member of the Antaeus Theatre Playwrights Lab and teaches playwriting at the University of Southern California's School of Dramatic Arts.

CANARY

Hanna Cormick

A true story, a fantasy, an allegory. For all the people, animals, insects, and landscapes whose bodies are on the line, voluntarily and involuntarily, through climate activism, climate displacement, climate disaster, climate illness; for those who leverage the safety and privilege of their bodies to stand in for those who cannot stand out or speak up due to risk of harm or persecution; for those who, through their small everyday actions, carry on the messages of those of us injured, disappeared, imprisoned, so that change will come.

> *Le cadavre est à terre et l'idée est debout.*[14]

> – Victor Hugo

NOTES:
For one or many performers. To be delivered with momentum. A bit of live electric bass and a fierce outfit would not go astray. Please do not wear scented products during performance.

~~~~~~~~~~~~~~~~~~~~~

I am standing here for a body that cannot stand here
I am speaking for the voice that is writing that is Hanna
This body stands here for her body
As we all should with our bodies that can stand here
For those that cannot

Coal
Was mined by hands
With soot under nails
A dark cramped cough
And the little sunny flicker of the canary

---

[14] "The body has fallen, but the idea still stands."

In its cage

This body is standing here for a body that used to stand on stages (like this
    body does now)
That used to dance to electroswing and jump into embraces and
Dig down into old quarries and catacombs

This body is standing here for a body that four years ago
Found an abandoned coal cellar under the streets of Paris
Untouched for years, the walls didn't reflect the torchlight
Consumed by the rich blackness

The canary was used as a warning signal
She said: get the hell out, you're breathing poisoned air
She sent it with the envelope of her silent corpse
This body stands here for that body
Sacrificed to send you a message
To keep you safe

I am standing here for a body that is [*insert distance to Canberra, Australia*]
    kilometers/miles away
This body is here for that body, her body, that cannot be here
And not just because of the distance

For a body that lies in a bed
Breathing through respirators
Unable to open a window to feel the breeze on
The skin of her body
This body feels the breeze for her body
This body stands in this public air for her body
That can no longer stand in the public air or under public gaze

I am standing here amongst you for that body
Whose genes have mutated, developed a warning signal
A body whose white blood cells attack petrochemicals
Treat them like an allergy, a poison
With a potentially fatal immune response

The canary thrashes its beak against the bars
Claws scratch at cheap gilding

Her cells, on a hair-trigger
Changing system pathways to explode at will
Stuck on a feedback loop until every single source of food and water and
    breath is lost to the rising tide of reactivity
A body injected with biologics and chemotherapy and pain
Just to only barely survive the uninhabitable spaces we create around it
A body whose throat swelled up because her nurse accidentally wore eyeliner
A body swollen with hives from a piece of plastic
A body shaken by 100 seizures daily because of the propylene glycol in your
    soap

A body that can smell your laundry powder from across the street
Smell what you ate three days ago through your skin
Smell bacteria
This body stands here for a body that doesn't know if it is an evolution or
    an illness

The last ink and paper book she read was *David Bowie Is Inside*
She had to wear a gas mask and sit far away

She wants to ask me not to wear scent when my body stands here for her
    body
She hesitates; what kind of climate activist's body would wear scent?

What kind of activist, when 90 percent of the chemicals that make up scent
    are petroleum derived?
She asks again, because the answer is: most of us
Unknowingly

And
Makeup
Hair product
Synthetic fabrics
Synthetic leathers
Moisturizers

Clothing detergents
Our bodies soaked and wrapped in fossil fuels

Because the media drives that tell us to ditch our straws don't let us know
that washing synthetic fabrics in our home is one of the highest sources
of microplastics in our oceans and in our lungs

Because we were never told that our indoor use of personal care products
and household cleaning supplies
Produces half of all outdoor city air pollution
More than cars

The little canary breaks out of the cage and yells:
Fuck you capitalist coal-junkies!
And flies off into the sky

This body stands for those bodies that are changing into bodies that cannot
stand here like this body
The 34 percent and rising of bodies that are noticeably injured by these
scents and plastics and beautifiers
We pretend we need, but we could be free from in an instant

Up high high like a cloud, all the canaries are free of their cages
Flashing bright yellow in the sun
Like a light

This body stands here for her body and breathes in and breathes and
breathes and breathes
Like her body cannot
And breathes in
what her body does not
Have to

I stand here for her body
In my body that is breathing all the poisons with you

And a rain of yellow feathers tumbles down
Soft on your nose and eyelids

And the canaries are stripping off their wings, they say
Never again will we be made to feel like our lives are lived for your profit
And on the dead branches, they stand gloriously naked

We stand here for their bodies

The canaries have dipped their little beaks in soot and scrawl
Fuck the Anthropocene
And
Oil is genocide
And
Drown the one percent
Across each other's tiny naked bodies
And welts and hives rise up around the letters

My body asks her body what it feels like
For her body to be so damaged by all the tiny personal choices of our day
Her body tells my body that she feels like the Earth
So this body here also stands here for the Earth that cannot stand here
And that cannot speak to us
Except through the envelope of silent corpses

The canaries drop themselves onto the bonnets of cars in New York
Onto department store skylights in London
Onto ferries full of tourists in Paris
Their bodies catch on the girders of the Sydney harbor bridge
Talons tangle in the hair of Hitchcock heroines
Tiny pink blistering bodies
Fill the chlorinated fountains

And I fill my lungs with this poison air
To shoot bullets of words through this poison air
Because my destruction will not be silent

In their death rattle
The canaries say:
This is the message we send with our bodies
We are not your warning signal anymore

You don't need a warning if you just
Stay the fuck out of the coal mine
Stay the fuck out of the coal mine

This body is here amongst their bodies and also stands for their bodies and
    the bodies that cannot stand here

Some lay struggling, not quite dead, on hot tarmac
Wing-bones broken
Beak shattered
And tiny manacles are placed around their ankles
As police gently scoop them up
To be put back in cages

The words are washed from their bodies
They are to send a new message
As their new cages are hung high
Outside shop fronts and town halls
Their broken bodies on display
A warning

But sullen silent stares seem to say something different
Than what their captors wish
Their caged bodies to be saying

And the corpses of the canaries that were not scooped up
By the policemen with their
Gently violent
Hands

Are trodden under shoes
Burst under the pressure of car tires
And fry very slowly in the sun

And you walk over that red smudge on the footpath
You have your car windshield replaced
A workman cleans your pool

And they are almost forgotten
In the silence of their absence
Forgetting also
That their silence
Is the warning

And
I will go home to my home
That is not a cage
I won't notice the air freshener on the bus
And the hidden petroleum ink embedded in my recycled toilet paper
And the plastics in the product in my hair
Or the scent that maybe I did or didn't wear today when the body I stood for
Asked me not to

HANNA CORMICK is a Finnish-born performance artist based in Australia with a background in physical theatre. She is a graduate of the École Internationale de Théâtre Jacques Lecoq in Paris, and has created works in Australia, Europe, and Asia. Her recent work, *The Mermaid*, a confrontation of the social model of disability and the climate crisis, was shortlisted for the 2018 National Award for Disability Leadership (Arts). Her current practice is a reclamation of body through radical visibility.

BLACKJACK

Derek Davidson

Last December I read the superb memoir *Extreme Conservation: Life at the Edges of the World*, by Joel Berger. Somewhere near the end, Berger – who was conducting a study of the recently introduced muskoxen on Wrangel Island, in the Arctic Ocean – made a passing reference to Ada Blackjack, the young Iñupiaq woman who accompanied the ill-fated expedition to the island in 1921. The reference intrigued me enough to compel me to read *Ada Blackjack: A True Story of Survival in the Arctic*, by Jennifer Niven. It was a riveting story, reminding me that environmental heroes surround us; they come from every corner of the planet, every epoch, most of them unsung. I decided to sing about one: Ada.

CHARACTERS:
ADA BLACKJACK, an Iñupiaq seamstress
JOEL, a conservationist
STEFANSSON, an explorer. He waves a little Canadian flag around from time to time.

/ indicates an overlap

~~~~~~~~~~~~~~~~~~~~

> *JOEL, pacing, ADA, and STEFANSSON, seated. All in parkas.*

JOEL, *reading from a book while pacing*: Says here: uh –

ADA: Could be one.

JOEL: Says here you were born in Spruce Creek, Alaska –

ADA: Or eleven.

JOEL: Married a Blackjack, Jack Blackjack, that was his real –

ADA: Yeah, that was his real name –

JOEL: And he left you –

ADA: I was 16, he marries me, then he runs off. I was stupid.

JOEL: Well. You were 16.

ADA: Oo, he was a gamble everybody says, didn't know nothing about gambling.

JOEL: What happened to him?

ADA: How do I know? I don't know. How do I know? Who cares? See this coat? Reindeer. I made it.

JOEL: Yeah, I'm just. So he leaves you and you walk –

ADA: Walked back to Nome. Slow. With Bennett.

JOEL: Ah – (*flipping pages*): your son. Whom you carried sometimes. Forty miles to Nome.

ADA: He was sick. He was just a kid.

JOEL: And no money –

ADA: And my sick boy –

JOEL: So when this show came along –

ADA: Show?

JOEL: The, uh, the expedition.

ADA: …

JOEL: When they posted the job, you took it.

ADA: Well.

JOEL: Good money. Let's see: *(flips to other section of book)*.

STEFANSSON: Planning a three-year polar expedition and am in need of skilled laborers and seamstresses drawn from the Eskimo community to accompany us.

ADA: Used the word "Eskimo" back then. More money than I'd ever seen. My boy was sick.

STEFANSSON: We set sail in September of 1921.

JOEL: 1921. And you were the only –

ADA: The only one showed up. They wanted more.

JOEL: More, um –

ADA: More Eskimos. To hire for the trip.

JOEL: So you, and four young men –

ADA: Almost turned back around. Four white men and just me? I got afraid.

JOEL: I don't blame you, one small woman among –

ADA: No.

JOEL: No what?

ADA: Victoria too, I told you.

JOEL: Sorry – Victoria?

ADA: Cat.

JOEL: Ah!

ADA: And bears.

JOEL: Bears?

ADA: Polar bears. Scared a them too. Afraid I'd be eaten by a bear I go on this trip. *Oi oi oi oi.*

JOEL: You weren't.

ADA: No.

JOEL: In fact – *(flips pages)*: you were the ONLY one to survive – *two years* on Wrangel Island –

STEFANSSON: Ah, Wrangel Island, its dangers over-dramatized. Given a healthy body and cheerful disposition, one may live as easily here as anywhere.

JOEL: Terrible. Three of the men set out away from camp –

STEFANSSON: *Easily*, I say! What does one stand to lose in the face of adventure, fame/ for country and –

JOEL: Tried to make it to Siberia –

ADA: Nobody saw them ever again.

JOEL: The other fellow stayed, died of scurvy –

STEFANSSON: I say any man with good eyesight and a rifle can live anywhere –

ADA: Tried to save him. Learned to shoot a gun by myself. Hunt. Took care of him, fed him soup of the gulls I shot. And a goose one time. He died in the tent and all of them were gone then.

STEFANSSON: Any man with good eyesight and a rife –

JOEL: All of them gone, just you, until – *(flips page)*: a ship shows up months later.

ADA: No.

JOEL: No? Says here – *(showing ADA the page he's looking at)*

ADA: Not just me. Vic.

JOEL: Vic? – Oh, / the cat –

ADA: The cat.

JOEL: Okay. And you lived a long time after.

ADA: Eighty-five. Way I figure it was just luck.

JOEL: Well, Ada, luck or no – *(closing book)*: you played an amazing hand.

ADA: Luck. The ace can be one or eleven, you just decide.

JOEL: The ace? – oh, *blackjack* –

ADA: Say, well, I'll make it eleven, I'll just go that way. And you hope and you hope like me, a boat comin and finally one did. You learn to shoot. You make a good coat out of reindeer: look.

JOEL: Well, hope or, or luck, whatever you choose to call it –

ADA: If that's gambling then just living is gambling. Where's the choosing?

JOEL: You could say "I'm not playing."

ADA: No one says that. You choose to hope, that's all. Anyways, I had to get back for my son, Bennett.

THE PLAYS | 111

JOEL: Yeah, see, that's interesting: the men go off, *you* stay put, take/ care –

ADA: The man who hired me. Stef, uh, Stef –

JOEL: Stefansson. Canadian, left you in the lurch as I understand it, all of you.

ADA: Made money on the story though –

STEFANSSON: "The Adventure of Wrangel Island," a powerful memoir I penned in 19 –

ADA: I didn't see no money from it and he wasn't even there.

JOEL: Your fellow adventurers died while the guy in charge is thousands of miles away telling lies about the "Gentle Arctic" and making a living off your misfortune. Uuggh. Charlatan.

STEFANSSON: *Tsk,* I offer *Romance.* The world gets daily poorer in Romance –

JOEL: Like I said: *charlatan.*

ADA & STEFANSSON: Who are you?

JOEL: Me? Nobody, just. Well, I'm here on the island, ya see, Wrangel Island/ and –

ADA: Why come here?

STEFANSSON: It is as easy to live up here as it is down home, if you know how.

JOEL: Shut up. You've never even been here. *(to ADA)* I guess you'd say I'm a modern explorer. 21st century style.

ADA: 21st –

JOEL: Reading about *you*. Anyway, I'm just a scientist. See, we've re-introduced a herd of muskoxen to the island,/ it's pretty fascinat –

STEFANSSON: Ah, musk-oxen and reindeer in vasty herds to the edge of the Arctic, the heart *swells* –

JOEL: Shut up please. There *were* muskoxen here once and we're hoping to see if they can survive –

STEFANSSON: Why, it is easier to survive –

JOEL & ADA: SHUT UP.

JOEL: Seriously. So due to changing climate they're in trouble, the musk – I mean/ we've found –

ADA: Changing...?

JOEL: Yes, the earth, and so that means Wrangel Island, it's getting warmer. Lots warmer.

ADA: Warmer is bad.

STEFANSSON: Warmer is good!

JOEL: Ugh, *no*, it's *not*.

STEFANSSON: Of course it is good, of course.

JOEL: NO – unless you want more – you name it, more extreme weather events, less drinkable water, less food –

ADA: Warmer is bad.

JOEL: In the case of the muskoxen there's dietary changes, new predation patterns –

STEFANSSON: The easier to hunt them.

JOEL: Not easier if they're wiped out. Ugh, you people.

ADA: Oof. So?

JOEL: So we're studying *them* because you know, the same might be said for us.

STEFANSSON & ADA: Wiped out.

JOEL: Gone.

ADA: I know gone. They all went to Siberia and he died in the tent. Then it's just me and Vic.

STEFANSSON: Brave boys, all. Heroes. Gone.

JOEL: Gone. The warming makes surviving a crapshoot. No water. No food. Tough odds and you're betting against the house.

STEFANSSON: I find these gambling metaphors distasteful.

JOEL: Buddy, you were gambling with *other* people's stakes all your life, weren't ya?

STEFANSSON: I have no idea what you're talking about.

ADA: We come to the island and four men gone and it was your plan and that is what he means by Ugh you people –

STEFANSSON: My dear, of course you wouldn't understand. We are men, men know what must be done, men are perfectly capable of living/ off the land –

ADA: So the animals die?

JOEL: Yup. But funny thing: when threatened, by wolves, whatever, the male muskox runs out, away from the herd, against approaching predators, you know, or. And the females stand their ground and circle around the young.

ADA: Stand their, oh, they stay by the the the calves.

JOEL: Yep, and in the long run taking care of the young is greater assurance of survival. So.

STEFANSSON: And yet something noble, uplifting: to *charge* headlong into the *unknown*, into *danger*, bodily harm, *death* perhaps, but –

ADA: I think he told you to shut up please. He said please.

STEFANSSON: How can you expect to understand what is necessary at times for survival?

ADA: What are you talking about? What is he talking about?

STEFANSSON: I'm talking about what must be *done*. You say no food? Go where there *is* food – *take* what you must, if you must – the lesson of nature: the survivors prove their right to survive by surviving.

JOEL: What does that even mean?

STEFANSSON begins to bluster.

No, it's your way of thinking that got us into this. Time for a change in strategy, bub.

ADA: 'Cause now it's getting warmer.

JOEL: Yup. *Lots* of things gonna change.

ADA: What do we do?

STEFANSSON: We charge ahead, full-speed, hearts pounding into the, the uh. The.

Coughs.

JOEL: Yeah, *no*. But whatever we do.

ADA: Whatever *you* do.

JOEL: Better do it soon. What – what's here? *(gesturing vaguely around)* What can I learn? From the muskox, or? What we got here? From you, Ada Blackjack. A real person doing hero-y things way back in '21.

ADA: Not hero: my son. Didn't know what to do, he was sick. Wanted good for him, that's all.

JOEL: Well, *you* survived. For your kid.

STEFANSSON: But it is all a gamble, isn't it?

ADA & JOEL: A gamble.

JOEL: How do we play our hand? Is the question we're lookin at. And what's it count for?

ADA: One?

JOEL: Eleven? What do we lay down?

ADA: Just to live?

STEFANSSON: What do we stand to lose?

JOEL: What indeed? While some tell lies and make money with other people's stakes.

ADA: One. Eleven. See this reindeer coat? I learned to shoot.

JOEL: Which do you choose? I have a kid, you know. A daughter. What to do here.

ADA: I learn to shoot and I hope and I live. And I choose hope.

STEFANSSON: One.

ADA: Eleven.

ALL: One. Eleven. Blackjack...

DEREK DAVIDSON teaches playwriting and theatre history at Appalachian State University in North Carolina. Davidson is also Artistic Director of In/Visible Theatre (a professional company in Boone, North Carolina), and is a playwright, director, and AEA actor. Before Appalachian State, he was an Associate Artistic Director for the Barter Theatre in Virginia and Coordinator for the Appalachian Festival of Plays and Playwrights. His solo pieces, *Ox* and *Furrow*, were part of Piccolo Spoleto and Asheville Fringe Festivals in 2018.

ABSOLUTELY NOTHING OF ANY MEANING

Sunny Drake

When Britain's former prime minister, Theresa May, criticized student walkouts for climate action as a waste of lesson time, Swedish high school organizer Greta Thunberg tweeted: "That may well be the case. But then again, political leaders have wasted 30 years of inaction. And that is slightly worse." Why are so many of us guilty of inaction?

NOTES:
1 & 2 can be any gender, race, ethnicity, or age. Please keep up the pace: there should be a constant flow of quick chatter, except in the moments indicated "silence" or "beat." ALL CAPS denotes heightened emotion, which doesn't necessarily need to be yelling, but could be.

Big thanks to dramaturgs Donna-Michelle St. Bernard and Kathleen Flaherty, and for feedback from Awilda Rodríguez Lora, Patri González Ramírez, Chanelle Gallant, and Isaac Lev Szmonko.

~~~~~~~~~~~~~~~~~~

> *In the dark (or if that is not possible, a creative solution that indicates the dark).*
>
> *2 speaks the **bolded words** together with 1.*

1: You have completely screwed up over and over again. I want to know if this catastrophic mess is from your total incompetence, horrible lack of motivation, willful disregard and selfishness, or refusal to see the severe consequences of your actions. Just in case for some unbelievable reason you missed the memo the first hundred times: THE DESCRIPTION IS **COMPLETELY WRONG** FULLY FOLDED OUT IT IS **FORTY-TWO INCHES WIDE** AND IS **HARD AS A ROCK** IN WHAT WORLD IS THIS "FULL SIZE" **YOU SENT US A TWIN SIZE SOFA BED, AMAZON**, AND IT SHOULD BE ILLEGAL TO CALL THIS **SALMON-COLORED** IT IS CLOSER TO

TUSCAN RED IT SMELLS LIKE A WET DOG AND IS HELD TOGETHER BY **STAPLES AND PRAYER** LIKE **LITERALLY** THE PACKAGING IS **EXCESSIVE AND ENVIRONMENTALLY UNFRIENDLY** AND WE WAITED **FOUR DAYS** FOR DELIVERY WE ARE LIVID STILL AWAITING RETURN INSTRUCTIONS IF WE COULD GIVE THIS A **NEGATIVE STAR RATING** WE WOULD. **DO. NOT. BUY. THIS. COUCH!**

2: Should we talk about it?

1: I already pressed submit – people deserve to know.

2: I meant about the... the...

1: The..?

2: Okay. Let's not discuss it then.

1: We always discuss everything.

2: We never discuss anything. Of importance.

1: True.

2: Are your ankles wet?

1: I already told you my knees are wet so what does that say about my ankles?

2: I wasn't sure if you might have stood on something. Maybe on the couch.

1: AS IF ANYONE COULD STAND ON THAT COUCH WITHOUT FALLING AND –

1 & 2, *together:* – BREAKING THEIR NECK!

2: I told you we should have bought the futon.

1: Are you gloating at a time like this?

2: Sorry. Was that another...? Could you turn the light on?

1: I can't reach.

2: The switch is right next to you.

1: But if I try and fail, then that could be emotionally devastating.

2: But it's right next to you.

1: Yes, but it might not work.

2: Well if it doesn't work then that would be good to know. So we can buy another one.

1: WE WON'T EVER BUY ANYTHING FROM YOU AGAIN, AMAZON!

2: EVER! What was that?

1: Nothing.

2: Was that you ordering something?

1: Amazon sent a Special on a flashlight.

2: But we have the light switch.

1: It was a really good Special.

2: What's the delivery time?

1: KNOWING AMAZON IT WILL PROBABLY TAKE –

1 & 2, *together*: – A WHOLE DAY!

2: Can't you just turn the light on? In the meantime?

1: Can't *you* turn the light on?

2: I don't have time to turn the light on.

1: What the hell are you doing?

2: Absolutely nothing of any meaning.

1: That *is* surprisingly time consuming.

2: Are you sure you can't just reach over? And switch the switch?

1: Fine.

2: Wait.

1: What?

2: It's just...

1: What?

2: Well, just...

1: What?

2: Do we really want to? See?

1: Good point.

2: We have tried that before.

1: Good point.

2: And we just turned it straight back off.

1: We do it multiple times a day.

2: The light goes on.

1: And then off.

2: And then on.

1: And then off.

    Silence.

2: You know what I think is a bummer?

1: What?

2: The speed of light.

1: Are you about to have one of your philosophical meltdowns?

2: No. I'm just saying. The speed of light is a bummer since – oh.

1: What happened?

2: I hate the part where your butt gets wet.

1: Would you prefer it was slower or faster?

2: I'd prefer to not have flood waters gushing through our home at all. Should we do something about that?

1: Yeah we should – I meant the speed of light: slower or – not that it matters since we won't switch it on.

2: We switch it on multiple times a day. We just discussed that.

1: We discuss complete lies all the time.

2: Good point.

1: There's just no point switching it on WHEN ALL YOU CAN SEE IS TUSCAN RED –

1 & 2, *together*: – YOU SHOULD BE ASHAMED, AMAZON!

2: Really there's nothing wrong with the dark.

1: The dark is very important.

2: Introspection. Intuition. Reflection.

1: But do we?

2: What?

1: Introspect?

2: We don't have time to just stand around and introspect.

1: I'm not exactly "standing."

2: Why are you not standing? The water must be filthy.

1: What defines "standing in water" versus "swimming" versus "drowning"?

2: Looks who's getting philosophical now.

1: *What's the meaning of life?*

2: *Who am I?*

      They both laugh a little.

      Silence.

1: So then, who are you?

2: I'm... I'm... I don't know.

1: Okay, who do you want to be?

2: Someone who – someone who switches on the light. Like a – like a person who... looks. And –and... sees. And then –

1: Hang on, is this metaphor a bit problematic for blind people: equating a lack of seeing with ignorance?

2: Good point.

1: We should be inclusive.

2: Definitely.

1: Let's keep the light off.

2: For equality.

1: Yes.

2: Definitely.

    Beat.

Although are blind people actually asking – oh.

1: What?

2: Was that another person floating by?

1: Probably.

2: Should we help them?

1: Probably.

2: Hello? Do you need help?

1: They're most likely dead.

2: I'm going to turn on the light.

A delivery drone arrives.

1: Wait – that'll be the flashlight delivery.

2: Hurry up so we can find them. Something smells strange. I hope you're not right that they're –

1: OMG AMAZON YOU SENT A FLASHLIGHT WITHOUT ANY BATTERIES?!

2: SERIOUSLY?!

1: WHAT THE HELL!

1 & 2, *together*: DISGRACEFUL!

1: AND THE PACKAGING?!

2: IT COULD FIT A DEAD BODY!

1: ZERO STAR RATING!

1 & 2, *together*: WE WON'T EVER BUY ANYTHING FROM YOU AGAIN, AMAZON!

2: Should we order batteries?

1: Just did.

2: So who do *you* want to be?

1: What?

2: Before when I said I wanted to be someone who...

1: I wish you were taller than me.

2: Why?

1: It's up to my armpits which means it must be nearly... Let's turn the light on – really this time.

> *Some nature sounds. A hypnotic voice.*

THE CORPORATIONS: Hello from your friends at The Corporations. Criminals have been apprehended for spreading fake news about the existence of "light switches." There is no such thing as a "light switch;" we are all already living in the light.

1: There's no such thing as a...?

THE CORPORATIONS: Any effort to find or activate this so-called "light switch" will cause catastrophic loss of jobs and plummeting economic prosperity.

1: I'm switching it on.

2: I don't want to lose my job.

1: You're about to lose your –

THE CORPORATIONS: You will be prosecuted to the full extent of the law.

1: You can't even swim – I'm turning it on.

THE CORPORATIONS: Or we may just kill you.

1: Oh.

2: Okay.

THE CORPORATIONS: So laze back in your luxurious indoor lake, salmon swishing swiftly by, gaze out at the Tuscan red sunset. This is *your* time. Finally. Relax.

The announcement cuts out. A few beats.

2: That does sound kind of nice.

The flick of a light switch.

2: AHHH! *(shielding eyes)* WHY DID YOU DO THAT?!

1: Oh my god grab onto something you're nearly –

2: TURN IT BACK OFF!

1: No.

2: TURN IT OFF!

1, *looks at audience*: Is that…?

2: PLEASE!

1: Look.

2: PLEASE?

1: LOOK!

An electric crackling. Black out.

SUNNY DRAKE is a playwright, theatre creator, performer and producer. His works have been translated into four languages and presented in over 60 cities across the world for a wide range of audiences, from elderly ladies in regional theatres to queers in underground warehouses. Born in Australia on

Jagera-Turrbal land (Brisbane), he has lived in Tkaronto (Toronto, Canada) since 2011, on the territory of the Two Row Wampum Belt Treaty.

THE WORD IS A SEED IS A WORLD IS A DEED

Clare Duffy

This play is inspired by Vandana Shiva and the links she draws between love, biodiversity, and the structures and powers of patriarchy and capitalism that work to separate things. I'm really interested in what a climate-just world would look like, feel like, sound like. What language would communicate such a radically different world? The play is also inspired by the loss of words of nature from the Oxford English Dictionary for children.[15] Finally, I'm inspired formally by Gertrude Stein's plays.[16]

NOTES:
Artists are given complete license to interpret the play however they wish. I'm hoping this is absurd, poetic, and that it might have some music in it. The words in the headings are all towns in Scotland.

~~~~~~~~~~

A IS FOR AIRDRIE

are you coming out?

in the rain?

yes.

my hair will melt.

it will grow again.

---

15   Flood, Alison. "Oxford Junior Dictionary's replacement of 'natural' words with 21st-century terms sparks outcry." *The Guardian*. January 13, 2015. https://www.theguardian.com/books/2015/jan/13/oxford-junior-dictionary-replacement-natural-words

16   Stein, Gertrude. *IIIIIIIIII* in *Geography and Plays*. The Four Seas Press, Boston. 1922. 189-198. https://www.gutenberg.org/files/33403/33403-h/33403-h.htm#IIIIIIIIII

and curly!

what's that?

what?

that high plain in the center of your neck

it's a pasture my love.

oh fuck. the sheep! the sheep! I forgot about the fucking sheep. baa! they'll be in bloody Glasgow by now.

B IS FOR BATHGATE

"boar wood" originally.

really?

oh aye.

it's a bastardization.

no.

oh aye.

you mean the word "boar" had sex with another word that it wasn't married to?! some slight-y, fly by night-y, bad seed and a few weeks later there was a "bath" baby growing in poor "boar"?

Nooooo.

so what happened to poor "boar," was she a single mother? did she live in the woods bringing up "bath" too ashamed to go show her face at the gate?

I think you're taking this a bit far.

far and away and over the hills?

yes.

I'm just saying.

b is also for bastard.

thanks. (*beat*) actually. "bastard" probably comes from "bastum," which probably comes from a French word meaning "packsaddle"… so once upon a time, there were some some-ones who used their packsaddles, off their ponies, for pillows and then in the morning they were gone again. It was a "wherever I put my packsaddle that's my home" kind-of-situation.

how idyllic, a packed bag under the stars, smelling the grass, the earth and the worms. It does make you want to get your head down.

or you might say that a packed bag is like a scrotum?

oh aye.

C IS FOR THE BEND BETWEEN THE HEIGHTS

Cromaty was always my favorite. a curved bay. curved like a "c." like the cu cu cu that the mouth makes. Cu cu cu.

"South Utsire: northwesterly 5 or 6. moderate or rough. occasional rain. good, occasionally poor. Forties, Cromarty: northwest 4 or 5, occasionally 6 at first. moderate, occasionally rough in northeast Forties. rain or drizzle, fog patches developing. moderate or good, occasionally very poor."

for me, before audio books and podcasts there was the radio shipping forecast at 00.48 every night. still. now. every night on BBC Radio 4. the seas of the British Isles, music: "Sailing By" and then the national anthem. God save the queen. it is the gateway to the world service and insomnia.

I knew if I was listening to the shipping forecast I was in trouble. I was about to embark on a flotsam night, watching stories from around the world floating by on the radio shock waves of British empire.

land and
body
grab
seeds
tongue
words
blood
seeds

rarely acknowledged and still enriching the mothership.

the shipping forecast lists the regions of the sea around the UK starting with most northerly.

viking, between Scotland and Norway, and then proceeding in a roughly clockwise direction:
North Utsire, South Utsire, Forties, Cromarty, Forth, Tyne, Dogger, Fisher, German bight, Humber, Thames, Dover, Wight, Portland, Plymouth, Biscay, Trafalgar, Fitzroy, Sole, Lundy, Fastnet, Irish Sea, Shannon, Rockall, Malin, Hebrides, Bailey, Fair Isle, Faeroes and Southeast Iceland.

D IS FOR DINGWALL

ding meant an assembly and then it became "thing." an object.

going to the ding tonight?
it meant a gathering of free people.

a riot.

nooooo. it's where the lawspeakers spake.

get out!

they did. they knew all the laws off by heart.

oral tradition.

no writing-it-down.

embodied.

words.

shared.

all together.

at the thing.

E IS FOR EDINBURGH

Eidyn might have been the burgh before Edin.

I can't help thinking of Eden.

what-ho utopia!

REAL LOVE IS THE ONLY THING

just because I don't want you to touch me, it doesn't mean I don't need your love.
just because I recoil from the squeak of skin touching skin
doesn't mean I don't need you.

just your too close breath fires splinters through every pore
but it doesn't mean I don't love you.

I know every crease inside your mouth, from the sound of you drinking your tea.
when you lick a smudge of chocolate from your lips, I lurch like a drunkard in a storm.
and your smile is my delight.

let our love stand naked in the sea and share the rocking of the waves.
let our love roll down mountains together.
let our intimacy sing through the crepuscular animals, beyond the table light.
just please don't ask to touch me. let me love you just as I am.

CLARE DUFFY is the artistic director of Civic Digits and co-director of Unlimited Theatre. She won a Pearson Award for her first full-length play, *Crossings*, in 2003. In October 2018, Clare's play *Arctic Oil* was presented at The Traverse Theatre, receiving four stars from the *Stage* and the *Herald*. She is an associate artist at Perth Theatre making *The Big Data Show*, which integrates ethical hacking, digital gaming, and live performance. Clare wrote and directed *Money the Game Show* for The Arches in 2011, which was remounted at The Bush in London and published by Oberon Books.

TWO VOICES

Brian Dykstra

I just read an article about a firm called Trillium Asset Management –
a "socially responsible investment firm" – which advocates, among other
things, divesting from companies that continue to add to the carnage of
climate change. Now, to be fair, I didn't investigate the company and don't
want to throw too much credit if it isn't deserved, but the concept was the
thing that inspired the piece.[17]

NOTE:

Some poets, or actors, are great at taking another poet's rhythms and speaking
them comfortably. Other times, even with a really talented performer, the
rhythm just doesn't fit in their mouth. This can be a sort of double-trouble with
a "team" poem like this one. Of course, it is totally possible that performers
chosen are on a similar heartbeat to the piece. But I can lay down a rough
recording of it in order to help the readers or performers with how it rings in
my ear. I have a director I work with who treats any spoken word section in
any play I write like a song the performer needs to learn. But, you know, maybe
you'll find the perfect duo to do this. Anyway, let me know what you need. By
my reading this should play around 4:20.

FIRST VOICE: Invested in our skies and seas
    Divesting from the companies
    That want us staying on our knees
    And praying old-school deities
    Will save our skins while / all of these
    Polluters argue needs
    That feeds their greed while / SEC's
    New rules kill opportunities
    That undermine the people's pleas

---

[17] Segerstrom, Carl. "Can the tools of capitalism curb climate change?" *High Country News*. March 27, 2019. https://www.hcn.org/issues/51.7/climate-change-can-the-tools-of-capitalism-curb-climate-change

To inoculate against disease
And / fight the fight for honeybees
While micro-plastic poison beads
Pollute us all with maladies
We never thought we'd ever see /
A hotter world for you and me
That / incubates the bugs that / leaves
Us lost for cures no one believes
Are even low priorities
Because we see the policies
Protecting businesses that seize
Our rights with tendencies
To treat us all like regencies
Treat serfs who / work the land for fees
Or / free while / kings and other royalties
Decree their emissaries
Carry profits even / robberies
Protected by the panoplies
Of profit, growth, twin knaveries
That lead us straight to eulogies /
I hate to say they put the squeeze
On not just us, but air that makes us wheeze
And waterways that can't appease
Our thirst. / It's chock-full of impurities. /
If we accept absurdities
Like these, with apathies
That overcooks our legacies
And overlooks that briberies
Get paid, / erasing boundaries
Protecting health or / wealth they're pleased
To seize / Deceived like patsies
Maybe we deserve our autopsies
Ignoring sorted butcheries
Because the casualties
Like everybody's families
Who die / before the factories
Will retrofit the shit they sneeze
Into the atmosphere like sleaze

That / squeezes us like nobodies.
We're not nobodies.
We Are The People.

SECOND VOICE: So, how do I know that nothing's ever gonna change?

FIRST VOICE: We're looking for the devotees

SECOND VOICE: Because we're human beings

FIRST VOICE: Who don't get scared by legalese

Or quake beneath attorney's fees

SECOND VOICE: And human beings take shit

FIRST VOICE: Who recognize the miseries

SECOND VOICE: Sometimes the shit we take is called an investment.

FIRST VOICE: Created by absurdities

SECOND VOICE: So, how is it I'm aware, *mon frère,* that polar bears can
    kiss their ever-less-chilly asses goodbye?

FIRST VOICE: Who stand up to barbarities

SECOND VOICE: How do I know that?

FIRST VOICE: And undermine bureaucracies.

SECOND VOICE: Because we all know what we're doing

FIRST VOICE: Embracing all the urgencies

SECOND VOICE: And we do it anyway.
    Because it's not supposed to happen for 50 years down the line. Right?
    Not really.

FIRST VOICE: But what about our families?

SECOND VOICE: And I never met nobody who gives the first shit about the great-grandkids they don't yet have.

FIRST VOICE: Innocent, those casualties.

SECOND VOICE: Let's face it, we take what we want. Feeling good when our mutual funds (holding just a little bit of company that spun off from Enron) outperform the market as a whole.

FIRST VOICE: Forgive us all our blasphemies.

SECOND VOICE: And who is it who stands between us and this uninhabitable planet

BOTH: While climate fleeing refugees

SECOND VOICE: Pop up all over the world?

BOTH: We do. – The Human Beings. – The People. – Me & You.

FIRST VOICE: We have these capabilities

SECOND VOICE: But we're going to count on the people?
On us?
We're going to count on us?
Really?

FIRST VOICE: We do have these abilities.

SECOND VOICE: Here's what I think. To those, those great grandkids, the ones who haven't been born quite yet: Let me be the first to tell you what my generation must to be thinking: Fuck you. You're on your own.

FIRST VOICE: Calamities.

SECOND VOICE: Because we got ours.

FIRST VOICE: And villainies

SECOND VOICE: And we're not done getting ours.

FIRST VOICE: Insanities.

SECOND VOICE: Just like human beings.

FIRST VOICE: Vulgarities

SECOND VOICE: Just like always. – Just under the wire.
  And, you? – Fuck are you going to do about it?
  See? This is more simple than poetry

FIRST VOICE: It don't require similes

SECOND VOICE: It's simple.
  We are standing directly in the way. And we do that until the day that
  we insist on some kind of reckoning. But we haven't done that yet.
  You know how I know what I know?
  I take a peek at your portfolio
  And if you're actually making cheddar

BOTH: Or any other kind of cheese
  Off any of these entities
  Belching methane, or refineries
  Then you're just a bunch of groupies –
  Who just know how to tease.

SECOND VOICE: If you can't

FIRST VOICE: Divest from all the companies

SECOND VOICE: Take that one simple step.

FIRST VOICE: That bite our backs like plaguing fleas

SECOND VOICE: If you can't

BOTH: Choke 'em out with currencies.

SECOND VOICE: You stay on the bench

BOTH: Embracing your hypocrisies.

SECOND VOICE: The Truth isn't difficult.

FIRST VOICE: Don't just be a bunch "visionaries."

SECOND VOICE: But we all gotta ask ourselves...

FIRST VOICE: Be revolutionaries.

SECOND VOICE: "How hard is that?"

BRIAN DYKSTRA is an actor, playwright, and HBO Def Poet. He is from Los Angeles and lives in New York City. This is his second play about climate. His first, *Clean Alternatives*, won a *Scotsman* Fringe First at the Edinburgh Festival Fringe, and played in a number of theatres in the U.S. It was about 100 minutes longer and had an intermission. Brian is married to Margarett and that fact makes him smile every single day.

SIX POLAR BEARS FELL OUT OF THE SKY THIS MORNING

Alister Emerson

I believe that comedy makes universal truths more palatable. I have always been inspired by the classic satirists such as Jonathon Swift, Molière, and Brecht, but I can't go past the modern comic masters of the absurd: Monty Python or Jon Stewart, who smack us in the face with the truth like a wet fish.

CHARACTERS (genders can be changed):
MADAME PRESS SECRETARY
ADVISOR TO THE PRESS SECRETARY
ADVISOR'S ASSISTANT
REPORTER

~~~~~~~~~~~~~~~~

MADAME PRESS SECRETARY, ADVISOR TO THE PRESS SECRETARY and ADVISOR'S ASSISTANT are in a corporate boardroom, the office of the PRESS SECRETARY.

ADVISOR: ... and then I said to my cleaning lady, "If everyone at my country club makes five hundred thousand dollars a year, it can't be that hard!"

PRESS SECRETARY, ADVISOR, and ASSISTANT laugh obnoxiously.

PRESS SECRETARY's phone buzzes and she is suddenly intently watching breaking news on her phone. She shows it to ADVISOR and ASSISTANT.

PRESS SECRETARY: Check out the breaking news. It's unbelievable.

Focus changes to a REPORTER speaking to the audience.

REPORTER: Residents of Wellington City [OR INSERT NAME OF LOCAL CITY] have awoken to a shocking and unprecedented event. According to eyewitness accounts, six polar bears fell out of the sky this morning. Despite falling from the sky, they miraculously landed unharmed and were last seen walking away in search of food.

Change focus back to PRESS SECRETARY, ADVISOR, and ASSISTANT.

ADVISOR: The greenies are going nuts and blaming climate change. Someone is going to have to do the press briefing and tell the public everything is okay. Just another day in paradise.

ADVISOR and ASSISTANT both silently stare at PRESS SECRETARY until she relents.

PRESS SECRETARY: Dammit. How can we spin this one?

ADVISOR: We could go with: no cause for alarm, it was a weather balloon.

ASSISTANT: Weather balloons go up; the polar bears fell down out of the sky.

ADVISOR: A weather balloon malfunction?

ASSISTANT: Or a satellite returning to earth that broke up into six polar bear-shaped pieces. Yes, that's good. But what about any eyewitnesses who saw the bears walk off in search of food?

ADVISOR: Unfortunately, the six polar bear-shaped pieces landed on six unlucky cows grazing near the city center. The cows were dazed by the falling space debris, but all were unharmed and walked away in search of food. In the confusion, drunken locals reported they saw polar bears.

PRESS SECRETARY: Plausible.

ADVISOR & ASSISTANT: Agreed.

PRESS SECRETARY, *looking at her phone*: Problem, one of the eyewitnesses posted photos of a polar bear walking away from the crash site. Already has 1.3 million likes.

ADVISOR: Okay... one of the polar-bear shaped pieces of the fallen satellite crashed into a visiting circus and landed on a polar bear cage, freeing the surprised but lucky polar bear. The circus was relieved to learn that their most precious bear... Mr. Fluffles, was unhurt, and looks forward to reuniting the bear with its dearest friend Bongo, the three-legged elephant, who has been crying all night since the polar bear went exploring around town.

PRESS SECRETARY: Plausible.

ADVISOR & ADVISOR: Agreed.

PRESS SECRETARY, *looking at her phone*: What? Apparently International Polar Bear Rescue already has people on the ground here with a video camera and just uploaded videos of four more of the bears wandering the city, climbing into dumpsters, snuffling through rubbish bins... and one of them just ate a poodle. 2.8 million hits on YouTube.

ADVISOR: Okay... okay... Excited and disorientated by the noise of falling pieces of polar bear-shaped satellite, a startled group of teenagers, who were out selling Girl Scout Cookies to raise money for an orphanage, and were dressed as polar bears, became confused and jumped into dumpsters to escape the noise. When they emerged, the youngest member of the group, little Sally...

ASSISTANT: ...who recently gave one of her kidneys to a complete stranger...

ADVISOR: ...realized she had dropped a contact lens during the commotion and asked the others in the group to help find it...

ASSISTANT: ...they combed the cold, lonely, city streets, even searching through rubbish bins for the precious contact lens...

ADVISOR: ...which used to belong to little Sally's dead grandmother and had been a gift to little Sally on her deathbed...

ASSISTANT: ...the teens were later surprised to learn that International Polar Bear Rescue may have inadvertently filmed them and are seeking damages for use of their images without permission.

PRESS SECRETARY, *hesitant*: Plausible?

ADVISOR & ASSISTANT: Agreed.

PRESS SECRETARY, *once more distracted by her phone but visibly rattled*: Son of a biscuit! What is wrong with these people? A helpful local has befriended the last of the fallen bears and has taken it home, giving it food, shelter, and a family who love it dearly. They will be appearing on a special episode of Oprah Winfrey at 8 p.m. tonight for the tell-all story of a bear that fell from the sky.

ADVISOR: We could discredit the bear, talk about how it was an alcoholic, seal pup-murdering savage, and fell out of a plane during a drunken bender while it was trying to snort coke off the air hostess.

ASSISTANT: Plausible.

ADVISOR: Agreed.

PRESS SECRETARY, *clearly exhausted by the mental effort*: Or maybe we could just tell the truth, the greenies are right. Admit that things are utterly out of control. The polar bears were flung halfway round the world by severe weather events caused by man-made climate change so rampant and so ridiculous that anything is possible.

> *PRESS SECRETARY collapses under the strain. ASSISTANT helps her off-stage, consoling her as they walk.*

ADVISOR: Come on Madame Press Secretary, you've had a stressful day. I think you need to go have a lie down and a nice cup of tea. Maybe some soothing music, and we can buy you a new puppy, and some new pajamas with pictures of rabbits on them...

> *ADVISOR gestures to the REPORTER to come onto stage, and whispers something in the REPORTER's ear. The REPORTER turns and addresses the audience.*

REPORTER: Residents of Wellington City [OR INSERT NAME OF LOCAL CITY] have awoken to a shocking and unprecedented event. A satellite containing poems written by children-from-around-the-world-who-were-lost-in-the-forest-as-babies-and-raised-by-wolves was returning to earth but unfortunately broke up on re-entry and crashed into government buildings. During the freak accident, a rogue piece of satellite smashed through a wall before landing in the office of the Press Secretary, killing six visiting orphan polar bears and decorated war hero Madame Press Secretary. Moments before tragedy struck, she was preparing to host a dinner in honor of left-handed orphan polar bears. Donald Trump has honored the late Press Secretary by promising that Mexico will pay for the wall.

ADVISOR: Plausible.

ALISTER EMERSON is a playwright from New Zealand and the Artistic Director of Duck Bunny Theatre, a small but feisty theatre company using satirical humor to comment on the absurdity of corporate stupidity, greed, and corruption. His recent plays include *The Fridge* and *Ed Sheeran Tastes Like Chicken*, a play about the plight of the endangered Māui dolphin which debuted at the Nelson Fringe Festival and was shortlisted for the NZ Playmarket Plays for the Young.

A DOG LOVES MANGO

Georgina Escobar

This play was inspired by the groundbreaking Dutch company Fruitleather Rotterdam, an innovative startup that uses principles of the circular economy to cut down on two environmental scourges: food waste and leather production.

~~~~~~~~~~~~~~~~~~~~

Lights rise on a special screening area at a small American town's airport security checkpoint. JEFF, a senior officer, and CLARA, his trainee, each hold a sneaker in their hand; they inspect it cautiously and almost comically meticulously – a swab around all parts, they smell, taste, pinch, and photograph the sneakers.

On a chair, with a bag by her side, LUCRETIA watches them, patiently.

A moment.

JEFF: You see Ms....?

LUCRETIA: André.

JEFF: Ms. Ahn-dreah, our dogs are highly trained and would never sniff you out if you had, well, if you had nothing on you that would alert the dog of the need to alert you to us and our staff. You see, Clara, we have highly trained dogs and they would never sniff, they would never accidentally *lick* a traveler's shoes if they weren't laced with – well with something dangerous.

CLARA: Mmm-hmm.

LUCRETIA: Did anything show up on your – what's on those cotton swabs anyway?

JEFF: Highly confidential... stuff.

LUCRETIA: Right. *(pause)* Well, I once heard a friend was detained in a similar room with, oh, I believe it was five of you trying to figure out why the dog nudged her.

CLARA: And what was it?

LUCRETIA: A beef rib.

JEFF: From where?

CLARA: She was traveling with a rib?

LUCRETIA: An artist. Needed it for an installation about – well about the amount of waste high-end restaurants produce? The rib was intact, you see, perfectly normal, perfectly edible –

CLARA: If you eat meat –

LUCRETIA: If you're an abomination and eat meat, yes, but the point is –

JEFF: You don't eat meat?

LUCRETIA: No. I'm afraid I am a lover of wildlife and well, I don't support the things that decimate the things I love. I did once. I was in a band with this guy that used to beat my sister up? In my defense I didn't know that, but when she told me I didn't believe her. Denial is our worst enemy, isn't it? We love the comfort of ignorance, it's not confrontational and that feels right. Well I learned my lesson so.... Anyway. I love wildlife and well, life in general so....

JEFF: You don't have to eat a wild boar, what about a cow? That ain't wild.

LUCRETIA: It's not what I meant, I meant that basically 90 percent of the destruction of, say, the Amazon, for example, is because of animal agriculture.

CLARA: I thought it was because of paper.

LUCRETIA: Because of… paper?

CLARA: Isn't that what they always say like when, you know what I'm talking 'bout Jeff, when Shila says "please don't print the entire email with all the threads and stuff, save a tree in the Amazon for fucks sake" she says, you know what I'm talking about?

JEFF: I don't know if she means the Amazon. I think she's more of a buy American hire American kind of gal.

LUCRETIA: Right…. Well. Anyway. No. I don't eat meat, but if the dog – the screening dog I mean – if it was able to find my friend's rib, I mean not her rib but the beef rib, well… you see where I'm going with this?

JEFF: Yeah I see where you're going with this.

Pause.

No I don't see where you're going with this.

CLARA: She means a dog's a dog and you can't tame nature and a dog's always gonna go after a bone, isn't that what you're saying?

JEFF: Our dogs are – they're staff members for one – and they're highly trained, highly skilled. You think our highly trained, highly skilled dog went to lick your shoe because it likes fresh I-talian leather? Where are you flying in from again?

LUCRETIA: Uh. San Diego.

JEFF: Exactly.

CLARA removes a piece of paper that the computer's spat out.

CLARA: Negative. Says she's clear.

LUCRETIA: Maybe your dog really likes mangos.

JEFF: Maybe our staff member wouldn't like it if you were talking smack.

LUCRETIA: I mean, I've known dogs that like fruit a whole lot.

CLARA: She's not wrong. My sister's dog eats oranges whole. Skin, pith and all.

JEFF: You know you're supposed to declare any fruits and vegetables you travel with Ms. Andrea?

LUCRETIA: It's André, and yes of course. But... I mean. It's dehydrated.

JEFF: Where is it?

LUCRETIA: Uhm. You're holding it in your hands.

> *JEFF eyes LUCRETIA suspiciously, he squints his eyes while CLARA drops the shoe as if it were suddenly a hot potato.*

JEFF: We don't take lightly being made fun of here at security.

LUCRETIA: No, please, I'm not. I mean that those sneakers? They're made of mango leather.

CLARA: Shut the front door!

JEFF: Clara.

CLARA: Sorry. You mean like, you mean like the fruit leather you eat?

LUCRETIA: Sort of. It's more – I actually don't know the specifics, I just know someone said this company from Rotterdam was making sneakers out of mango leather instead of real leather and I was like Sign Me Up! I mean so much fruit never makes it from farm to table, but rather from farm to trash, you know?

CLARA: Is it true elephants get piss drunk off of rotten mangoes?

JEFF: That's monkeys.

LUCRETIA: Uhm I'm not too sure actually if there's, like, mangoes wherever elephants are but – I don't know actually. But I just know this company's also like created a bunch of jobs for troubled youth? I mean could you imagine that here? You get a kid giving you trouble you send them to take the pits out of mangos or you're like "goshdarnit Josh I'm tired of you not doing your homework, this weekend you get to mash the mangos!" instead of like, I don't know, sending them to work at slaughterhouses and traumatizing them for life.

JEFF: My cousin Nelly worked at a pig farm. Then moved to the slaughterhouse. A promotion they said.... Ain't never been the same since.

LUCRETIA: She eat bacon?

JEFF: Come to think of it... I only ever see her eating fruit...

LUCRETIA: Yeah well fruit's abundant. That is, if we can keep it from being decimated. It's all one big cycle.

CLARA: Does it smell like mango?

LUCRETIA: I mean I've had these for a –

CLARA takes a deep whiff.

Oh okay... uhm...

CLARA: They most definitely do NOT smell like mangoes.

LUCRETIA: Yeah they're my travel shoes? So... Anyway, so is it okay for me to go?

JEFF: We gotta talk to Smalls about Kiki. Maybe Kiki really likes mangoes....

LUCRETIA: Yeah maybe. I mean. I don't blame Kiki. And honestly, these shoes? They really are a treat for your feet.

CLARA: Oh ha ha! That's funny! That's punny!

LUCRETIA: "If you've been looking for a pun to run with, try shoe puns"

JEFF: You're good.

LUCRETIA: I'll be here all night.

Pause.

No, but seriously – I won't be here all night, right?

GEORGINA H.L. ESCOBAR is an artist and play-maker based in New York City. She employs multiple mediums including performance, visual art, puppetry, and music to create impossible narratives for the stage. She has participated in residencies including the MacDowell Colony and the Djerassi Artists Residency, and is a recipient of the Theatre For Young Audiences National Award from the Kennedy Center. Her work has been exhibited throughout the U.S. and in festivals internationally (Denmark, Sweden). Artistic partners and presenters have included Milagro (OR), Clubbed Thumb, Lincoln Center, INTAR, Aurora Theatre, Bushwick Starr, Dixon Place, The Flea, and the Latinx Theatre Commons, among many others.

THERE ARE A LOT OF STORIES YOU CAN TELL ABOUT HUMANITY

David Finnigan

You know what, I got deep into writing a traditional playscript format with *characters* and *stage directions* and, y'know, *subtext*, and then decided that that's not what I wanted to do, that was not the best way to treat this subject. So this, this is literally two stories, and I trust you guys to perform them any way you choose, however you feel, there are no wrong moves.

~~~~~~~~~~

There are a lot of stories you can tell about humanity. Here are two of my favorites:

Humanity was born in the Rift Valley in Kenya. It spent its infancy and most of its childhood in East Africa.

It had siblings, other hominid species it grew up alongside, and who one by one passed away. Mysteriously or not.

There was a moment late in humanity's childhood when it came close to expiring. 75,000 years ago, during the last Ice Age, the Toba Volcano erupted. A huge eruption that blocked the sun from the sky for three years and locked the earth into a horrific deep freeze. Humanity lost all but 15,000 individuals living in the Ethiopian highlands. The species had a very tough time of it, it came very close to going extinct altogether.

That's, my grandparents, yours, everyone you've ever met, all of us trace our ancestry back to that community of 15,000 people in the highlands.

After the weather warmed again, humanity spread out of Africa into Europe and the rest of the world.

And then, a few thousand years ago, the Ice Age ended. The species came out of its childhood and it began to develop very suddenly. Population growth, technological growth. It became rapidly stronger, more intelligent. You could say the species hit puberty.

But like a lot of adolescents, its emotional development hasn't caught up with its physical and mental growth.

As in: it hasn't yet learned to empathize and collaborate with others, it's still on occasion thoughtlessly cruel and abusive. Still bewitched by material technology. Still unconcerned about planning for the future.

And in order to make it to adulthood, humanity will need to survive what looks like some pretty tempestuous teenage years.

Another story:

Imagine a ship sailing from the past into the future. We are the passengers on this ship, we are also the crew.

We have limited resources, and there are no other ships out there. We are completely on our own.

Every decision we make, every action we take, slightly alters our course.

For a long time, let's say the last 12,000 years, we were sailing in one direction, at a steady speed, and that course seemed pretty safe.

About 200 years ago, give or take, we started to change course. We took on new passengers at an exponential rate. And we started accelerating in this new direction faster and faster.

Right now we're in unfamiliar waters. As far as we know, no one's ever been here before.

There are some people who think we're steering into danger. If there's a safe operating space, we're not in it any more. There are signs that we may have sailed into a hidden reef and there are rocks ahead of us and around us that we can't see. We could be about to rip a hole in our hull at any moment and start taking on water.

We can't turn around and go back the way we came. A ship with nearly ten billion passengers, you can't just put it in reverse or do a U-turn.

We have to navigate through somehow. We have to pick our way between the rocks and make it back out to clear seas.

And if we get in trouble – if we hit a reef and start sinking, in the middle of the ocean, there is no one coming to help us.

DAVID FINNIGAN is a writer and performer raised on Ngunawal land in Australia.

OWN NOW!

David Geary

I'd like to thank Dr. Scott Sampson, the CEO of Science World in Vancouver, Canada, for his inspiring talk about the great disruption between Humans and Nature. I'd also like to acknowledge the Spinoff article by Danyl Mclauchlan, "The Subtle Art of Not Giving a Fuck About Jordan B. Peterson," which references Scott Alexander and his short story "Sort by Controversial," which introduces the idea of "'Scissors': ideas or arguments or scenarios algorithmically designed to tear people apart."[18]

SETTING:
A large auditorium, arena, community hall, church, house of commons…
If possible, a large screen with images of a world in conflict and the ravages of climate change. If not, no sweat.

CHARACTERS:
SCISSORMAN, a modern day shaman/charlatan/self-help guru/politician
JC, Jesus Christ herself, trickster

~~~~~~~~~~~~~~~~

Powerful stadium anthem music plays, builds to a crescendo.

ANNOUNCER: It is time. He is here. Raise your hands. Put them together and Own Now!

SCISSORMAN bounds onto the stage, slick and professional, carrying a briefcase. Tumultuous applause. The screen changes to flashing "OWN" "NOW" "OWN" "NOW" "OWN" "NOW."

---

18   Mclauchlan, Danyl. "The Subtle Art of Not Giving a Fuck About Jordan B. Peterson." *The Spinoff.* February 18, 2019. https://thespinoff.co.nz/books/18-02-2019/the-subtle-art-of-not-giving-a-fuck-about-jordan-b-peterson/ Alexander, Scott. "Sort By Controversial." *Slate Star Codex.* October 30, 2018. https://slatestarcodex.com/2018/10/30/sort-by-controversial/

SCISSORMAN: Own! Now!

> *He makes the local sign language symbols for "Own" and "Now."*

Own! Now! Thank you! I own you now!

> *He makes the local sign language symbols for "Bull" and "Shit."*

Bull! Shit! No one owns you. Brothers, look under your seats, you will find my new book! Are you looking? *(pause)* Look harder! *(pause)* Okay, it's not there. Why not? Because we burn books. Books kill trees. My latest book, *OWN NOW!*, is a download from here *(points to his head)* to here *(makes heart over his heart)*.

Let's talk about decadence and dog videos.

> *Screen shows cute dog videos.*

Save the Planet – Eat your pets. Nod, nod, smile, nod, make heart symbol.

> *Nods, nods, smiles, nods, makes heart symbol.*

Yes, I'm reading an autocue, folks. It's my direct line to the Lord. Hallelujah, are you bored, Brothers? Tired of information overload – well, the tedium is the message. And I'm here to get you excited about The Great Disruption. Man vs. Nature vs. Nurture vs. Nietzsche vs. the Creature Feature Monster Movie that is the international political shitfight cluster fuck – forget-about-it, and Own Now!

I am the Great Disruptor. And *(does his James Brown impersonation)* and I feel good! Because we're going to capture The Rapture in my next chapter.

And let me tell you there is no left or right, or right or wrong. No center. The center cannot hold. Let's make a Quantum Leap together.

He does a spectacular leap, roll, and pose, or jumps on the spot.

Why are we so afraid of bombs? The universe is a bomb! And I am the Big Bang. Think about that. Own now.

Pauses. Freezes. Makes head exploding gesture

Questions! Questions? Are the mics ready? But first we got some housekeeping, or maybe housecleaning to do. How was the meal? Nobody eating with anyone other than their wife, am I right? Their surrendered wife? Brothers, are there any Sisters here? Because we've had some sinful sinister Sisters sneaking into these events, wondering what the men are talking about. They get curious, but you know what, curiosity killed the cat, and that's not all... Who wants to see a holy relic?

He holds his briefcase up as if a holy relic. He opens it towards himself. He's hit by a divine glow from inside.

I received this gift from a special brother from the Middle East.

SCISSORMAN pulls out a gold bone saw and holds it aloft.

A Prince of a Man. Ah-huh. You know who I'm talking about. It's the real deal. Did the damage. Cut through the Istanbullshit! You know the story. The journalist who went into the consulate to get his marriage papers, and ended up at his funeral. You might have read one of his pieces. Badummcha!

Punctuates joke. Pause.

Too soon? *(pause)* No! No, we follow the Chinese proverb: Kill the chicken to scare the monkeys. Journalism is Dead! Long live the Bloggers! The trolls! The hackers! The robo-callers. Long live the Disruptors, the Dividers, the bi-polarized bears unable to escape the binary: Good vs. Evil vs. Funkier Than A Mosquito's Boll Weevil Tweeter. Let's talk about The Rapture.

These fires and floods, typhoons and hurricanes, that are engulfing us all, don't be afraid, because they are part of "The Grand Plan" – The End of Days: They are the cleansing fires. Noah's flood come back to rid the world of the D-Generation of Degenerates. Only when we hold life sacred again, only when we build walls from the cement made from the pulverized bones of the Unbelievers, and the barbed wire drips with the blood of the hordes who would rain down their foreign diseases upon us, and we're not just talking measles… Only when we lock up those who would falsely accuse us, only when Hollywood burns will we truly own now! And be free to tell our truths.

Then He will come back to lead us…

From the audience a cloaked figure slowly rises.

… to Paradise. But first we must develop some immunity to community. Stop listening to the Global Village Idiots. And the self-help, self-hate, self-harm charlatans with their chicken soup for the arsehole Russell Rebrand new age guru Devil worship at the Church of New Me-dia. Who put the "me" into me-dia! Tweet that #ownnow Post that! Like that!

And own Easter! We got to crucify that cute bunny that is Mother Nature. Only then can He truly rise again. Sorry, are you feeling triggered? I'll show you a trigger.

Makes finger guns, points them at either side of his head and then suddenly at the audience. He mimes shooting them.

We needed our guns because the Sheriff was a long way away, but, Brothers, now we are the Sheriff, and no one is taking our guns away!

He finally stops to take in the standing figure.

Brother, Brother, are you ready to ride? … or do you need the bathroom? *(to wings)* Where are the bathrooms?

JC, *to audience*: Behold…

SCISSORMAN: Where is um... Security?

JC: ... Scissorman!

> *Pause. A loud sound of lightning striking. Lightning strikes SCISSORMAN. A light show... or whatever you can manage. SCISSORMAN rips off his corporate gear to reveal the superhero costume of SCISSORMAN, complete with logo. He takes large scissors from his briefcase and poses with them.*

JC: Everything Scissorman says is designed to divide us, to cut us. To dominate the news cycle so you can't hear any other voices, can't hear the voices of reason.

SCISSORMAN: No, voices of Treason! Fear me. For I am Scissorman, and... I'm running with scissors!

> *SCISSORMAN runs menacingly around the audience with his scissors.*

Get out your phones. Shoot me now. Livestream me! Own now!

> *JC takes out their phone and livestreams SCISSORMAN on FaceTime or YouTube or whatever platform you want. It comes up on the screen(s). SCISSORMAN runs around the audience snipping scissors and improvising lines about the issues that would work as scissors and instantly polarize the local audience, e.g.:*

Vaccinations cause autism and/or "What never grows old? Dark humor and unvaccinated children," ban cars, more bike lanes, smoke-free city, eat your pets, stop the pipeline, stop paying taxes, free university tuition, #metoo, #noteveryman...

> *SCISSORMAN stops, breathless, to check a device on his wrist.*

JC: He's checking his ratings, his Fitbit for his soul. You know he has an earpiece under his hairpiece. He's a puppet.

SCISSORMAN: I am no one's puppet! I am the real deal – the truth and the light. Whereas you, Jesus, you are the one who has divided the people far more than me. Remember the Crusades, the Witch Trials, the Doctrine of Discovery, the... Schools. All done in your name.

JC: No, they used me –

SCISSORMAN: You are –

JC: ... used my name to –

SCISSORMAN: You are the Scissorman!

JC: No, you are the Scissorman!

SCISSORMAN: Rock, paper, scissors!

> *They jump into a game of rock, paper, scissors but do scissors every time.*

JC & SCISSORMAN: Scissors! Scissors! Scissors! Scissors! Scissors! Scissors! Scissors!

JC: Rock!

SCISSORMAN: Paper!

> *SCISSORMAN celebrates. In slow-motion, he wraps his paper hand around JC's rock hand. JC winces in pains.*

SCISSORMAN, *after a pause*: I don't like playing the bad guy.

JC: I forgive you, my son.

SCISSORMAN: Oh fuck you!

> *SCISSORMAN goes for his scissors and makes to snip JC. JC scrambles to grab the bone saw. They battle – snipping*

and sawing bits off each other, taking grievous wounds, until both are exhausted, near death.

SCISSORMAN: How does it end?

JC: The sun flames out, everything that we know and love is gone... forever.

SCISSORMAN: Ashes to ashes.

JC: Stardust to stardust.

SCISSORMAN, *to audience*: I'm sorry I said those bad words before. Everyone knows this is just a show, right? And I was acting? I'm ... [*Actor's real name and what they do personally about climate change, e.g.: I have a metal straw, and a glass straw, and a metal drink container, and a bus pass, and I went on the march, and...*]

JC: And I'm not really Jesus, but we can own right now!

SCISSORMAN: She's actually my wife.

> *JC and SCISSORMAN kiss, get out their phones, and go out into the audience. They encourage the audience to do the same. The names and phone numbers of local representatives appear on the screens.*

JC & SCISSORMAN: We can get out our phones. Get out your phones. Find the number of our local representative, local MP, local Council, Mayor, Prime Minister, CEO, and tell them we want to meet and talk to them about Climate –

JC: Change.

SCISSORMAN: Crisis.

JC & SCISSORMAN: Emergency. Right now. That's our gift. The present is the present. Own now!

SCISSORMAN: And while you are there, head to the App shop. Install JC & SCISSORMAN and our new download:

JC & SCISSORMAN: Capture the Rapture!

SCISSORMAN: You've been a wonderful crowd. It's been real. And so, Brothers... and Sisters, let's dance!

> *Curtain. Blondie's "Rapture" plays. The cast lip sync, dance & encourage the audience to join in.*

DAVID GEARY is a playwright, screenwriter, documentary maker, director, actor, teacher, and writer of haiku on Twitter. He is a member of the Taranaki Māori iwi-tribe and grew up in Aotearoa (New Zealand) enthralled by the trickster stories of Māui. He has now found a new home among the Raven and Coyote tricksters of Turtle Island (in Canada). He's rapt to be part of CCTA again, after creating *Morehu & Titi* and *Science is Dead!* for previous iterations.

YOU'RE DAVID SUZUKI, AREN'T YOU?

Nelson Gray

Scientist, author, media host, and the most prominent environmental activist in Canada, David Suzuki is, as they say, a force of nature. All his life, he has combined an unquenchable curiosity for the empirical wonders of the physical world with an unwavering defense of this blue-green planet. Like anyone in the public eye, he has his detractors – those who call him sanctimonious, arrogant, cranky, and hypocritical – and he himself has been quick to admit that he too often shoots from the lip. Yet Suzuki's tireless work on behalf of the biosphere, along with his commitment to environmental justice, has made him one of the most admired and trusted public figures in Canada. In what follows, I imagine the elder Suzuki, among those who curse, cajole, bless, and love him: one person who has made a difference in the world, and around whom an entire community has formed.

CHARACTERS:
DAVID SUZUKI, 83 years old
ADMIRING VOICE
A WOMAN and HER DAUGHTER
DAVID'S GRANDSON, a young child of six
Four ACCUSING MEN
THE GHOST OF DAVID'S FATHER
A REPORTER
TARA, David's wife
SEVERN, David's daughter
ANOTHER GRANDCHILD
DAVID'S BEST FRIEND
GHOST OF HIS MOTHER
TAMO, David's grandson

DAVID SUZUKI appears, center stage, in a pool of light. He is alone at his computer, working feverishly on a campaign for ocean protection, when voices begin to speak to him.

ADMIRING VOICE: David Suzuki.

DAVID continues to type.

ADMIRING VOICE: You're David Suzuki, aren't you?

DAVID continues to type and to look at his screen.

ADMIRING VOICE: The scientist? The environmental activist?

DAVID, *continuing to type and look at his screen*: I'm just one person.

A WOMAN *appears, in silhouette far upstage, with her young daughter*: You are, though, aren't you – so (*holding out a book for an autograph*) ... would you mind? My daughter is a very big fan.

DAVID, *standing up and addressing the woman as if she is someone in the audience*: Well, thank you, yes, that's very nice, but I'm really just one person.

DAVID'S GRANDSON appears, standing far upstage, very small.

DAVID'S GRANDSON: You're famous, though – right, Grandpa? That's what the kids at school say.

DAVID: Is that what they say?

GRANDSON: They say you're on TV.

DAVID: Well, yes, that's true – but being famous is not... I mean that's not something you should ever strive for.

A MAN appears, far stage left.

MAN, *accusing*: David Suzuki – I don't believe it!

DAVID: I'm sorry?

A SECOND MAN appears, center left.

SECOND MAN, *accusing*: You know how impossible it is to get to you!

DAVID, *looking up, a little bewildered*: Excuse me – do I know you?

A THIRD MAN appears, far stage right.

THIRD MAN, *accusing*: Over a hundred letters I sent to you, and not even one bloody answer!!

DAVID, *starting to get irked*: Well, I'm very sorry, but if you're that *salmon farmer...*

A FOURTH MAN, the CEO of a lumber company, appears, center right.

A FOURTH MAN: You know, Suzuki, what tree-huggers like you don't get is who the hell's going to pay for all the –

DAVID, *getting more pissed off*: Look – what do you want from me, because –

FIRST MAN, *interrupting*: And unless you flew here in a solar-powered jet –

DAVID, *protesting*: – because I pay for every mile I fly to offset the carbon!

ALL THE MEN TOGETHER, *attacking*: Oh yes – because you can, can't you. Because you're such a rich, famous, and powerful man!

DAVID: Oh, piss off! You think I care about that!

THE GHOST OF DAVID'S FATHER appears.

THE GHOST OF DAVID'S FATHER: That's right, son.

DAVID: Father?

THE GHOST OF DAVID'S FATHER: If all you care about is getting people to like you, you won't stand for a goddamned thing!

DAVID: I suppose so, Father, but sometimes I –

A REPORTER: Dr. Suzuki.

DAVID: I beg your pardon?

A REPORTER: I'm from the *National Post* and...

DAVID, *somewhat impatiently*: Yes, and?

A REPORTER: And our readers are curious: What will you care about *after* you're gone?

DAVID: What? When I'm dead?

A REPORTER: Yes –

DAVID: When I'm *dead?* I can't even believe you're asking me that. When I'm dead I won't care about anything! Because I'll be *dead*!

> *TARA appears.*

TARA: But you care now, don't you, David?

DAVID: Tara?

TARA: You remember when we first met?

> *As TARA, in extreme slow motion, begins to approach him, the other characters on stage do so as well, drawing closer and closer to him in a semi-circle.*

DAVID: Of course – how could I forget about that!

TARA: And that huge snowy owl flew in and perched at the window.

DAVID: And the light that singled you out from the crowd.

TARA: And after all these years later, your greatest achievement...

> *More and more people, of various ages, sizes, and ethnicities*
> *begin to appear now, and, like the others, move in extreme*
> *slow motion toward him.*

DAVID: Getting you to marry me, Tara!

SEVERN: And you care about your grandchildren, don't you, Dad.

DAVID: Severn? Where are you calling from?

SEVERN: Haida Gwai!

> *ANOTHER GRANDCHILD comes in, holding a crab.*

ANOTHER GRANDCHILD: Bampa – look! A crab.

DAVID, *like a little kid himself:* Yes, yes! Can you see what kind it is?

DAVID'S BEST FRIEND: And you care about me, don't you, David, my oldest and dearest friend? Do you still have the handle I carved for your door?

DAVID: I think of you every time I touch it.

GHOST OF HIS MOTHER: And is the clematis still in the front yard, where my ashes are buried?

DAVID: Yes – yes, of course, Mother.

TAMO: And you cared about me, grandfather, when I got arrested at the Kinder Morgan protest.

DAVID, *angry and protesting:* They had no right to drag my grandson across that line!

Because he had the guts to do what was right.
And because this is the 59th minute of our last Earth hour
and because now that I'm in the death zone I can say
whatever I think without holding back
and because my grandchildren
and the clematis in the front yard
and because what I was taught to believe in
and the handle you carved for the front door
of the only home I enter
still remain
and the sweetness of the atmosphere
and the sparkling sea
and the sun's bright light on me
and the hydrological cycle that became
the first science lesson I learned
and the sacred Earth I was
am
and will soon, in some new way, remain

> *Speaking to everyone that has surrounded him now and to
> the audience.*

and because of the world we must all know now
we must now all hope to imagine together

EVERYONE AROUND HIM, *speaking at once*: David Suzuki. You're
   David Suzuki, aren't you?

> *Pause.*

DAVID: Yes, yes – but I'm just one person.

NELSON GRAY is a writer and director, and a professor of English at
Vancouver Island University. His interdisciplinary performances, co-created
with Lee Eisler, have been produced nationally and internationally, and he
was the co-founder, with Beth Carruthers and DB Boyko, of the SongBird

Project, one of the first eco-art projects in Canada. Nelson's play *Talker's Town* was recently published in a volume with Marie Clements' *The Girl Who Swam Forever*, and he is currently working toward the production of *Here Oceans Roar*, a contemporary opera for the Anthropocene.

THE DONATION
(FOR CHRISTOPHER FRY)

Jordan Hall

Climate change needs a different kind of heroism. You see it when you look at organizations like Project Drawdown: a heroism of endurance, of everyday work.[19] I was thinking this when I stumbled on an *Atlantic* article about climate anxiety and suicide,[20] which promptly smashed into Fry's glittering springtime comedy, *The Lady's Not for Burning*, and here we are.

CHARACTERS:
JEN, practical, overworked
TOMMY, good-hearted, if a little drunk

NOTES:
Though this is (hopefully) a comedy, climate anxiety and depression are serious, and I'd love for you to post a resource for anyone who might be affected at the end of the performance. Finally, I've written Jen and Tommy as a woman and a man in homage to Fry's characters. I invite you to recast them freely as any combination of genders and adjust pronouns accordingly.

~~~~~~~~~~~~

JEN sits at her desk. She's an overworked nonprofit kind of girl.

JEN: Alright. So if we lower the thermostat by another two degrees...

TOMMY, a discharged soldier, a little drunk, starts hammering on JEN's office window.

---

19 Hawken, Paul. *Drawdown: The Most Comprehensive Plan Ever Proposed to Reverse Global Warming.* Penguin Books, New York, 2017.

20 Meyer, Robinson. "Climate Change May Cause 26,000 More U.S. Suicides by 2050." *The Atlantic.* July 23, 2018. https://www.theatlantic.com/science/archive/2018/07/high-temperatures-cause-suicide-rates-to-increase/565826/

TOMMY: Anyone?

JEN: ...and get Alison to wear a goddamn sweater instead of using that bloody space heater...

TOMMY: Hello? Anyone?

JEN: That could save us another fifty kilos or so...

TOMMY: I can see you there ignoring me!

> *With a sigh, JEN opens the window. Just a crack.*

JEN: We aren't open. If you're here for a canvassing job, there's another intake on Monday.

TOMMY: I'm here to make a donation.

JEN: That's terrific. You can do that on the website.

TOMMY: It's not that kind of donation.

JEN: Oh. No. We don't accept gifts-in-kind. We're a nonprofit so we don't have the infrastructure –

TOMMY: I want to give you my life.

> *There's a beat. TOMMY pushes the window open the rest of the way and hops inside.*

JEN: What?

TOMMY: I want to donate my life.

JEN: Do – you mean you want to volunteer? God. If I had a nickel for every guilt-ridden drunk who rolls up wanting to save the world. Look. I'm just the office manager. There are pamphlets outside, you sign up and – you might not get to kayak in front of an oil rig right away, but –

TOMMY: No – I mean, the kayaking sounds exhilarating. But I want to donate my life.

JEN: I'm missing something, aren't I?

TOMMY: I thought if I came here the donation could be properly recorded. And you could advise me about the most carbon-neutral way to do it? Because I was thinking about pills – but then I might be sending toxins into the groundwater? And there's always a gun – but that would mean supporting weapons manufacturing and I'm not really comfortable with that.

JEN: Are you – are you talking about killing yourself? Can I call somebody to help you? Like a friend? Or a therapist? Or a hotline?

TOMMY: This isn't a suicide thing.

JEN: It kinda sounds like one.

TOMMY: No. I know. I get it. But think of it like this. If we were in a foxhole, taking fire, and I could cover you to get to the Jeep – but laying down cover was gonna get me shot? If I did that – knowing I was gonna get shot – that's not suicide. Not really.

JEN: But you aren't talking about –

TOMMY: Of course I am. I've seen the UN Report. Droughts. Sea-level rise. Climate change casualties are at 400,000 per year, and it's gonna get higher. And in order to stop it, we need to hit net zero by 2050. That's how we get to the Jeep. I'm 25. Say I've got 50 years left, that's 900 tons of carbon. I can give that back to you. I can give you that much cover.

JEN: That's oddly noble – and – I can see you've thought about this – but neither I nor the organization I represent want you to do that. There are – there are better ways for you to help.

TOMMY: Not really. Not that'll save us 900 tons.

JEN: Green living. Public transit. Vegetarian diet.

TOMMY: 300 at best.

JEN: Well then, make a bigger difference. Protests, lobby for green candidates

TOMMY: Because that's been a roaring success for the last 50 years, hasn't it. Look. I'm not here to make you feel bad. You seem lovely. With your night school law books, here at 7 a.m. If you really don't want my life, I'll just nip over to Greenpeace –

JEN: No!

TOMMY: It's really no trouble.

JEN: No. You should stay here. Stay here, and I'll make a cup of tea, and we'll talk.

TOMMY: You're just going to keep trying to talk me out of it.

JEN: Well, I – Yes. Please. Have some tea. Things always seem better after a cup of tea. Give me that long. And if I can't talk you out of it, I'll let you go... donate to Greenpeace.

TOMMY: ... Alright.

JEN: Alright. Alright. Now you just stay... Stay...

> *Keeping her eyes on him at all times, she nips offstage for a second, and then dashes back on.*

JEN: There. Kettle's on. So. So-so-so. How did you – how did you think of your – donation?

TOMMY: Oh. Well. I was down at the pub. Nowhere else to be. And the news came on with the UN report and I looked at my beer – leaving this half-moon of wet on the bar – and I wondered how much carbon went into it? Into me. All the cold beers and steak pies and my Da's car.

What had I done to be worth so much? What had I done at all? Except get discharged –

JEN: Discharged?

TOMMY: That's not the important part. And anyway, it all comes back to this.

JEN: Comes back to this how?

TOMMY: All of it. Army. Police. We say democracy. Human rights. But mostly we help old men say where the money goes. Or the oil. Or the mine. You know it because when it really is about democracy or human rights, they tell you to protect the pipeline, and not the people.

JEN: Is that what happened?

TOMMY: I told you that doesn't matter. What matters is I can do this now. And it will save lives. 900 tons. That's five people in South America. Fifteen in India. Thirty-six in the Maldives.

JEN: Or one here.

TOMMY: Pretty much my point.

JEN: Well then, maybe I should do it too.

TOMMY: Do what?

JEN: Donate my life.

TOMMY: But – no. I don't want you to do that.

JEN: Oh. I see. It's fine for you, but not for me?

TOMMY: Yes. I'm a grotesque waste of resources, and you're – you're –

JEN: What? I'm worth at least 600 tons. And what am I doing, really? Looking for improvements in heating technology and paperless office procedures? Going to law school at night so that in five years I can intern for a lawyer who supports Indigenous land claims or environmental class action suits? Band-Aid on a bullet hole. Your way is much better – all the good I'm ever going to do, all rolled up into one moment. And best of all, I don't have to stick around and find out the hard way if it doesn't work. Or – y'know – for the cleanup.

TOMMY: No. You are deliberately twisting –

JEN: How so?

TOMMY: This isn't some kind of escapist – this isn't me trying to get away from –

JEN: Whatever it is you don't want to talk about?

TOMMY: I told you, that isn't –

JEN: Then why not just tell me?

A beat. She's got him. TOMMY takes a deep breath.

TOMMY: It wasn't a big thing. There was this protest, downtown. They said we were there to maintain order. But we weren't. We were there to scare them. To remind them what would happen if they really got in the way of the money. We knew it, and they knew it. There was this girl – in one of those "Got Land?" t-shirts – and she got in my friend Nick's face. Yelling that he was a "Corporate Colonial Thug." Just yelling. But it's getting under Nick's skin and he tells her to shut up. And she won't – she keeps going "I will not be she who betrayed her people." And Nick – Nick's got a baton – so he hits her in the face, and they drag her into the van. And I didn't do anything. I just watched. Then later, in the locker room, Nick's making fun of her. Doing this voice: "I will not be she who betrayed her people. I will not be she – " Except we were. Because that girl is trying to get us all to the Jeep. And what were we doing? So I hit Nick in the face, and he cracked his head on a locker. And they discharged me.

JEN: And so you thought, if you couldn't be a hero that way, you'd find yourself another.

He nods. She sighs.

Why do people always think some grand gesture is how we save the world?

TOMMY: I don't – wait. What?

JEN: I know the big sacrifice looks romantic – but don't you think we might be better off if the sort of person who'd donate his life would stick around? To lobby for green policies and better public transit and even to lower the bloody thermostat. Because heating efficiency represents a potential nine billion tons in carbon savings for the planet, thank you very much.

There's a moment between them. Then TOMMY recoils.

TOMMY: Oh. Oh no no no no – I can see what you're doing here. You're trying to save my life by making me fall in love with you!

JEN: What? No. That's – even *if* I thought you were... charming? You are clearly unhinged!

TOMMY: Charming? You think I'm – ? Oh! Shameless! Here I am, set to give my life for the planet, and you come along with your blandishments of incremental change and the nobility of thermostats! I will not be swayed by some siren office manager! I'm going to Greenpeace!

He starts climbing back out her window. JEN casts about for a way to stop him.

JEN: No! You can't! I won't let you! I – (*a moment of desperation*) I accept your donation!

They both freeze. TOMMY's half out the window. A beat.

TOMMY: But – I haven't made it yet.

JEN: Yes. Yes, you have. You came to donate your life and I've accepted it and now – now, you have to do what I say. And I say you have to do the work. To come back on Monday, and apply for a canvassing job. To eat vegetarian and ride buses and go to protests and to *live*.

TOMMY: But there's still all of it – melting ice caps, and climate change deniers, and the old men, killing people for greed. Still those 900 tons – how am I supposed to carry that?

JEN: The same way we all do. As best you can. One day after another.

A beat. She takes his hand.

C'mon. Life's not so bad if you squint at it just right. Let's get you that cup of tea.

JORDAN HALL is a playwright and screenwriter based in Vancouver, British Columbia, Canada. Her work focuses on climate change, inequality, and the development of the fully-realized female protagonist. She is the author of *Kayak* and *How to Survive an Apocalypse*. As a screenwriter, Jordan co-created *Carmilla: The Series* (Winner: CSA, Digital Fiction) for Shaftesbury Entertainment, and was *Carmilla*'s lead writer for three seasons and the subsequent movie. She teaches screenwriting at Capilano University.

THE OLDE WOMAN WHO LIVED IN A SHOE

Kamil Haque

On the 26th of December 2004, several countries in Asia and Africa were struck by a tsunami and I experienced loss on a magnitude I had never felt before. A week later, I moved to Los Angeles to start my life anew. On August 23, 2005, five days after my 23rd birthday, Hurricane Katrina hit Florida and Louisiana. On both occasions, I grieved for many days for the hundreds of thousands of people who lost their lives.

I have wondered for many years since then: What is it like to be a survivor? What do they hold on to? Where do they go from there?

In the writing of this piece, I chose to fracture an innocent fairy tale and fill in the gaps with the horrors of surviving a disaster of epic proportions.

~~~~~~~~~~~~~~~~

There is a woman who is a mother.
She pledges her allegiance like me and you.
Under the power of the Almighty,
The Government, that is.
She is blessed and promised a right to life, liberty, and The Pursuit of Happyness.
In return, she promises to work hard, work tough, work strong to earn her keep.

Boy does she work.
Works so hard, the calluses on her hands prevent her from feeling the face of her child.
How she hates her hands. Hands-on to make her new home grow.
"Grow big and strong and tall so you can look after me one day" she says to her littlest little one.
He looks up at her and blinks as if to say yes.

Each day when night falls, she kneels by her bed and counts her blessings.
Day in, day out, she bows her head in sweat or religion.

One Tuesday, without warning,
AHHHHHHHHHHHHHHHHHHHHHHHHHH!!!!!

A silent scream.

Her eyes close, her eyes open, she can barely stand.
What just happened? Where is her Almighty?
The Government, that is.
She remembers walking her son to school. Her son!
She feels for it, where once his little hand held hers.
She grasps, she grabs, she clutches.
She holds nothing.
He left without saying goodbye.
She ages 70 years in this moment.
She blacks out.

As if waking up for the very first time in an Eden of Hell, all she can see
are nameless faces buried in the levee walls and God's tears.
She looks up.
The sunshine sparkles like an array of diamonds, shimmering against the
twisted metal and broken glass.
Her throat is dry with a brackish tang.
Her voice is hoarse with anguish as it echoes off the splintered trees.
She weeps alone.

The expanding smell of silence.
Her withered hands are crimson from the digging.
"Where are you?"
The vultures of fate circle around her as they mock her cawing.
From the fields to the source, she searches for life.
Her legs bloat with the lack of warmth.
Then she sees it.
All that remains is one solitary shoe.
The shoe drifts toward her as if walking on water.
It bobs oh so gentle and nods at her as if to say:

"Don't worry mama, I'm fine now."

She wraps her withered olde fingers around the shoe.
She takes in the dirty white canvas with black laces.
She recognizes where a small hole reveals where his little toe would poke through.
She knows now it is his. Where he is, he has no need for shoes.
She empties the shoe of black water and fills it again with her white tears.
She sways to the memory of his voice in the hollow remains of a playground.
She looks down at the shoe.
She lives her life now in this shoe.
She waits for a Savior to swoop down and save her.
Her Savior, the Almighty,
The Government, that is.
The olde woman who lived in a shoe.

KAMIL HAQUE is the Artistic Director of Haque Centre of Acting & Creativity (HCAC), Singapore's first professional acting studio. As a Singaporean of multi-ethnic origin, Kamil is the only coach in Asia experienced in teaching the Lee Strasberg method of acting. Kamil has coached actors to appear in leading and supporting roles in major Hollywood films and TV shows around the world. Bringing theatre into the workplace, Kamil also trains corporate leaders and employees.

VANILLA ICE CREAM

Monica Hoth, translation by Georgina Escobar

Vanilla Ice Cream looks to question the absurdity of "ecologically sound" politics in our times in Mexico, and to open the field for discussion of what is absolutely necessary to stop climate change. It also explores the idea that it takes the smallest question to launch an entire journey of change.

~~~~~~~~~~~~~~~~~~~

> *A ton of trash to separate and recycle. A mature-aged WOMAN is engaged in the work of separating the recyclables from a pile of trash; meanwhile, a radio plays. Through a small slit in the upstage center door to the collection center, another person peeks in. The WOMAN is pleasantly surprised and speaks to her. We never see the other person.*

WOMAN: Come on in. Are you here volunteering too? I've been working now for many years at this collection center. Come on in, now. Don't be shy. Did they explain to you how this works? I'll explain.

…

Fine, you can stay out there, if you want. You'll come in when you come in…

…

No, it's not hard, and truthfully in doing it you'll feel so much better, you'll feel like you're part of a common good. Because every day the news gets worse and worse, it's either El Niño, or the polar vortex, or global warming, or the sad polar bears whose ground is literally melting from under them… Look, pay attention: in order to recycle plastics you have to figure out what type they are and where they belong, you can see it here in this little triangle here or, hold on, where is the one on the bottles, ah yes, here it is. You see how there's a number here? Once you get familiar with that, you can separate them into groups. Like this. Oh look, here's a plastic cup, let's see, let's see, what number is it. Aha! So then we put it over here. You see how simple it is? It's important that you teach your children this.

...

Why don't you have children? They're so beautiful.

...

Wow you're pessimistic. I'm of the thinking that if we are the problem, we too have to be the solution and in motherhood, you can educate your children so that they can become good citizens. Conscientious citizens.

...

Yes, I know there's too many of us. Some people even say we are a plague, the worst plague that has ever ravaged Earth. I don't like to hear that, even if it's a little bit true, but look, these caps can be recycled too, and by group. I organize them by colors, that way they're easier to recycle.

...

But how can you think that? How can you think that the best thing for Earth is the extinction of the human race? You really are in the wrong, woman... You can say that because you don't have children, but think about the newborns, they have a right to live a fulfilling and happy life. I want to live to see my grandchildren. But that's what I'm saying: we have to be part of the collective good. We have to recycle. The colored caps, I donate to a foundation that takes care of children with cancer. Oh and recycling paper is also a thing, we just have to make sure it's clean, and glass too... although not all collection centers accept them. But look, to me, the problem, the biggest problem we have is plastic. Have you seen those videos that are all over the internet? I was very affected by one, even made me not want to ever use straws again, it's a video of a turtle, almost as big as this bulk of trash that I'm separating. The poor thing had a straw up its nose, can you imagine? How painful! And of course, it couldn't breathe. They had to remove it with such care, with these, like, surgeon's pincers, poor thing... and of course, since then, every time I get a straw, I give it back... and the same with Styrofoam cups and plates, which, by the way, I hear are forbidden in certain countries, but in others, like mine, they give you a Styrofoam cup or plate for everything. For tamales, here's your little Styrofoam plate, quesadillas, another plate, some churros, another plate, every snack we consume comes in one of those damn things and god knows in Mexico we eat delicious snacks all the time... although they're saying that at the university, they've invented a machine that can recycle Styrofoam. But I prefer not to buy it, because you know, it's all about consciousness.

...

I know that's not going to solve the problem, but at least I'm doing something.

...

Radical? No, I'm not radical. But look, like the other day, it was very hot, and I thought I should buy myself a gallon of vanilla ice cream. You know the fancy, tasty ones that they sell outside the cathedral, and I thought I'd take it home with me. But they would only offer me a Styrofoam container for it and well, no, I didn't buy it and we didn't enjoy dessert.

...

Oh, no? So then according to you, what is it to be "radical?" You expect us to, say, go and murder the owners of the plastic factories or those who contaminate the air or poison our water or kill the tiger hunters or...? To you that's what it means to be radical?

...

No, no, no, I'm not mad. It's just horrible to see all these bad things happen and then do your best to change them... but in spite of all your efforts, nothing seems to change. It's this feeling of impotence. That's it. It's the impotence that makes me mad. You say we have to be radical, but I don't understand what you mean by that. It's as if everything was way too complex and so no one is willing to do anything to make even the smallest difference, like choosing not to buy ice cream if it comes in a Styrofoam cup.

...

Of course! It would be better if they just stopped producing it, and I'm not just talking about those materials but about everything and anything that is putting the future of our planet at risk. But no one is going to make that call, even if we argue that this crap is killing us, the flip side would be that people would be left without jobs and that the economy would plummet. It's just us, changing our consumer habits, that could change the whole thing but it has to be all of us – it is our collective responsibility.

...

What do you mean that's not the way? If all the studies say it: we humans have to think of new ways of sustaining life.

...

What about them?

...

Government, I have no idea what they are doing there, but –

...

Well, yes, the point of government is to preserve the common good, but in reality they're just protecting the interest of the rich and the powerful.

...

Of course, that's not their job, we don't pay them to do that.

...

That. We have to require them to work for the good of human life. I totally agree.

...

Where?

...

There's a rally? A rally to demand regulations for... gas emissions and toxic waste!? Yes let's, let's, let's do it and – what else can we do to demand that the government do its job?

You didn't come here to volunteer with me today, did you? You came here to invite me to help put pressure on our leaders to make them act on this... All right, very well. Let's go... I'll come back later to finish separating this trash because for as long as things don't change, someone has to keep doing it.

She exits. Blackout.

MONICA HOTH von der Meden was born in Mexico in 1958. She is a playwright, a puppeteer, and a cultural manager who has received a variety of prizes and accolades, notably the *Premio Nacional* for Literature by INBA/Conaculta (2001) – Theatre for Young Audiences for the play *Marina and the Bird Men*, Citation of Excellence in the Art of Puppetry by UNIMA USA for *A History of Elves and Other Realities*, and a variety of regional prizes for literature in narrative and theatre (2005, 2010) . She is currently a member of the National System of Creators-FONCA, 2018-2021.

GEORGINA H.L. ESCOBAR is an artist and play-maker based in New York City. She employs multiple mediums including performance, visual art, puppetry, and music to create impossible narratives for the stage. She has participated in residencies including the MacDowell Colony and the Djerassi Artists Residency, and is a recipient of the Theatre For Young

Audiences National Award from the Kennedy Center. Her work has been exhibited throughout the U.S. and in festivals internationally (Denmark, Sweden). Artistic partners and presenters have included Milagro (OR), Clubbed Thumb, Lincoln Center, INTAR, Aurora Theatre, Bushwick Starr, Dixon Place, The Flea, and the Latinx Theatre Commons, among many others.

THERE GOES MY BOW TIE WITH THE STORM

Zainabu Jallo

My research interests include intersections of theatre performances and transcendent performances within the practices of *Bori*, *Candomblé*, and *Sufi*. My major focus is on the theatricalities they possess, their mythologies and oral performances, especially in West African, South American, and Native American cultures. With this play, I experiment with bringing together deities from ancient Yoruba, Roman, and Aztec cosmologies, who share somewhat similar interests and obligations.

SETTING:
Riding in a fierce storm, on thunderbolt and on a large piece of obsidian, are IANSÃ (pronounced "yan-sah"), the goddess of the winds and storms; TEMPESTAS ("tem-pes-tas"), the goddess of lightning; and TEZCATLIPOCA ("tes-kaht-li-poh-kah"), the smoking mirror of violent storms. Their forces have blown off the roof of the grand opera house during a performance. They have a few things to say before journeying on.

CHARACTERS:
RALI
WOMAN IN BROWN
MAN IN TUXEDO
A TERRIFIED PERSON
PERSON 2
PERSON 3
IANSÃ
TEMPESTAS
TEZCATLIPOCA
WOMAN IN BLUE
WOMAN IN RED

Darkness.

Radio Fuzz.

Woolly sounds of a radio report: "...*with that said, the campaign has turned out more successful than the federal administration anticipated, the political storms were overemphasized.... And now to news on another potentially devastating storm. Rali, how is it looking?*

In the dark:

RALI: Not good, I am afraid. The National Hurricane Center has warned that the storm is going to be centered around 80 miles south-southeast of us. Following landfall, it is foreseen to charge internally on Wednesday. This storm is likely to transform into a hurricane by –

Sound of radio tuning frantically.

WOMAN IN BROWN, *frenzied*: Darling... darling? We must leave, we cannot risk everything for the premiere!

MAN IN TUXEDO, *from within*: Heard that... there's one week before it hits. Premiere's in two days... tickets are sold-out... the other shows have been cancelled. Did you try on the dress? Do you like your brown frock? ...darling? Are you there?

Loud sound of thunder and torrential rain. Three beats.

The flashes of lightning reveal an opera house with everyone glamorously dressed. This happens four to five times until there is absolute silence for about five beats.

Lights on.

A grand opera house. There is loud applause with the curtain call, which includes three glamorously dressed women and a man in a tuxedo. Then a loud hurricane sound and sounds of people in panic and disarray. The lights flicker and there is a loud bang.

WOMAN IN BROWN: Darling the roof is gone!!

MAN IN TUXEDO: My bow tie! The storm's snatched it away!

There is an uproar and lots of screaming. Darkness.

Lights stabilize. In the opera house, a group has huddled together on the stage. The roof has been blown off. The storm, though subsided, still rages and everyone is disheveled. There is a strange sound. Two women clasp their ears, a man kneels holding his chest, others hold on tightly to each other. Someone lets out a cry. MAN IN TUXEDO's bow tie is gone and he has a cut on his forehead. Suddenly, through the open roof, fish of all sorts fly in.

A TERRIFIED PERSON: It's raining fish!

A blinding light pours through the open roof along with the fish, so bright, they can barely look up.

MAN IN TUXEDO: The apocalypse... in my lifetime!

PERSON 2, *quavering*: Iansã, Lady of the Passions, Queen of Lightning, Cyclones, Hurricanes, Typhoons....

PERSON 3: You have come on your own winds, powerful warriors. Tezcatlipoca, Tempestas, Iansã.

MAN IN TUXEDO: What is happening to us? Who is –

IANSÃ'S celestial voice startles everyone.

IANSÃ: The storms of transformation have come upon you.

MAN IN TUXEDO: Who are you? What is transformative about all this destruction? Look at all the mess!!! Look what's become of our grand opera house!!!

TEZCATLIPOCA: From the beginning, we have journeyed ceaselessly through the oceans and seas.

TEMPESTAS: We have embraced the entire 6.6 sextillion tons and all of the 260 billion cubic miles. You have your own roles to play... It goes beyond the slaughtering of black sheep...

IANSÃ: ...or offerings of black she-goats...

TEZCATLIPOCA: ...or donations of flowery songs.

CELESTIAL TRIO: We have ridden on millions of lightnings and innumerable thunders
We are the wind that eases the heat
We are many volcanos waiting to erupt
We are the sacred Earth

MAN IN TUXEDO: Stop with the daunting platitudes!

CELESTIAL TRIO: In the beginning... you pledged to honor and uphold the sacred bond between the elements of nature and human beings.

MAN IN TUXEDO: What beginning?! We are not a part of that beginning... your pact was not with us. We are eons away from them, what has that got to do with my bow tie? It has come through five generations. This was the last time I was going to wear it before handing it down to my son for his wedding next year. It saddens me incredibly. Take my shoes, my jacket... not the bow tie!

CELESTIAL TRIO: You have fashioned us into a dumping ground.

WOMAN IN BLUE, *confused*: We separate our garbage just as we are told!

Once again stormy winds are heard and people scamper about, holding on to rails and just about anything.... There is a loud bang, screaming, and then darkness.

WOMAN IN BROWN: Darling, you don't want to upset them with a bloody bow tie! Don't you see we are on the verge of losing our lives?

Lights come on revealing three WOMEN in their bedraggled glamour, and the MAN IN THE TUXEDO looking more ruffled, his tuxedo in tatters. They all sit on the stage where drops of rain soak them. They speak as though they were in some kind of trance. Their gaze is focused on nothing in particular. Some of the fish flutter about them.

MAN IN TUXEDO: That was a fifth generation bowtie, on the cusp of the sixth!

WOMAN IN BLUE: Iansā rode on a water buffalo.

MAN IN TUXEDO: I could barely see anything. I was upset... I still am.

WOMAN IN BROWN: Tempesta rode on a lightning bolt.

MAN IN TUXEDO: The lights were blinding. I am distressed.

WOMAN IN RED: Tezcatlipoca rode on a large obsidian.

MAN IN TUXEDO: There was too much light. I am distraught.

Fish flutter about as rain continues to pour. No one makes any attempt to move. They all still appear to be in a trance.

WOMAN IN RED: Many elements are being added to that dumping ground tonight.

WOMAN IN BLUE: The vortex eats them up and vomits them back at us.

MAN IN TUXEDO: Then... then it might come back to me by some miracle.

WOMAN IN BROWN: Tonight, we are the dumping ground.

MAN IN TUXEDO, *runs towards the open roof where rain continues to pour in and yells*: HELLLLLLLLLLLLLLLLLP!!!!!

ZAINABU JALLO is a Brazilian-Nigerian-Swiss scholar, playwright, and portrait photographer. Her academic and creative work have been conveyed through fellowships at the Sundance Institute Theatre Program, The Institute for World Literature, Harvard University, the Institute for Cultural Diplomacy in Berlin, Residenztheater Munich, Château de Lavigny, and the House of Writers in Switzerland. She is a Fellow of the Royal Society of Arts England, and the UNESCO Coalition of Artists for the General History of Africa.

THE STORY OF THE BOUNTIFUL WINDOW AND THE LAST ROPE

Vinicius Jatobá

The inspiration for this short play was the first image that came to mind after reading the word "light" in the invitation to this project: a man looking at a spot of light far away without knowing what it is. From there, the line "All those broken bones" appeared. The whole writing process involved figuring out what those words meant to the characters.

~~~~~~~~~~~~~~~~

> *A very old and messy office. CHARACTERS A and B are sitting in rotten office chairs. Upstage, a spot of light, indiscernible. A third chair has been abandoned, downstage left. It sits near a window. Silence.*

CHARACTER A: Oh, do you remember?

CHARACTER B: *That* was glorious. All those broken bones.

CHARACTER A: *Severely* broken, I must add.

> *Pause.*

Can you believe that when it's cold some of mine… still hurt?

CHARACTER B: You're lucky I'm not jealous, you damn bastard.

CHARACTER A: We were wonderful, so wonderful.

CHARACTER B: Oh yes.

> *Pause.*

What a poison. Sweet poison I would dare say if I was still brave –

CHARACTER A, *interrupting*: Oh dare, please. *Dare*. We're among friends after all.

CHARACTER B: All right, I'll dare. Sweet poison. Sweet. So... much... optimism.

CHARACTER A: So much –

CHARACTER B, *interrupting*: A lot –

CHARACTER A, *interrupting*: More than a sane mind could ever –

CHARACTER B, *interrupting*: Sane mind. A *sane* mind, you say. Who was the last sane mind around here?

CHARACTER A: Here. *Here*.

> *Pause.*

Well, let's see... maybe Jesus?

CHARACTER B: This is why I can't imagine life *without* your sweet innocence. But, really... let's have some perspective: He... And forgive me for bringing up this sensitive subject at our present conjuncture but... Well, He... How can I put it –

CHARACTER A, *interrupting*: Just spit it out, dear.

CHARACTER B, *treading lightly*: He... Well, *okay*, damn it... He *walked* on water –

CHARACTER A, *interrupting emphatically*: That's a lot, yes, yes, I agree, that's a *lot*! The audacity of this act –

CHARACTER B, *over each other*: Well, you know, I'm just saying –

CHARACTER A, *over each other*: After all, we know *that*, as a fact –

CHARACTER B, *over each other*: And I feel bad for –

CHARACTER A, *over each other*: It's science, dear, science –

CHARACTER B, *over each other*: Reputation is as important as –

CHARACTER B, *interrupting emphatically*: We know that only *dogs* walk on water.

Long silence.

CHARACTER B: I love the way... you enlighten my mind.

CHARACTER A: Guess what.

Pause.

This may last forever.

They look at the light in the back of the stage.

CHARACTER B: I still remember the day we got here.

CHARACTER A: That first moment. I cried at the door.

CHARACTER B: We all cry, it seems. Then we laugh. But in the beginning, we cry. That's for sure. Here, there. On every floor, in every department, every office. Then some more happens. More crying, I mean. But first we laugh, then we cry. And then comes the late stage, the full-fledged development of our... *career*. First, we cry after laughing, and then we cry *while* laughing. We need a lot of skill to get to that point. A lot of effort and concentration. And then, the glorious moment arrives... the moment when we cry... *after* crying. That's very hard...

CHARACTER A: We could never do that without eating properly.

CHARACTER B: Of course not. We need a balanced diet at this advanced stage of our career. Some of us even get dentures, you know... to add bite, as the youngsters used to say in the hallways when there were still youngsters around... or even hallways for that matter...

Long silence.

CHARACTER A: Let me tell you a story to cheer you up.

CHARACTER B: Oh yes, please.

CHARACTER A: Did I ever tell you the story of the rabbit who found himself inside the lizard's mouth and –

CHARACTER B, *interrupting*: I know that one.

CHARACTER A: All right, let's see.

Pause.

I assume I've told you the story of the elephant who married the moth –

CHARACTER B, *interrupting*: Yes, so lovely! I know it by heart. That's a shame. Some stories I would love to unhear so I could hear them fresh again.

CHARACTER A: That would make my daily storytelling so much easier.

CHARACTER B: You're the king of making something out of nothing. That's *your* talent.

CHARACTER A: You're far too kind, dear. Far too kind.

Pause.

Oh, I know. Yes! Did I ever tell you the story of the apple and the immovable table?

CHARACTER B, *enthusiastic*: No, never. Go for it. I'm all ears.

CHARACTER A: Okay, so.... Once upon a time, there was an apple. It was as red and round as the happiest of all apples *because* – oh lucky, lucky apple – from tender infancy it was fed with all the caring maternal light the Sun used to bestow upon our good old Earth. In those days, so immemorial that words barely existed, birds sang, fishes swam, lions ran, and every mouth smiled as not even death had been invented. The apple was put on the corner of a very beautiful table. A wooden table. The perfect table. But there was a problem: the table was immovable. And we all know apples become restless when they're on immovable tables. Watermelons can find happiness near such perfect tables, and so can oranges and strawberries, not to mention grapes and the unflagging pineapples. But for the red apple, it was too much. Had it had a mouth, it would have screamed; arms, it would have fought; eyes, it would have blinked and used Morse code to signal to birds that it needed to be rescued. But all the apple could do was wait, wait to be eaten.

> *Pause.*

To this day, the apple hasn't been eaten. It's still there. The table hasn't moved. The table is there, like a mountain. The perfect table. And.... *This* is the story of the apple and the immovable table.

> *Long silence.*

CHARACTER B: I *too* am very restless near immovable tables.

CHARACTER A: Who isn't?

CHARACTER B: I'm sure there's a deep moral lesson somewhere in there.

CHARACTER A: Once you grasp it, do me the favor of telling me what it is.

CHARACTER B: I will, I promise. But only if you keep telling me stories.

CHARACTER A: It seems that's my job around here.

They look at the light in the back of the stage.

CHARACTER B: Do you think it's getting any closer?

CHARACTER A: Sometimes I feel it's farther.

CHARACTER B: That might be good.

CHARACTER A: It makes no difference. Closer, farther. It will catch up with us.

> *Pause.*

And after all these years… it's beyond good. It might even be *worse*. But worse is better. Worse is always better.

CHARACTER B: I hope it is. Anyway, anyway… the last time… it was sweet to believe it might be –

CHARACTER A, *interrupting*: A message for us, sure. The light was different. Strong. Stronger than this one.

CHARACTER B: At least now we know *how* to recognize a train.

> *Silence.*

CHARACTER A: So many broken bones, so fast… The other times… The flood was an adventure: swimming can relax your mind and it's fabulous for cholesterol. And the earthquake! Jumping around, running and –

CHARACTER B, *interrupting*: The earthquake was the *best*!

CHARACTER A, *dispirited*: I didn't like the fire.

CHARACTER B: Me neither. The acrid smell, everything distorted, misshapen.

CHARACTER A: Fate has exquisite taste when it decides to give you the punishment you deserve.

CHARACTER B: Oh yes, always so... *fickle.*

Pause.

The train was a blast: heavy, fast... Dare I say... *thunderous?*

CHARACTER A: Dare.

CHARACTER B: Thunderous.

CHARACTER A: You nailed it. Thunderous.

Silence.

CHARACTER B: It's sad our friend didn't make it.

They look at the abandoned chair.

CHARACTER A, *treading lightly*: I don't want to say bad things about such a great soul, but...

CHARACTER B: I know...

CHARACTER A: Did he *really* have to jump out the window with the rope? I mean: either you jump out the window or you use the rope. That's protocol. You don't jump out the window *with* the rope. That's rule number one. You signed – on the dotted line... You signed *even before* you first cried.

CHARACTER B: Such a generous soul he was... That was the ultimate act of selfishness... Despair. Despair can destroy reputations.

CHARACTER A: It sure can. But now we're a little short on options.

Silence.

CHARACTER B: Sometimes I wonder if we're responsible for it... somehow.

CHARACTER A: That's *ridiculous*, dear. How so?

CHARACTER B: When we thought that... You know, the light... We thought: now it's going to be different. It was a *message*, for us. And we all got so... happy.

CHARACTER A: And then the train came.

CHARACTER B: Yes, I mean, what we experienced then. Sheer optimism.

CHARACTER A: Do you think it was too much for our friend?

CHARACTER B: Hearts can be broken in so many different ways. It's... poison. But I think that he somehow kept his optimism... *intact*.

   Silence.

CHARACTER A: He jumped.

CHARACTER B: Sure. But... with the rope.

   Pause.

   I'm sure he thought he could use the rope midway through his fall... he could use it to... *come back*...

CHARACTER A: That... makes... total sense...

CHARACTER B: I know.

CHARACTER A, *pointing at the window*: That man... that man *deserves* a statue.

CHARACTER B: Yes.

They look at the light in the back of the stage.

CHARACTER A: It's closer.

CHARACTER B: A little farther.

CHARACTER A: A lot farther.

CHARACTER B: Definitely closer.

Silence.

CHARACTER A: I have a story for you... for tomorrow.

CHARACTER B: I don't want to wait until tomorrow to listen to the new story.

CHARACTER A: Well, tomorrow is the first day after today. I know it might sound dreadful but... *Think* about it: tomorrow, today will be yesterday. Was it worth the wait for today's story?

CHARACTER B: Of course. *Of course,* it was. I'll think fondly about the apple for a long time.

CHARACTER A: So we wait. *Together.*

Silence.

CHARACTER B, *dispirited*: Walk *on* water.

CHARACTER A, *agreeing*: Yes, I *know.*

Slight pause.

I know.

VINICIUS JATOBÁ was born in Rio de Janeiro, Brazil. He is a fiction, essay, and theatre writer. He was chosen as one of the Best Young Brazilian Writers by Granta Magazine. His short stories have been translated into English, German, French, and Spanish. His theatre sketches have been read and performed in France, the United Arab Emirates, Austria, Italy, and Germany. He won the 2017 Portuguese Criar Lusofonia fellowship. In 2018, he won a fellowship at Akademie Schloss Solitude, in Stuttgart, Germany and he is a 2020-21 artist-in-residence at the Freiburg Theatre, Germany. He holds a Ph.D. in Comparative Literature.

FAILED EXPERIMENT

Vitor Jatobá

My inspiration for this play came from my feeling about humans' ability to deceive themselves. We can see but we prefer to ignore. We can act but we prefer not to. We are aliens on our own planet.

~~~~~~~~~~~~~~~~

Looking at Earth from a spaceship, two alien creatures act concerned.

ALIEN 1: There's no hope this time. As Director of Research Division for New Species, I must recognize that this planet is moving straight toward self-destruction.

ALIEN 2: What leads you to this tragic conclusion, sir?

ALIEN 1: This *dominant* species we put out there... They can't harmonize with any other beings, it's obvious. They simply poison every environment they inhabit.

ALIEN 2: But they are a very young species, sir.

ALIEN 1: The planet is running out of time.

ALIEN 2: We too were a very young species once. We needed time to evolve, sir. Everything takes time, sir.

ALIEN 1: Rookie, I respect your enthusiasm. I really do. But they have enough intellectual awareness by now to identify their problems – problems that they themselves created – and find solutions. They're clearly conscious of the consequences of their actions.

ALIEN 2: But with all due respect, sir, we shouldn't give in to pessimism.

ALIEN 1: Sometimes I wonder if you ever listen to anything I say, rookie.

ALIEN 2: I've been learning from you all my young life, sir. Centuries listening to you. The new species is gaining awareness of what it must do. The numbers show it.

ALIEN 1: But will they ever do something about it?

ALIEN 2: Maybe they just need more trust from us. Sir.

ALIEN 1: It's going too slow. Some of them are very enlightened. We know. They're trying. But there aren't enough of them. And they don't have the power to address all the shit –

ALIEN 2: Oh sir, you just said a bad word.

ALIEN 1: That's how upset I am! Don't you get it? What these few individuals do isn't enough. They destroy way more than they preserve. They drink water, a very simple formula: H_2O. And even though it's essential for their survival, they pollute and poison it. Knowingly. They put poison on their own food. Tell me, rookie, what other species have we created that has poisoned its own food?

ALIEN 2: Not a single one, sir.

ALIEN 1: This is a failed experiment!

ALIEN 2: There are *homo sapiens* discussing these issues right now, sir, all over the planet. Sir, I understand your frustration but we weren't that different from them when we started off. We weren't better than them.

ALIEN 1: I know that, rookie. You're impossible.

ALIEN 2: Should I take that as a compliment, sir?

ALIEN 1: Whatever, rookie. Whatever! Listen, we gave them autonomy: they think, they write, they have concepts, they can even achieve more than us – their planet is perfect for life. Every species we have thrown out there has found a way. But this one, all it cares about is money. Power and money. And the few enlightened individuals, what happens to them? Put in jail, killed, and exiled. It's useless.

ALIEN 2: Sir, have you ever thought about an *intervention*? Like, we go there, and point them in the right direction?

ALIEN 1: Be honest with me: Do you think they would understand that it's for their own good?

ALIEN 2: I'm not sure, sir.

ALIEN 1: And rookie, the way they are, I'm not sure it would be wise to reveal our existence. They can find our planet. We're very close. It has been thousands of years since we've had any weapons. How would we defend ourselves?

ALIEN 2: Sir, can I propose something that could bring some excitement to this dire situation we find ourselves in?

ALIEN 1: What?

ALIEN 2: A bet.

ALIEN 1: Oh yeah baby, let's go for it, rookie!

ALIEN 2: This planet is our responsibility. But this Solar System is not the Corporation's main concern right now. Am I right? The Corporation even talks about cutting our budget and shutting down operations.

ALIEN 1: I'm listening.

ALIEN 2: I'll sign the Reboot Protocol and –

ALIEN 1: Are we talking...?

ALIEN 2: Yes, sir.

ALIEN 1: My dear and beloved –

ALIEN 2: Oh yes, sir, I'm afraid so.

ALIEN 1: Dinosaurs? We're talking dinosaurs?

ALIEN 2: We're talking dinosaurs, sir.

ALIEN 1: What's *happening* to my face, rookie?

ALIEN 2: That's… That's a smile, sir. You're very happy.

ALIEN 1: Dinosaurs.

ALIEN 2: I bet that humans will evolve, and survive, and prevail. They'll survive, find a way. The few who see and understand what's necessary will be embraced by the rest of humankind and carve a path toward light and wisdom.

ALIEN 1: Oh rookie, and to think I once was idealistic like you. They'll disappear because they're too smart for their own good. And we reboot. Reboot Protocol: my two favorite words side-by-side. That's the bet. And then we return to my dear and beloved dinosaurs, a project that, *by the way*, should never have been discontinued.

ALIEN 2: They were very short on arms, sir.

ALIEN 1: That's no excuse.

ALIEN 2: They could never write and create language with those tiny fingers, sir.

ALIEN 1: That was my first project, give me a break. Fingers. Fingers are something new.

ALIEN 2: I know, sir. I don't mean to upset you.

ALIEN 1: I know, rookie. And what do you want if a miracle happens and you win this bet?

ALIEN 2: A dinner at Galactic Star, sir.

ALIEN 1: That's a very expensive place. You sure know how to make a bet.

ALIEN 2: Do I feel a shade of doubt in your voice, sir?

ALIEN 1: Don't be sillier than you already are, rookie! You should know that Galactic Star is way overrated. I hate that place.

ALIEN 2: Do we have a bet, sir?

They shake hands.

ALIEN 1: Oh yeah baby!

ALIEN 2: So let the bet begin, sir.

VITOR MARTINELLI JATOBÁ is a Brazilian educator, producer, director, and writer. He is currently researching the relationship between classical philosophy and contemporaneity, seeking to understand happiness and wellness. He is an educator and a life coach trying to make himself and the world a little better.

ENGLISH PLEASE

Marcia Johnson

A friend of mine raises Monarch butterflies every year in honor of her late mother, who taught her how to do it. She grows milkweed and posts her progress. I think that it's a beautiful way to remember her mother while helping the Monarchs, who keep losing more and more of their habitat every year.

~~~~~~~~~~~~~~~~~

A sunny room in a big house. SUSAN is making notations on bits of paper and attaching them to small jade-colored objects from a plastic storage container. She speaks to the objects as she does this.

SUSAN: I'll call you Dana. And you're Taylor. Now *you* look like a… I don't know. I'll give
Scott the honor. *(calling)* Scott!

A teenaged boy enters, using his phone.

SCOTT: Yeah.

SUSAN: Oh, I forgot to shut it off last night.

SCOTT: Yeah, thanks for that.

SUSAN: You know the house rules.

She goes to her computer.

SCOTT: Five minutes.

Susan types on her computer and hits return.

Grandma!

SUSAN: Now, five caterpillars went into J-hang yesterday, so the chrysalides are hard enough to hang this morning.

SCOTT: English please.

SUSAN: You can name the last one.

SCOTT: No thanks.

SUSAN: Something gender neutral.

SCOTT: Why?

SUSAN: Because we won't be able to tell if they're boys or girls until they emerge.

SCOTT: Grandma, I have to read the print on your pill bottles. You're telling me that you can see a male butterfly's di –

SUSAN: Scott!

SCOTT: Just saying.

SUSAN: The males have two black dots on their wings.

SCOTT: Oh.
Rowan.

SUSAN: What?

SCOTT: The butterfly name.

SUSAN: Good choice. *(as she writes down the name)* Your grandpa and I planted that rowan tree over there when we got back from our honeymoon. Do you know the symbolism of that tree?

SCOTT: I didn't even know rowan was a tree.

SUSAN: Just attach the chrysalides and I'll turn the internet back on.

SCOTT: Awesome.

> *She moves a stepladder over to a string that's hanging across the window. SCOTT moves it aside. He's tall enough without it. She hands him the chrysalides and he attaches them in silence.*

SUSAN: When I was a girl, there would be a time of year when we'd walk home from school and all the trees and bushes were covered with monarch butterflies.

SCOTT: Really?

SUSAN: It was an amazing sight. I just want to give them a chance to get their numbers back up. After all, they do help to pollinate and those poor honeybees need all the help they can get.

> *He's finished with the chrysalides.*

That was fast.

SCOTT: What now?

SUSAN: They'll come out of their chrysalides in about 11 or 12 days, dry their wings and fly away.

SCOTT: Cool.

SUSAN: You'll be happy to know that your job with them is done.

SCOTT: It wasn't all bad.

> *She turns the internet back on.*

SUSAN: A promise is a promise.

SCOTT: Thanks.

Susan starts cleaning out her plastic containers.

SCOTT: I bet you were a great teacher, Grandma.

SUSAN: Well, I tried.

SCOTT: So...

SUSAN: What is it? Isn't the internet working?

SCOTT: Yeah, I was just curious about the rowan trees.

SUSAN: Can't you find out about them on your phone?

SCOTT: I'd rather you tell me.

SUSAN: Oh, Scott! Really?

She hugs him.

SCOTT: Come on, Grandma. Don't turn this into –

SUSAN: I know. I know. I'm harshing your mellow. I'll be right back.

SCOTT: You need props?

SUSAN: Just make yourself comfortable.

> *Scott sits. He looks at his phone for a moment, then puts it away so that he doesn't get caught up in it. Susan returns with a large shopping bag.*

SCOTT: What's that for?

SUSAN: Your mother wants an Aran for Christmas and I need to wind the skeins into balls.

SCOTT: English please.

SUSAN: Hold out your hands like this.

> *She demonstrates. He follows. She places the skein on his outstretched hands and sits across from him.*

SCOTT: Grandma.

> *She begins winding.*

SUSAN: Back in ancient times, people began planting rowan trees next to their homes. It's known as the tree of life. Try to keep the same tension, honey.

SCOTT: Like this?

SUSAN: Yes, perfect.

> *Scott's phone pings.*

Do you need to get that?

SCOTT: No, I'm good. Keep going.

SUSAN: The tree is a symbol of courage, wisdom and protection.

SCOTT: Is that why you won't move?

SUSAN: It's why I don't have to move.

SCOTT: You rock, Grandma.

SUSAN: I know, Scott. I know.

> *They continue winding.*

MARCIA JOHNSON is a performer and writer born in Jamaica and raised in Canada. Marcia directs audiobooks, including *The Night Piece* by Andre Alexis, *Petra* by Shaena Lambert, *Lear's Shadow* by Claire Holden Rothman, and *Close to Hugh* by Marina Endicott. She also narrated *The Waiting Hours* by Shandi Mitchell and *Policing Black Lives* by Robyn Maynard. She acts in theatre, film, TV, and radio, and performed in the world premiere of her play *Serving Elizabeth* in 2020.

BIRTHDAY SUIT

MaryAnn Karanja

My inspiration comes from the late Nobel Peace Prize winner Wangari Maathai, whose unwavering fight for environmental justice and spreading of the tree-planting gospel through her organization, The Green Belt Movement, continues to impact thousands of people.[21]

SETTING:
Police cell.

TIME:
Day.

CHARACTERS:
RIZIKI, female, 60 years old
PAM, beautiful young lady, 24 years old
POLICE OFFICER, can be played by any gender, 40 years old

~~~~~~~~~~~~~~~~~~~~

The small cell room has a tiny metal bed, thin mattress, an old blanket, a rusty and dirty metal bucket, and an old stool with a plastic cup, plate, and empty water bottle on it. The floor is dirty with empty plastic bottles, fruit peels, etc. scattered all over. There's a single bulb and the light is on.

PAM, dressed in a bright mini-dress, one high-heel shoe and no jewelry, is seated on the tiny bed chewing gum; she stares at the entrance. The POLICE OFFICER, with a chain and padlock in one hand, pushes RIZIKI (also in one shoe and tip-toeing on her bare foot) into the cell. RIZIKI breaks from the OFFICER's push a few meters from PAM. Confused and shocked, RIZIKI rolls her eyes at the dirty floor, the rusty

---

[21] The Green Belt Movement: http://www.greenbeltmovement.org/

bucket, and then at PAM who is now wearing a sarcastic grin. She turns to look at the OFFICER, who turns around and leaves. We hear the noise of a door, chain, and padlock banging.

PAM, *with a chuckle*: Welcome to wonderland.

A startled RIZIKI takes a step back as she turns around to face PAM. She accidentally knocks the bucket with her leg but quickly holds it back up before it rolls over. She's shocked to see the content of the bucket. Almost throwing up, she steps away with her hand over her nose. PAM busts into laughter.

PAM: You disturbed it. Washroom!

RIZIKI swallows hard, her eyes fixed on the bucket and her bare foot still on tiptoes.

PAM: First time here?

RIZIKI: Mmmhh.

PAM, *chuckles*: You'll get used to it, although mine doesn't stink as much. You should have met my former cellmate; she's got a sewage for a stomach.

RIZIKI: We are not discussing...

RIZIKI points at the bucket.

PAM: What? Poop? Pee? C'mon, unless you don't poop or pee.

RIZIKI, *firmly*: Okay, enough.

PAM hums a song; RIZIKI is awkwardly silent, then she tiptoes to the bed and sits on the edge, keeping a safe distance from PAM. PAM stretches her hand for a handshake.

PAM: Sex trafficking, spiking people's drinks, and robbery. You?

RIZIKI: Protesting an... and... ind... indecent exposure.

PAM: Even you?

Chuckles.

My mum calls me an outcast and thinks that our business is for immoral youths; she should meet you and realize that anyone can do it and I don't have to retire early.

RIZIKI: I'm not a prostitute.

PAM, *surprised*: Oooh sorry, I thought you said indecent exp –

RIZIKI, *interrupting*: I undressed in protest. To make a statement to the government that I'm ready to do anything to ensure that deforestation and grabbing of Karura forest stops.

PAM, *excited*: You're that environmentalist who stripped naked outside Statehouse? Ooh my gosh, I can't believe I'm seeing you live. I'm your fan.

Pause.

I don't mean coz of the stripping.

RIZIKI: I know.

PAM: My mum says that it's a curse to see your elder in their birthday suit!

RIZIKI: It is.

PAM: Isn't the whole country cursed now?

RIZIKI: My birthday suit protest was only directed at those greedy and corrupt politicians who are slowly killing our planet. *(getting agitated and louder)* How stupid can one be to steal a forest so that they can build a mall? You know what? The level of ignorance in this country, in this continent, in this world, is driving me crazy.

Notices that the bulb is on.

Why the hell is the light on?

PAM: It's not on my bill.

RIZIKI: That! That is the kind of ignorance I'm talking about, young girl. Nobody cares as long as it doesn't cost them. But how long will it not cost you? When will you realize that those little things that you ignore really matter? That with time, the little non-significant looking things will eventually grow into one major problem that humanity cannot control?

She tiptoes to the socket on the wall and turns off the light.

RIZIKI: It only takes a second to save energy, save essential natural resources, and reduce pollution. It may not be your bill but it is your environment, our planet. Lemme ask you, how would you feel if I did this?

RIZIKI moves towards PAM and holds PAM's nose to block her breath; PAM pushes RIZIKI's hand away.

PAM, *angry and breathing hard/loudly through the mouth*: Do you want to kill me?

RIZIKI: That is what we are doing to our environment. Every time you turn away from a good cause or watch as others abuse the environment just because it does not directly affect or cost you, remember that you could be slowly killing Mother Nature. But you and I can make up for our previous mistakes; we can try to mend what has been broken and make our planet a better place.

PAM: You cannot save the world all by yourself.

RIZIKI: I will do the little I can; it's better than doing nothing.

PAM: I love your energy but you should not do things that cost you happiness. Just enjoy today, tomorrow may never come.

RIZIKI: Who said that if I die today, I'll take the whole of humanity with me? Won't my children and grandchildren be there tomorrow?

PAM: If you put it that way then it makes sense.

RIZIKI: And for your information, everything I do for the environment gives me happiness and satisfaction. Even being here means that somebody somewhere heard my voice.

Short silence.

PAM: It's funny how different we seem yet we are so alike! You strip, I strip. You strip for trees, I strip for men; the only difference is, men pay instantly, trees pay later.

They both laugh, then their laughter is interrupted by the sound of door chains coming loose. The POLICE OFFICER walks in carrying a door chain, padlock, key, and a typed letter.

POLICE OFFICER: Riziki?

RIZIKI: Yes, ma'am!

The OFFICER gesticulates to RIZIKI who tiptoes over to her. She is handed the letter. She reads it as a smile broadens.

RIZIKI: They've fired the Environmental Cabinet Secretary?

POLICE OFFICER: Seems like you know people in high places. C'mon, let's go.

The OFFICER places her hand on RIZIKI'S shoulder to lead her out. PAM shouts…

PAM: I can strip.

The OFFICER and RIZIKI turn to look at her.

PAM: ...for trees!

They laugh as they leave. PAM shrugs her shoulders as she watches them disappear.

MARYANN KARANJA is a Kenyan playwright, screenwriter, producer, and actress. She has written and produced three plays at the Kenya National Theatre. She also wrote a play for Climate Change Theatre Action 2017. As a screenwriter, she has co-written and written over 20 TV shows, 11 short films, and one feature film. She is currently writing her second feature film.

IF NOT NOW

Andrea Lepcio

Molina and Rowland's discovery added years of life to the planet. I want to make sure folks remember them, their brilliance, and their courage.

~~~~~~~~~~~~~~~~~~~~

> *The four characters enter. They can remain on stage, stepping forward and back as needed.*

DUPONT EXECUTIVE: I am an unnamed, but very powerful executive at Dupont. We make CFCs. A lot of CFCs. These guys are about to put us out of business.

CYNICAL SCIENTIST: I am a forgotten Cynical Scientist dedicated to making the world safe for Dupont and industry. These guys are about to ruin my life. And you want to know the most annoying thing? After years of having their funding cut off, their scientific credentials questioned, their status negated, they win the goddamn Nobel Prize. Yea, I never got one of those.

DUPONT EXECUTIVE: Without further ado, we return to 1974 and the meeting of Professor Sherwood Rowland, Professor of Chemistry at the University of California, Irvine.

CYNICAL SCIENTIST: And this Chemistry postdoc, if you can believe, is from Mexico. Isn't that where all the drugs come from? Name is Mario Molina. What's wrong with Mark?

> *CYNICAL and DUPONT step back as ROWLAND and MOLINA step forward. ROWLAND offers his hand to shake.*

ROWLAND: Sherry.

MOLINA: Mario.

ROWLAND: Welcome.

MOLINA: I've been following your research, sir, I am delighted to join your team.

ROWLAND: Delighted to have you. We're working on a number of research topics. You can have your pick. There is ongoing work with radioisotopes. You might continue your work with chemical lasers. Or, I've been thinking to follow up on Lovelock's research on CFCs in the atmosphere.

MOLINA: I also read the research. A billion pounds of manufactured CFCs in the earth's atmosphere in both hemispheres even though these gases are only in use in North America and Europe.

ROWLAND: There is the general belief that CFCs remain nonreactive, and therefore, do little harm.

MOLINA: The chemical industry has a saying: "Colorless, Odorless, Non-Toxic, Non-Flammable, Energy-Efficient, Low-Cost, and Safer than Mother's Milk."

They chuckle.

ROWLAND: You can let me know at your convenience which topic you choose to research.

MOLINA: Without question, I choose to investigate the consequences of CFCs.

ROWLAND: Agreed. I have some funding from the Atomic Energy Commission that could support our research.

Molina pulls on a chalkboard. They begin to scribble formulas and diagrams.

ROWLAND: Okay. What if CFCs migrate to the stratosphere? What happens?

MOLINA: Is it possible ultraviolet radiation reacts with CFC molecules, altering or breaking them apart?

ROWLAND: ...releasing chlorine atoms?

They scribble more math.

ROWLAND: Can it be that all the CFCs we release into the atmosphere are broken apart by ultraviolet radiation into free radical chlorine atoms that destroy ozone?

MOLINA: It would appear there is a recycling, the chlorine is generated and regenerated. My calculations are that one molecule of chlorine can destroy up to 100 thousand molecules of ozone.

They each write out equations as they figure this out.

ROWLAND: Catalytic Destruction of Stratospheric Ozone.

CYNICAL SCIENTIST pokes his head in.

CYNICAL SCIENTIST: Is this the post-doc? Is this Molina?

MOLINA: I am Mario Molina.

CYNICAL SCIENTIST: Well, I am a fully tenured professor and I blame you.

ROWLAND: Mario and I are working together.

CYNICAL SCIENTIST: Admit you are wrong about CFCs and get to work on something that benefits industry.

ROWLAND: Ultraviolet radiation breaks CFCs into free radical chlorine atoms.

CYNICAL SCIENTIST: CFCs are "Colorless, Odorless, Non-Toxic, Non-Flammable, Energy-Efficient, Low-Cost –"

MOLINA: And Safer than Mother's Milk. We've proved those are all lies.

CYNICAL SCIENTIST: Watch it, Post-Doc. Be the scientists beloved by industry like me.

CYNICAL SCIENTIST storms out indignantly.

MOLINA: I'll re-check our calculations.

ROWLAND: I'll call *Nature* and get started with approval to publish our findings.

MOLINA: You think we are ready to publish?

ROWLAND: I think we must.

They exit.

DUPONT EXECUTIVE enters followed by the CYNICAL SCIENTIST.

CYNICAL SCIENTIST: I want you to know that I am doing everything in my power to protect DuPont's market and promote the wide use of CFCs despite these insane accusations.

DUPONT EXECUTIVE: We're putting out an ad questioning this "hypothesis."

CYNICAL SCIENTIST: Uncertainty about science and fear of job loss just might get public opinion on your side. I wonder if the scientists defending tobacco can help us raise doubt?

DUPONT EXECUTIVE: Let's stick with the story that Rowland and Molina are talking nonsense. As if the sky is falling!

CYNICAL SCIENTIST: Rowland and Molina are the new Chicken Little. *Aerosol Age* magazine already accused Rowland of being a Soviet agent.

DUPONT EXECUTIVE: They're worse than communists. They're environmentalists.

CYNICAL SCIENTIST: Nothing is more American than apple pie, motherhood, and aerosol hair spray.

DUPONT EXECUTIVE: Is the Mexican here legally?

CYNICAL SCIENTIST: Unfortunately, but just being Mexican is enough to turn some against him.

DUPONT EXECUTIVE: Leave it to me. The Mexican is getting blacklisted and Rowland's money is getting cut off. Governor Ronald Regan heads the Regents of the University of California and is no friend of those who question industry.

Off the bad guys go.

ROWLAND and MOLINA re-enter the lab.

ROWLAND: Our funding has been cut.

MOLINA: I am amazed. We put forth an important scientific theory and we are considered biased because the business implications are unpopular.

ROWLAND: I'm tenured. I realize this is much more difficult for you because you are at the beginning of your career and have no job security. If you need to get another job...

MOLINA: Thank you for your concern, but without question, we must continue.

DUPONT and CYNICAL come up on either side of them.

CYNICAL SCIENTIST: They get invited to speak at the American Chemical Society. That's my gig!

DUPONT EXECUTIVE: The speech gets a lot of press.

MOLINA: People all over the country start throwing out aerosol cans.

ROWLAND: My wife Joan threw out 30. We don't miss them.

DUPONT EXECUTIVE: I hire an atmospheric scientist – not this guy – and get him to work on finding alternatives to CFCs. I can see the writing on the wall.

CYNICAL SCIENTIST: I look for a new client. Always some industrialist with cash to burn.

MOLINA: Without funding, we continue our research.

ROWLAND: I came home, one day, my wife greeted me asking how the work was going. I answered. "Very well, except it looks like it might be the end of the world."

MOLINA: It took 13 years, but finally, in 1987, the world ratified the Montreal Protocol agreeing to phase out CFCs.

DUPONT: We were one of the first companies to quit making them. Our scientist, Mack McFarland, was a leader in finding alternatives.

CYNICAL: If that agreement had failed, if I had succeeded, climate change would have occurred much sooner. What was it about these guys? No funding. Real suffering. And yet they persisted.

ROWLAND: If not us, who?

MOLINA: If not now, when.

ANDREA LEPCIO is an American playwright who writes and worries about climate change.

ABOUT THAT CHOCOLATE BAR...

Joan Lipkin

What if we really asked where our food comes from? Who benefits? Who or what is sacrificed? *About that Chocolate Bar...* is a short play about a presumably little thing like chocolate that unfolds to reveal whole landscapes of privilege, naïveté, responsibility, and environmental justice. What we think is small is actually very big.

NOTE:
It is preferable to use the language in the script, including some of the more commonplace vernacular. If this is a problem for a particular community, "fuck" can be replaced by "screw," "hell" by "heck," and "shit" by "stuff."

CHARACTERS:
A middle-aged WOMAN, preferably white
A SPIRIT of the Amazon, gender non-specific, preferably a person of color, age mid-20s and up

~~~~~~~~~~~~~~~~

The scene opens when the WOMAN excitedly anticipates, then begins to unwrap and take a bite out of a chocolate bar. She is practically orgasmic. The SPIRIT, whom she does not initially see, exclaims for different reasons. Every bite hurts.

WOMAN: #LoveMyChocolate. #TreatYourself. #SelfCare. Ahh.

SPIRIT: Oh!

WOMAN: Ahh.

SPIRIT: Oh!

WOMAN: Ahh.

SPIRIT: Oh. Oh, Oh, Oooooh! *(This does not feel good!)*

> *WOMAN perceives that someone or something is present, close to her, but cannot yet see them.*

WOMAN: What the hell?

SPIRIT: Yes. What the hell?

WOMAN: I mean, who, what...? I know I shouldn't eat carbs but it's a cheat day. At least it's dark chocolate.

SPIRIT: How very white of you.

WOMAN: Um, excuse me? I'm not white. I'm a Jew.

SPIRIT: This, I think, is what they call a technicality.

WOMAN: Tell that to the alt-right. And who the fuck are you, anyway?

SPIRIT: I'm the Spirit of the Congo. I am the Spirit of the Amazon. I'm the Spirit of the −

WOMAN, *interrupting*: − Amazon?

SPIRIT: Rainforest. Well, what's *left* of it, anyway.

WOMAN: The spirit?

SPIRIT: A representative of sorts. What, you don't like spirits?

WOMAN: I've always prided myself on direct communication. I mean, no offense, but I'm not so sure about talking to spirits. It makes me feel a bit crazy, to tell the truth. Like, am I imagining things? Am I talking to myself?

SPIRIT: Hell's bells. We're all a little crazy, don't you think? It's the state of the world. The what of the what. And who doesn't talk to themselves?

WOMAN: True, but I prefer to talk to a person.

SPIRIT: Well, that person, or rather, the physical manifestation of a person, can't be here. He/She/They/It are too busy fighting the powers of deforestation caused in part by your little chocolate bar.

WOMAN: Seriously? *My* chocolate bar.

SPIRIT: Where once I/We/Us/They/It was covered in lush green forest – oh so lush, so very lush – and home to chimpanzees and elephant herds, now it is more common to see the skeleton of a tree.

WOMAN: The skeleton?

SPIRIT: Trees burned to plant cocoa. Or hacked.

WOMAN: Ouch.

SPIRIT: Yes, hacked. Or burned to the ground to make room for more and more cocoa to be harvested. To make your precious chocolate bar.

They pause to take this in.

WOMAN: Oh.

SPIRIT: Yeah. Oh. More than 80 percent of rainforest cover has been reduced since 1960 in the Ivory Coast alone.

WOMAN: But this is awful. I mean, why don't we know this?

SPIRIT: I don't know. Maybe you don't want to know this. Like, maybe it benefits you *not* to know. You dig?

WOMAN: Or maybe, fake news? Hey, aren't there regulations to deal with this sort of thing?

SPIRIT: Tell that to Mars and Nestle. They say they are trying, but...

WOMAN, *reads wrapper*: Well, this is 72 percent cacao. I mean, fair trade. Organic.

SPIRIT: So you think it's pure? What percentage of the 4.5 million cocoa farms on the planet do you think are actually sustainability certified? Seriously.

WOMAN: Ummm...

SPIRIT: You *have* heard of false advertising?

WOMAN: But I bought it at Whole Foods.

SPIRIT: Whole Foods. The same Whole Foods that was bought out by Amazon – *no* relation – that force of nature that has *destroyed* small independent bookstores and businesses worldwide? Fuck you, Jeff Bezos, fuck you.

> *The SPIRIT has a point. But now what?*

WOMAN: Well, what do you expect me to do? The world is unbelievably shitty right now.

SPIRIT: Tell me about it. I'm tired. My land is tired. You all need to do something.

WOMAN: Look, I went on the Women's March. I'm calling my senators. Well, *almost* daily. I'm trying not to drink. I recycle. I need something... I need *chocolate*. And that sustainably sourced shit is expensive. But I'm trying!

SPIRIT: That's your patch of the world, Petunia. What about the rest of us? Let us revisit. Goodbye, green, green hills of Africa. Goodbye, you gorgeous chimpanzees and elephants. Goodbye, *my* Amazon. Goodbye, rainforest.

WOMAN: Goodbye?

SPIRIT: A little more action would be nice. A little mobilizing?

WOMAN: So I guess, #ProtectTheRainforest?

SPIRIT: Uh, yeah. Because #By2030ThereMayBeNoRainforest.

WOMAN: Got it.

The SPIRIT takes the chocolate bar as she yearns for it.

WOMAN: Goodbye?

SPIRIT: Burned!

WOMAN: Burned.

SPIRIT: Hacked!

WOMAN: Hacked.

Could she finally be getting it?

Oh. Oh! #DownWithClimateChangeDeniersAndYouColonizing
LandPoachingBastards and #WeLoveOurRainforest

SPIRIT: Well, yes! You go, girl.

WOMAN: And, #EvenThoughILoveYourProductsFuckYouJeffBezosFuckYou
#WhatAreYouReallyDoingForThePlanet

Beat.

SPIRIT: #Woke *(beat)* #NotWokeEnough

JOAN LIPKIN is the Artistic Director of the U.S.-based That Uppity
Theatre Company and an award-winning playwright, director, producer,
educator and social activist. She specializes in devising and producing work
with underserved populations, helping people to tell the stories of their

lives that have both individual and collective relevance. Her plays are widely anthologized, have been both produced and published internationally, and are included in several other rapid-response theatre projects, including *Every 28 Hours* and *After Orlando*.

WARRIOR OF THE HEAVENS

Philip Luswata

Polythene bags are a real menace in Uganda and they contribute to dangerous flooding in the city. The ban on their use remains unsuccessful due to the myriads of people who benefit from their purchase, sale, and discarding, in spite of the now scientifically proven reality that they are considerable contributors to global warming (in addition to the traditionally recognized culprits).

CHARACTERS:
ANASTASIA, a burly middle-aged woman. A bully, flamboyant and colorful.
JOE KAKA, a thin middle-aged man. Smart with a colonial touch. Striving for aristocracy in his poor way.
RAYMOND, a street-wise youth dressed and visibly adapted for menial street jobs.

~~~~~~~~~~~~~~~

> *In a dimly lit but neat backstreet drinking den, JOE KAKA, faded but smart in a tie, is fast asleep on the lone sofa, a book covering his face. Central to the space is a fully stocked bookshelf. Nearby are a stove, a pot with drinking straws sticking out, a few Jeri cans, a bench, and a sack of charcoal. Enter ANASTASIA, calling out.*

ANASTASIA: Joe Kaka! Joe Kaka! He is always sleeping! How does he manage this bar business?

> *She moves over and covers him caringly with a leso (wrapping cloth for women) she has come with. She wears a grand headgear with a flowery dress to match. She settles her various bags down and retrieves their contents, in the form of paper bags of different sizes and shades, all filled with different kinds of food, including a full roasted fish, which she lays out on the bench. RAYMOND enters, struggling with a sack full of plastics that is much bigger than him.*

ANASTASIA: You light the charcoal stove and boil some water. I want to drink millet beer.

RAYMOND: But I don't even drink... Why am I the one to prepare your millet beer?

ANASTASIA: I don't want to disturb Joe Kaka. Use some of his polythene bags to get the fire lighting faster.

> *She moves over to JOE KAKA and removes the book from his face as RAYMOND lights the stove.*

ANASTASIA: This book could even choke him in his sleep.

RAYMOND: That's if he hasn't already choked himself enough with all the plastics he burns in here to light his stove...

ANASTASIA: What?

RAYMOND: I didn't say... I'm talking about what fumes from these burning polythenes do up there in heaven... even when they are not burning... they affect the heavens... less rain... hotter days...

ANASTASIA: Make the water hotter by lighting the stove...

> *She approaches him menacingly as smoke begins to rise from the stove.*

RAYMOND: These are things I also hear! Think about that full fish you are going to eat...

ANASTASIA: I eat because I have problems!

RAYMOND: That fish is from the river where the women wash the plastics, how much plastic has that fish eaten? And now you are going to eat it!

> *She grabs him and begins to squeeze him.*

ANASTASIA: I may be a woman of God but I don't take well to being insulted!

RAYMOND: Please Sister! You are squeezing my neck...

ANASTASIA: And this is why I was expelled from the convent!

The squeezing has stopped when we hear JOE KAKA cough and choke because of the fumes coming from the stove.

ANASTASIA: Joe Kaka is coughing! Quickly take the stove outside!

RAYMOND quickly obeys and darts out with the smoking stove as ANASTASIA hurries to JOE KAKA.

ANASTASIA: Kaka! Kaka! Joe Kaka!

JOE KAKA: Don't leave me alone! I think I am dying!

ANASTASIA: No! You have just woken up...

RAYMOND returns.

RAYMOND: Maybe he is having a heart attack! These fumes can make that worse! May be asthma... even you may find his kidney is already gone... burning plastics is death!

ANASTASIA: Stop jabbering and bring water...

RAYMOND brings the water but JOE KAKA can't drink.

RAYMOND: Joe Kaka... do you feel like vomiting... headache... he is not drinking the water... you forget him! If these plastics can finish the world, even when they are not burning, they are slowly eating the environment because of heat and light! Now you used fire! How do you expect poor Joe Kaka to survive? He is a historical case! You have killed him... and I told you Sister Anastasia! I told you! Now this is a police case!

ANASTASIA: What police?

RAYMOND: I am taking you to police! Even though you are the one who supplied the police station with the plastic tiles they used to construct their floor, the law is above you and your relationship with them! You are going to jail, Sister! All I am waiting for is for him to lose the last heartbeat! Is it even still there?

> *He leans over to feel the heartbeat, which startles JOE KAKA.*

JOE KAKA: Hey!

ANASTASIA, *really excited and relieved*: He is alive! Now go and report to your mother!

RAYMOND: Even if he has woken up, it is a fact that you burnt fumes that you knew could kill him! Joe Kaka... you are a survivor of environmental abuse! We can report to the National Environment Management Authority!

ANASTASIA: Go and "National" somewhere else! Silly! Dear Joe Kaka... don't listen to this one...

RAYMOND: Today you have increased the poisons in the air by forcing me to burn plastics, every other day you increase the poisons in the water by paying the women at the river to wash your plastics and dump the bad ones in the water! Now you want poor Joe Kaka to drink that poisoned water! Just like your full fish there! Joe Kaka, she should pay you!

JOE KAKA: How much has she drunk?

RAYMOND: She is a rich woman, Joe Kaka! She makes floor tiles out of these plastic bags and they are in high demand! Ask for money because of what you have gone through!

ANASTASIA: Ask for money for what? I collect plastics and use them to make something people are needing! Is that killing anyone?

RAYMOND: What are you saying?

ANASTASIA: Would you rather I leave all these plastics to be dumped all over the place and let people suffer? Here! Have money!

She hands him cash.

Take those plastics and dump them back where you picked them! See if the world will be better!

RAYMOND: Sister Anastasia...

ANASTASIA: No! I will not have you make me look like a fool in front of Joe Kaka... Joe, I play my part, dear... when people don't play their part by reusing these plastic bags, I pay people like this ungrateful ingrate to collect them and I make floor tiles out of them so that they are not littered all over the place. Is that bad, Joe Kaka?

JOE KAKA: Who said it is bad?

ANASTASIA: Joe, I have been watching you suffering here every day... I have been coming every day to support your bar business... I don't want you to continue suffering burning plastics to light your charcoal stove to make beer for your customers...

JOE KAKA: It is poverty, sister... poverty... even me, I know the dangers...

ANASTASIA: Leave the dangers behind you Joe Kaka... come with me and we work. Let us not be part of the problems of this world but part of the solution with my recycled plastic floor tiles...

RAYMOND: Joe Kaka...

JOE KAKA: You also keep quiet and they tell me! Yes, dear Sister...

ANASTASIA: I am taking these plastics to the factory... We can go together and I show you how we do the work... *(seductive)* We reduce, we reuse, and we recycle...

JOE KAKA, *reading mischief:* We reduce, we reuse, and we recycle... I don't know about the reducing... but the reusing and the recycling...

RAYMOND: What are you people talking about?

JOE KAKA: Ah! You keep quiet also!

> *JOE KAKA quickly gets up and lifts the plastics that RAYMOND came with.*

JOE KAKA: If anyone comes, tell them I moved! It is time I made my contribution to saving the world with the dear Sister!

RAYMOND: Shameless! You are off to fill your pockets!

JOE KAKA: As I save the world...

ANASTASIA: Bye bye, Warrior of the Heavens!

> *ANASTASIA and JOE KAKA exit. RAYMOND looks around, tries out the empty sofa, places the book over his face, and takes a nap just like JOE KAKA.*

PHILIP LUSWATA is a Ugandan living in Uganda. He has written for television, radio, and stage. Key stage dramas produced at the Uganda National Theatre include *Crazy Storms*, *Get Away from Me*, and *Nasty Good Story*, among others. Popular radio dramas include *Quiet and We Hear* and *Pay* for BBC Radio. He has also written for popular TV series and films in East Africa.

THE ARROW

Abhishek Majumdar

This play is a tribute to those many Indigenous populations who are fighting for their forests in the deep jungles of India. These are climate warriors, people who live close to nature but are today facing the wrath of big corporations wanting to mine, and the apathy of the larger middle class, who does not care for their wellbeing. These are climate warriors who are at the forefront of this struggle and yet have the least empowerment or support.

~~~~~~~~~~~~~~~~~~

A hot room.

A man, A, sits blindfolded.

Another, B, is sitting in front of him with a gun.

An old fan moves slowly.

This image is held for 15 seconds.

B walks up to A. Undoes his blindfold and comes and sits in his chair. A opens his eyes with great difficulty. Notices B.

A: You?

B: Water?

A feels the back of his head.

A: Oh…

B: Does it hurt ?

A: You hit me?

B: No. I brought you here

A: Who hit me?

B: Them

Pause. A looks out the window.

A: You are making a mistake

B: I don't think so

A: They will burn it all

B: They are buying it

A: To burn it

B: No. They are looking under the earth

A: So they'll burn whatever is above

B: We have to sell it

A: It's not ours to sell

B: It's the law

A: What is?

B: More than 70 years, if we till the same part of the forest, that part is ours

A: That part is ours to keep not ours to sell

B: If you had placed your thumbprint, this wouldn't be required

A: The forest isn't mine to sell

B: The forest is ours

A: Ours to protect. Not ours to sell

B: They'll kill you

A: No you will

B: I'll have to. Don't make me do it

A: How much?

B: Enough for our three generations

A: What will they do with it?

B: Go to the city

A: Then?

B: Then I don't know. Live. Perhaps

A: That money won't be enough. Not even for a decade

B: They've signed contracts with the government. We can sell or be evacuated

A: I'll go with the forest

B: They are a large corporation. They have a private army

A: I know

B: Your revolt will come to nothing

A: If they burn the forest and dig mines, at least they should have to bury my bones

B: You are being insane

A: You are my brother

B: But I want to live. Here or in the city, wherever. But I want to

A: Are you afraid?

B: Once we leave, they will begin work

A: Yes

B: If we stay, they will crush us with trucks. And then begin work

A: You are holding me hostage

B: I don't want you to go there and die

A: When did they come?

B: Two nights ago

A: Then?

B: You weren't there, in the village

A: You were

B: Yes

A: You sold the land

B: They took her

A: Who?

B: My wife

A: Oh

Sits with his head in his hand, on the floor.

B: I couldn't do anything. They dragged her. I chased them, they stripped me, beat me with the backs of their rifles and tied up me to a tree. They took her away. We screamed. The forest heard us

A: We are the last

B: Yes, everyone else had left

A: Then?

B: Then. Then they came back in the morning and untied me. Took me away

A: The cutting machines?

B: They came with the cutting machines and started chopping the area clean

A: Your wife?

B: She was there. In tattered clothes. We looked at each other. We bled together. We...

A says a prayer in silence.

B: Where were you?

A: I was on the other side of the river

B: There? On that bank?

A: Yes

B: What were you doing there?

A: I was preparing my bow and my arrow. I was poisoning the tip

B: Do we need to kill to save our forest?

A: Yes

B: Why?

A: They want what is under the forest. Not what is in it

B: It is foolhardy

A: To prepare a bow and arrow to save a single tree in a forest?

B: Yes

A: But that tree is our family. You were born under it, our grandfather died under it, our mother prayed around it, our sisters −

B: They killed my wife for the forest

> *Pause.*

And then when I came back with them in the trucks

> *Pause.*

You stood, embracing the tree

A: I turned around and pointed my arrow, right under his head

B: With a blindfold. What were you trying to −

A: That even with my eyes closed, I could give my life for my forest

> *Pause.*

B: They were many

A: Yes but I pointed at the owner, the one who had bought everything

B: I said, he will give his tree. He will give his land, don't shoot him

A: They did. My arrow went... zip! Killed him

B: And you?

A: Spot dead

B: What?

> *Looks at him carefully.*

A: I tried. I tried. I tried.

B: Who is with us?

A: No one. No one will fight for our tree

B: But –

A: No one will. If they really wanted, they would have by now

> *Pause.*

A: Before they cut that tree, do me a favor

> *Pause.*

B: You are alive. Tell me you are

A: Bury me. Under that tree

> *Pause.*

Bury me, I will go with my forest. I will go with my tree

B drops the gun.

B: Bury you?

A: Can you hear it ?

They listen. Sounds of people outside.

B: The villagers. Are returning!

A: What?

B: With bows and

A: Arrows

A smiles.

Pause.

A: Bury me under my tree. Let the war to save our forest begin.

Sounds grow louder. People arrive in large numbers.

ABHISHEK MAJUMDAR is a playwright and theatre director based in Bangalore, India. He is a Visiting Associate Professor of Playwriting at New York University Abu Dhabi and the Artistic Director of Bhasha Centre in Bangalore. He writes in Hindi, English, and Bangla, and his work has been performed in several leading theatres such as the Royal Court Theatre in London, Deutsches Schauspielhaus Hamburg, Theater Freiburg, Yale Rep, Prithvi Mumbai, and Ranga Shankara Bangalore, to name a few.

A HOLIDAY ON ICE IN A WARM CLIMATE

Julie McKee

A few years ago, an enormous iceberg floated by New Zealand. As there is a bit of a housing shortage there, I wondered if people could live on it and for how long. Later on, I wrote a play about seaweed. So when I was asked to write this play, I asked myself "what if?" and "why not?"

CHARACTERS:
MACK, any age, any ethnicity
MAVIS, any age, any ethnicity

/ indicates an overlap

~~~~~~~~~~~~~~~~~~~~

> *A coastal town in any Pacific Island or country. Indoor space with a large picture window. MACK tastes something on a plate.*

MACK: I can't tell anymore. My taste buds are so fucked up.

MAVIS: What?

MACK: I burnt my tongue! I'm a chef and I burnt my tongue!

> *Beat.*

What is that?

MAVIS: An iceberg. A giant iceberg.

MACK: A what?

MAVIS: Floating past our window.

MACK: Good god.

MAVIS: There's people on it.

MACK: Waving.

MAVIS: Wave.

MACK: Who are they? What are they doing on that iceberg?

MAVIS: They're on holiday. I think they might be glampers.

MACK: What's a glamper?

MAVIS: A tent with a wood plank floor, Persian rugs, a four-poster bed, and lots of cushions. Probably began their holiday in Antarctica. They wait for the ice shelf to calve, they helicopter in, put up tents and… and the currents take them where they take them.

MACK: What happens when the berg breaks up?

MAVIS: The tents go under and they get rescued! Let's do it! A newer, more exotic, more dangerous, exciting form of tourism. I'd rather do that than bungee, sky dive, or suicide by river.

MACK: I'd rather stick this fork in my eye.

MAVIS: Look at them enjoying themselves.

MACK: Are they waving or signaling for help?

MAVIS: I've never been to Antarctica. And a bit of it is just floating by. So fresh, clean, pure.

MACK: Yeah but. But always in the back of your mind is the moment when the "melt" causes the berg to roll over. Cause it will, and when it

does. No fun. And cold. Think Titanic. Here. Taste this. I'm including
it on the menu, but my buds are, I dunno I I I can't taste anything
anymore –

MAVIS: We don't take fun holidays anymore.

MACK: This chef is too busy, Mavis, too busy saving the planet.

MAVIS: What is that?

MACK: Dulse, sweet. Nutty. Crunchy. Supposed to taste like bacon. If
I don't come up with a bacon tasting seaweed, I'm in deep doo doo. The
planet is in deep doo doo.

MAVIS: The planet is going to be okay. And because it's going to be
okay, we have to book a glamp/berg holiday sooner rather than later.
Because once the scientists get climate all under control, and they will,
the calving will stop and that will be the end of a holiday on ice in
a warm climate.

MACK: Yeah but lots of glare, I don't think you'd be doing your skin any
favors. Your melanoma count is up to six.

MAVIS: The ozone's been taken care of. Which is exactly my point.

MACK: Not until 2065. That hole is still healing.

MAVIS: If they can fix that, they can fix the climate thing too.

MACK: Climate change is a bigger, different problem.

MAVIS: Different yes, bigger no, and just as deadly.

MACK: Exactly. So I'm determined to do my bit as an unsung hero and
put delicious, scrumptious seaweed on the menu.

MAVIS: You're going to save us from the second greatest man-made threat
to our planet's environment, by putting that on the menu?

MACK: If it tastes like bacon, YES, I am. On every menu in the country, YES, I am. I have to give these sea veg farmers, formerly known as fishermen, a chance to sell their produce. So I ordered tons of it.

MAVIS: There goes our holiday.

MACK: What happens when all the coastal areas flood and the farmlands disappear? What is the population going to eat? Huh? Seaweed, that's what! Requires no fresh water, fertilizer, feed, or arid land to grow. Protein, fiber, vitamins, calcium, and potassium.

MAVIS: Don't talk to me anymore, I'm watching our holiday float by!

MACK: How about a holiday house built with seaweed bricks instead?

MAVIS: How about an igloo built with ice blocks instead?

MACK: I'd rather not. Would you taste this for me. Please?

MAVIS: I'd rather not.

MACK: They're building a seaweed farm the size of Australia in the Pacific, it's going to sequester billions of tons of carbon dioxide. That could be an interesting spot?

MAVIS: You know what I love about you?

MACK: What?

MAVIS: I'm thinking.

MACK, *hurt*: Nice.

MAVIS, *silence, then*: Oh come on! I'm teasing, let me taste it?

MACK: No too late, I don't want your support, I don't need...

    MAVIS grabs a little and eats.

MACK: Well? WELL?

MAVIS: Hmmm. Hmmm. The food of last resort when famine arrives for good reason.

MACK: Except for Asians and Maori. For 13,000 years, civilizations have been eating it.

MAVIS: You keep at it darling, I love you, I have faith in you.

MACK: I love you, but fuck you too / Mavis.

MAVIS: I'm kidding, look I'm eating it, I'm EATING – Oh. Not bad, not great. YET. Good after taste. Good substitute for bacon, babe.

MACK: BACON! Did you say bacon? YES! Who doesn't love / bacon?!!

MAVIS: I like the nutty crunchy thing. A lot! / Now can we –

MACK: After I crack this baby, I'm doing seaweed pasta. Pasta, bacon, bacon, pasta. Can't go wrong.

MAVIS: There goes our holiday just floating on by. Where's your sense of adventure?

MACK: In my palate. Sorry. I know. But it's all I can think of. And so underrated. AS AM I! As was the ozone hole, Mr. Molina, Mr. Rowland, the sounders of that alarm. ALL OF US!

MAVIS: I rate you very highly darling. But you just never want to vacation where I want to vacation. Wave. And you have to have one, you need to get your taste buds back in working order, no?

MACK: Truth. I suppose… I suppose… I could consider an igloo. If you like.

MAVIS: It's a start.

JULIE MCKEE is a U.S.-based playwright from New Zealand whose plays have been performed all over the U.S., New Zealand, and Germany. The Sloan Foundation of Science and Technology/EST Project commissioned *The Secret Life of Seaweed*. Her plays are published by Smith & Kraus and Playscripts Inc. Julie has received fellowships from New York Foundation for the Arts, Sundance Playwrights Lab, MacDowell Colony, Virginia Center for the Creative Arts, and St. James Cavalier in Malta. She is a graduate of the Yale School of Drama.

AMERICA'S FIRST ENVIRONMENTALISTS

Mary Kathryn Nagle

The movement at Standing Rock significantly undermined the systemic erasure of Native Peoples from the dominant American narrative. At a time when most Americans continued to believe that Native Americans and Nations no longer existed in the United States, Americans were presented with a movement that forced a new conversation around values, identity, and our collective connection to the Earth around us and the lands we live on.

For several months from August 2016 until February 2017 – and during a Presidential election – millions of Americans and a global audience witnessed a powerful story unfold, told through grassroots activists, citizen journalists, social media, alternative media, and then ultimately mainstream media. Tens of thousands of individuals and hundreds of Tribal Nations traveled to Cannonball, North Dakota, to stand with the Standing Rock Sioux Tribe in its opposition to a pipeline that threatened to destroy the Tribe's drinking water, historic treaty lands, and sacred sites.

Suddenly, Native Americans were no longer simply characters from the past that occasionally popped out of oblivion and into a western or a museum. Instead, Americans watched as contemporary Native Americans populated the daily news diet with articulate, powerful narratives concerning the sovereignty of the Standing Rock Sioux Tribe – and all Tribal Nations – as well as the collective threat that climate change and losing our drinking water poses to us all.

~~~~~~~~~~~~~~

A bar in downtown Bismarck, North Dakota. Late August 2016. CAROL (Hidatsa) is working.

STEVEN (a white man who works for an oil company) sits at the counter, drinking. The TV plays in the background.

STEVEN, *looks up at the TV*: You watch Rachel Maddow?

CAROL: And Lawrence O'Donnell, yeah –

STEVEN: Why do you watch MSNBC?

CAROL: I need to stay current, you know, up to date, on what's happening in the world.

STEVEN: You can't do that by watching MSNBC.

CAROL: I take it you watch Fox.

STEVEN: Yeah. I do.

CAROL: So we both watch what we watch.

STEVEN How can you watch MSNBC?

CAROL You really wanna have this conversation?

STEVEN: They're so biased.

CAROL: And Fox isn't?

STEVEN: Fox reports facts.

CAROL: You know, I never thought about that, but now that you mention it, you have completely persuaded me.

STEVEN: I have that effect on women.

CAROL: Especially women who mistakenly watch MSNBC.

> *STEVEN gestures for another drink and she pours him one more. She pours herself a drink as well.*

CAROL: What are you doing here?

STEVEN: Talking to you.

CAROL: I saw your license. You're not from here. Out of state.

STEVEN: I work here. For now.

CAROL: On what?

STEVEN: The pipeline.

CAROL: You work on the pipeline.

STEVEN: Does that make me evil?

CAROL turns to the TV.

CAROL: Oh my god!

STEVEN: What?

CAROL: He's talking about us!

CAROL points him to the TV.

STEVEN: What do you –

CAROL: Shhhhhh!

CAROL grabs the remote and turns it up.

LAWRENCE O'DONNELL, *on the TV*: Every once in a while, there is a painful and morally embarrassing reminder, as there is this week in North Dakota near the Standing Rock Sioux Reservation, where hundreds of people have gathered and camped out in opposition to an interstate pipeline being built from North Dakota to Illinois. The protest is being led by this country's original environmentalists, Native Americans. For hundreds of years they were our only environmentalists.

CAROL: Holy smokes.

LAWRENCE O'DONNELL, *on the TV*: And so we face the prospect next month of the descendants of the first people to ever set foot on that land, being arrested by the descendants of the invaders who seized that land. Arrested for trespassing. That we still have Native Americans left in this country to be arrested for trespassing on their own land is testament not to the mercy of the genocidal invaders who seized and occupied their land, but to the stunning strength and the 500 years of endurance and the undying dignity of the people who were here long before us, the people who have always known what is truly sacred in this world.

CAROL is in tears.

CAROL: He just told the whole world we still exist. We're still here. We have the RIGHT to be here. And no matter how hard you try, you will never take it from us.

MARY KATHRYN NAGLE is an enrolled citizen of the Cherokee Nation. She previously served as the first Executive Director of the Yale Indigenous Performing Arts Program. She is also a partner at Pipestem Law, P.C., where she works to protect tribal sovereignty and the inherent right of Indian Nations to protect their women and children from domestic violence and sexual assault. Nagle is an alum of the 2013 Public Theater Emerging Writers Program.

THE BUTTERFLY THAT PERSISTED

Lana I. Nasser

An ode to Nature, the ultimate warrior, that persisted to exist and abound –
in spite of everything. And to the human being that persisted to envision
and strive for betterment, taking action no matter how small.

SETTING:
Anywhere and everywhere. Intentionally left open as an invitation to the
director(s): where does this take place?

STAGE/LIGHTING:
Minimal. Let the light serve as the décor.

NOTES:
While written for one female performer, the piece could be staged as a two-
person play or a dancing chorus. The *elemental* voice(s) begins to speak:
lyrical – a rhythmic ebb and flow. The *human voice* emerges in a burst:
reactive, staccato, inflating, deflating, changing. The elemental and the human
voices eventually become one.

These instructions are merely suggestions – a director cannot help but direct as
she writes.

~~~~~~~~~~~~~

> *Darkness. A shimmer of light shines on a face that begins to*
> *talk, slowly brightening and expanding into a large circle.*
> *The play begins quietly and works itself up – accompanied by*
> *expanding movement in the spotlight, circling it, stepping out*
> *of it… stepping back in.*

I am the butterfly that persisted…
Fluttering my wings
Even when the flowers were no longer
Sending messages far and beyond…

A cloud forms above dry land
It rains.

I am the rain… the droplets that fall on the scorched surface – your heritage
On soil you killed and wells you dried – I let myself fall
Onto the crust that threatens to break – I did not desist
Pouring into rivers where once things lived – murky
I persist…
To flow into the crevices of the earth and find my way
To the seas of plastic – between bottles and bags I persist
Trying with all my might to dissolve your toxins
Too much, yet…
I persist
To dance with the wind and make waves
Crashing against the shore time and again –

Are you listening?
I am here.
Under your feet
I am the body you raped and raped and raped –
Strong words you don't like to hear.
You punctured my core and sucked me out dry.
A vessel of light – you filled me with filth.
I wanted to erupt but
I desisted and desisted until ENOUGH.
Volcano. Burn *everything*.
Are you listening?

> *(bursts)* I am listening, damn it, but what can I do.
> I inherited this mess. I did not commit the crimes.
> I'm doing my best here and you know it. Do I have to list things!?

> *Beat.*

What can I do against the machine? It's not even about you to begin with.
(rants) It's about greed. Buying, consuming, botoxing, bombing, "liking," fucking, GPD.

> *Beat.*

Slavery. Empower the people! Are you kidding me?
They'll tax the wind and buy out the sun before they give it gratis.
(inflates) It's too much of a burden to carry.

My vertebra tectonic plates, they slide no longer.
They collide
Collide collapse collapse –
What are you willing to let go of to save me?
To save yourself...

Pauses. Thinks.

Take preemptive measures.
(like a mantra) Lie down before I faint. Breathe –

I am the breath that persisted
To get knocked out of you
And to come back in –

Withdraw from society. Move to a forest.
Grow my own greens –

I am the wind that will persist
To storm and uproot your trees

Why are you punishing me?

I am the tree you cut down

Beat.

I had no choice. You threatened to fall.
(broken) I heard you weep under the chainsaw...

I want you to hear. Don't close your ears.
Let me guide you.
You don't trust me.
You interfere at the wrong time

Plucking away, epilating your gardens, calling my medicines weeds

Begins to say something –

I am the thorns, the nettle, the bees that persisted –

To prick

I am the prickle that persisted
To wake you up before the dawn
But you persisted to turn your back on me

I –

I persisted to rise and set
Wax and wane
Sending you signs with the birds and beasts.
My songs you no longer hear –

I listened. I wrote. I tried –

Why did you stop?

Beat.

No one was reading.

I am the inspiration that persists
The thoughts that never die
The words that force their way into existence

Covers her eyes and face.

I am the vision that persists
To penetrate the darkness
I am the dream –

(cutting) Naïve! Failed. Unheard

Persisted!
I am the simple soul that persists in believing
But you were busy playing important
Set your ego aside and let me speak
I am you, but you have forgotten...
Ignorant of what I taught you – blind to what you know

Beat.

Mother knows best.

When will you learn, child?

Touching her belly.

I... the child that chose not to be born
In an overpopulated planet
The spirit that never became –

Or did it...

Beat.

I'm listening.

(together) It's time.

LANA I. NASSER: telling stories on the page and the stage. Born and raised in Jordan, she studied and lived for many years across the U.S. In 2013, she planted her roots in Limburg, Netherlands. She is an ecofeminist with a background in Psychology and Consciousnesses Studies, specialized in dreams; a performing and voice artist and a workshop facilitator; a writer with publications in Arabic, English and Dutch; a mythology buff in love with language and nature... a *fellaha* and beekeeper. She is the founder of Maskan: Aat Theater in the Netherlands.

BREATHING SPACE

Yvette Nolan

Two decades ago, walking down a Montreal street with a friend, I said I thought we should not be allowed to make anything new, that there was enough stuff and we should all just learn to make do with what already existed. She thought I was being extreme. Also, two decades before that, Marvin Gaye warned us.

~~~~~~~~~~~~~~~~

MOD is sorting things. RAN enters with sack or bag of some sort. They are both dressed in a motley assemblage of clothing and fabric.

MOD: abundance

RAN: and to you

MOD: good kill?

RAN: extremely

MOD: good work

pats space beside her

right here

RAN empties out the bag. There is an assortment of salvaged things. They could be an old cookie tray or tin, one end of a tool — a hammer? An axe head? A spade? A metal rack of some sort, an old piece of clothing, a long piece of rope, or wire, or chain. They could be a hundred years old, or ten.

MOD sorts through them. She picks up the tool and grunts approvingly.

RAN: remember when you could just go into a store and buy a new one of these?

MOD: hush. blasphemy

RAN: it's not blasphemy, Mod, it's just memory

MOD: the kids might hear you

RAN: so what if they do? they know it hasn't always been this way. I think Ker remembers more than he tells. don't you think it's important they know why we aren't allowed new things?

MOD: there is nothing new under the sun

RAN, *laughs*: I love it when you quote scripture at me

> *RAN moves in for a cuddle.*

RAN: talk dirty to me… if you could have one brand spanking new thing, what would it be?

MOD, *pushing him off gently*: you'll be getting a spanking if you don't stop it

RAN: oooh, more, more! come on, what would it be, a new stainless pot? a white linen shirt?

MOD: Ran, get off me, the kids'll be back any minute

RAN: come on, my love, dance with me

MOD: dance with – what has gotten into you?

RAN: Mod, Moddie, Mod, have you even been outside today?

MOD: I was out this morning to get water. I've been busy

RAN: it was a beautiful day

MOD, *skeptical*: a beautiful day

RAN: I swear, the sky was almost blue

MOD, *after a beat*: really?

RAN: I swear, Mod. and the air – well, I actually can't recall what the air was like. that's a good thing, right?

> *RAN stops and thinks.*

RAN: yep, nope. no smell. the air had no smell today

MOD: or else you're just so used to it

RAN: or else it's almost fresh again

MOD: huh

RAN: maybe it's working

MOD: of course it's working

RAN: but so quickly – ?

MOD: they always said mother earth could regenerate if we just gave her a chance

RAN: if we just stopped making things

> *MOD is thoughtful.*

RAN: which is why, old woman, I think you should dance with me

MOD: old woman?

> *RAN takes MOD's hands and helps her up. He embraces her and starts to dance, singing.*

RAN, *sings*: *oh mercy mercy me*
   oh things aren't what they used to be

MOD: you know, I have a piece of wood that is almost the right size to be a handle for that axe head. If you were to –

RAN: tomorrow. tomorrow. there's lots of time to work tomorrow. relax for a minute, melt into your loving partner's arms

MOD: the kids

RAN: that's right, this is how we made kids

MOD: oh you're bad

RAN: but I can be very very good

   MOD softens, maybe giggles.

RAN, *sings*: *oh mercy mercy me*
   oh things aren't what they used to be

   They dance, gently. Perhaps MOD joins RAN in the song. Still dancing...

MOD: I can't think of a thing.

RAN: what?

MOD: I can't think of a single brand new thing that I want

RAN: huh

MOD: isn't that amazing

   They dance, RAN still singing or humming.

MOD: is it really almost blue, Ran?

RAN: almost blue, Mod

MOD: I would like to see that

RAN: maybe tomorrow

MOD: maybe tomorrow

They dance.

YVETTE NOLAN is an Algonquin playwright, director, and dramaturg. She has written dozens of plays, long and short, including *Annie Mae's Movement, Alaska, The Unplugging, Prophecy*, and the libretto *Shanawdithit*. She loves the short-form play. Her book, *Medicine Shows*, about Indigenous theatre in Canada, was published by Playwrights Canada Press in 2015, and *Performing Indigeneity*, which she co-edited with Ric Knowles, was published in 2016. She is an Artistic Associate of Signal Theatre.

STARING HER DOWN

Matthew Paul Olmos

I was inspired by a book called *The Wave*, which discusses the history and current research on rogue waves; strangely, it also discusses big wave surfing. But with this piece, I was interested in looking at something macro like rogue waves and their potential increase as caused by climate change, but from a micro lens, i.e., two individuals staring one down.

~~~~~~~~~~~~~~~~~~~~

> *CAPTAIN, female of color, 40s, is dressed as though on a ship. She stands looking out at something vast.*
>
> *A POLITICIAN walks up next to her.*

A POLITICIAN: I didn't think they were real.

> *CAPTAIN hands him a pair of binoculars, he doesn't take.*

CAPTAIN: I guess you don't really need them. Now.

A POLITICIAN: A tidal wave… it sounds like some movie.

CAPTAIN: Rogue.

A POLITICIAN: Pardon?

CAPTAIN: They're more scientifically called rogue waves, as our understanding of them is finite.

A POLITICIAN: What's to understand. They're a freak of Mother Nature. And one of them is about to… clear us out of her way.

CAPTAIN: For generations they were like old wives' tales passed down from ship captains who'd run into one while lost in the center of the ocean. But as they've become more common, as of late, some of them have actually been recorded by human instrument. Like finding Atlantis.

A POLITICIAN: And now? Are we... recording?

CAPTAIN: Oh yea. That's the only fact that's giving me comfort right this very moment. That the world will have further footage, and actual measurements of... what it is you and I are staring down right now.

A gust of wind, wet. They both get pushed back a bit.

A POLITICIAN: I would think the human life aboard this vessel would be what matters most. That's what people truly care about.

CAPTAIN looks at A POLITICIAN.

CAPTAIN: And how about when a rogue just like that one rolls in closer. When they are no longer a freak occurrence, but a common one. When they begin crashing right up on our coasts.

A POLITICIAN: I thought they only occurred out in the middle –

CAPTAIN: We're not so far out. What you and I are looking at right now is the closest rogue wave in recorded human history.

A POLITICIAN: ...I find it eerie how you're able to say that so calm. In fact, you seem...

CAPTAIN: Tell me.

A POLITICIAN: I don't know what it is, but something in your voice, in your whole... way of being here, feels... satisfied or –

Beat.

CAPTAIN: When I look out there, I don't see just only death. I see an alarming. A sounding bell for all mankind to finally hear.

A POLITICIAN: Perhaps that's the difference between you and I. I see human tragedy and loved ones that will suffer such horrible loss. You see...

CAPTAIN: Apparently, this is what it takes. Mountainous waves to reach up to the heavens, their crests lit by the sun or moon, as they barrel towards human life. That's how enlarged our world has to react, to all we've done to her, for us to finally take notice.

But my question to you: In a few moments, when your life is drowned alongside mine, what will our loved ones react? Will they spend all their prayers on you and this un'convenient research trip you decided to ride along on, or will they even consider what it is that caused the catastrophe you and I are about to be forever caught in?

Sounds of something massive closing in. A POLITICIAN backs up scared, CAPTAIN admires in awe.

A POLITICIAN: ...how can you even... discuss... that... when... JESUSCHRISTLOOKATHER...

CAPTAIN: Well, what choice do I have...?

A rogue wave lands, swallowing them both up along with everything that they've been standing on.

MATTHEW PAUL OLMOS is a three-time Sundance Institute Fellowship/Residency recipient, Humana Festival Commissioned Playwright, Cherry Lane Mentor Project alum as selected by Taylor Mac, New Dramatists Resident, Center Theatre Group LA Writer, New York Theatre Workshop Fellow, Oregon Shakespeare Festival Black Swan playwright, Princess Grace Awardee in Playwriting, and La MaMa's Ellen Stewart Playwright Awardee as selected by Sam Shepard. Mentored by Ruth Maleczech through Mabou Mines/SUITE, his work has been presented nationally, internationally, and is published and taught at universities.

ANG DIWATA SA BUNDOK BANAHAW, OR THE GODDESS OF MT. BANAHAW

Giovanni Ortega, adapted from a story by Abelardo Molina

SETTING:
Magat River, Cagayan Valley, in the Isabela province of Luzon, Philippines

CHARACTERS:
DIWATA, SA INANG KALIKASAN, Goddess, Mother Earth
ENKANTO, SA IMPONG MAGAT, Grandfather Magat, a Spirit in human form
PULITIKO, POLITICIAN, president of a corporation
KA INGGO, a tribal leader
KATUTUBO, narrator, an Indigenous person from the Cagayan Valley of Luzon

KATUTUBO sings a lullaby. Kumakanta.

KATUTUBO: *Sana'y di nagmaliw ang dati kong araw*
   Nang munti pang bata sa piling ni nanay
   Nais kong maulit ang awit ni inang mahal
   Awit ng pag-ibig habang ako'y nasa duyan

   I hope my former days don't fade away
   When I was a young child in Mom's arms
   I want Beloved Mother's song to repeat
   Song of love while I was in the cradle

   On the mountaintop of Banahaw.

IMPONG MAGAT: I've done all that I can do to stop the politician from building a high-rise, but he continues to cut down trees. So many of the people from here cannot do anything. They have protested and some have died because of it.

In anger, DIWATA speaks to IMPONG MAGAT.

DIWATA: Go down from the mountain and send them the message that a storm is coming as punishment for treating nature in such a manner. No one can stop this from occurring as the heavens have approved it.

KATUTUBO, *to audience*: The storm continued for a week and the rain never faltered, endangering the people of the Valley.

IMPONG MAGAT: I know that your patience is at its limit, but please stop the punishment. Please give me strength to save them. I promise that I will save the land and all its creatures.

KATUTUBO, *to audience*: Goddess puts an amulet with a key on Impong Magat.

DIWATA: This necklace will help open people's minds in order to save humanity. Be careful of the key so that you can return to being a spirit after your job is accomplished.

KATUTUBO, *to audience*: *Kadiliman.* Darkness.
Thunder and the sound of the wind.
It comes closer and becomes louder.
Until the rain falls and the storm arrives.
Uulan. Rain. A mountainous landslide occurs.
Ilang araw matapos gumuho ang bundok.
The sun never shone. Days passed and the landslide continued.

She sings.[22]

Sa aking pagtulog na labis ang himbing
Ang bantay ko'y tala, ang tanod ko'y bituin
Sa piling ni nanay, langit ay buhay
Puso kong may dusa sabik sa ugoy ng duyan

In my sleep that's very peaceful

---

[22] Here is a link to the song, *Sa Ugoy ng Duyan*, as performed by Lea Salonga in 2016: https://www.youtube.com/watch?v=PpdAzjYwGss

The planets guard me
The stars watch over me
In Mom's arms
Life was like heaven
My heart that's hurting
Yearns for the sway of the cradle.

IMPONG MAGAT: *Bayan Ko*. What happened to our surroundings, they've become a cave of death. I can hear the pain and feel the suffering of my home. Home.

KATUTUBO, *to audience*: Impong Magat goes to a corner, gets down on his knees, and starts digging. He goes from one area to another, hoping to find what the landslide covered. He continues to look incessantly and digs with his bare hands.

PULITIKO enters.

PULITIKO: *Ano ang hinahanap mo?* What are you looking for?

IMPONG MAGAT does not respond.

Halika na. Come on, let me help you find what you seek. Just tell me if it's the gold of this land or something cheap and unnecessary.

KA INGGO enters.

KATUTUBO, *to audience*: It's true that there is gold in our land but we will not admit this to him.

PULITIKO: *Tanda.* Leave this place, old man, because I've bought and now own this land, so whatever has been buried here is mine.

KA INGGO: Since you've arrived, you've lowered our people's morale and have done nothing but ruin our land. What you've demolished has caused this landslide.

PULITIKO: *Wala kang utang na loob.* You lack gratitude

I've done nothing but help your people succeed.

KA INGGO: The landslide took our home.

PULITIKO: *Wala akong pakiilam.* I don't care.

KA INGGO: My child was inside that house!

> *KA INGGO attacks POLITICIAN, but he takes his gun out and points it at KA INGGO.*

KATUTUBO: *HUWAG!* STOP!

> *KA INGGO leaves. PULITIKO turns back to IMPONG MAGAT.*

PULITIKO: *Lumayas ka na.* I know that what you're looking for must be a shining item.
Get out of here.

IMPONG MAGAT: I'm not leaving.

KATUTUBO, *to audience*: The politician's ears burn and his smile is like a dog's. The politician suddenly looks in a specific direction. He sees something on the ground. He will grab and hide it in his hands, and will show it to Impong Magat with his clenched fist. The politician has what he's looking for and puts it behind his back.

IMPONG MAGAT: You're trying to fool me but I know that you're a liar.

> *Silence.*

What are you hiding in your hand?

PULITIKO: *Wala.* Nothing.

IMPONG MAGAT: Give it to me. It is mine. *Akin na, sa akin 'yan.*

PULITIKO: *Nasaan ko mahahanap ang mg ginto?* Where can I find the gold?

IMPONG MAGAT: I don't know.

> *POLITICIAN takes out his gun and points it at IMPONG MAGAT.*

IMPONG MAGAT: If I am shot, you will lose the election.

KATUTUBO, *to audience*: The politician puts his hands down but Impong Magat tries to grab the gun away from him. Gun shot. The politician looks up. Ka Inggot is holding the gun and runs away once Impong Magat sees him. The politician falls with his fist still clenched. Impong Magat slowly opens his hand and sees nothing there. He cries like a child.

> *DIWATA appears.*

DIWATA: *Anak.* My Child.

IMPONG MAGAT: *Ina.* This is the ground where I was trying to save...

> *IMPONG MAGAT does not hear KATUTUBO.*

KATUTUBO: ...me from the landslide. I grabbed his necklace instead and ripped it from his neck until I disappeared into the ground. He saved many, but feels that he didn't save enough.

> *DIWATA touches KATUTUBO gently.*

IMPONG MAGAT: This is my fault, and now I cannot go back to being a spirit.

> *IMPONG MAGAT kneels towards DIWATA. KATUTUBO watches.*

Para nyo pong awa. Patwarin n'yo po ako. Please forgive me.

DIWATA: We will now return to Mother Earth's home. You will be rewarded for your kindness to people.

> *KATUTUBO hands DIWATA the necklace, which she places around IMPONG MAGAT's neck. KATUTUBO appears to IMPONG MAGAT.*

IMPONG MAGAT: Katutubo?

KATUTUBO: *Salamat po.* Thank You.
Impong Magat.

DIWATA: *Engkanto.* Spirit.

KATUTUBO, *singing: Sana'y di nagmaliw ang dati kong araw ang munti pang bata sa piling ni nanay*

> *IMPONG MAGAT stands.*

ALL: *Nais kong maulit ang awit ni inang mahal*
Awit ng pag-ibig habang ako'y nasa duyan.
Nais kong matulog sa dating duyan ko, Inay.

I hope my former days don't fade away
When I was a young child in Mom's arms
I want Beloved Mother's song to repeat
Song of love while I was in the cradle
I Would like to sleep in my old cradle, Mother.

> *Ngingiti silang lahat at lalakad papuntang likod hanggang tuluyang didilim.*

> *They all smile at each other and walk away until they disappear.*

274 | LIGHTING THE WAY

ABELARDO MOLINA is a Filipino playwright who won the Carlos Palanca Memorial Awards for Literature with his one-act plays *Daigdig Dinaig ng Makamundong Pananalig* (1992) and *Ma-Te!* (1998) .

GIOVANNI ORTEGA is a Filipino-American playwright, translator, and professor at Pomona College. He has been involved with Climate Change Theatre Action since 2015 with his *plays El Pescador y La Lluvia – The Fisherman and the Rain* and *Fugaz de La Piel Canela – Fleeting Cinnamon Skin*. In addition, he produced and directed short films entitled *Green Shorts: Films (re)Imagining Our Troubled Environment* as well as Caridad Svich's *Upon The Fragile Shore*. Giovanni was recently commissioned by National Poetry Festival Singapore to write the poetic plays *Benches* (2018), *Palindromes* (2019) and *Belonging* (2020) . His second book, *Ang Gitano – They Gypsy*, was published by Carayan Press.

NIBI (WATER) PROTECTORS

Corey Payette

NOTE:

The Royal Canadian Mounted Police (RCMP) is the federal and national police force of Canada. The RCMP provides law enforcement at the federal level.

~~~~~~~~~~~~~~~~~~~~

> *This winter. NEEKO, an Anishinaabe woman in a long fur coat and fur hat sits behind a wooden barricade positioned over a bridge. The sound of water gushing beneath her. She holds a feather in her hand. It is dark and she's gently singing a song her Nookomis (Grandmother) used to sing to her as a child. She's cold so she sings it softly beneath her breath. ERIC enters running and is out of breath.*

ERIC: Neeko, the RCMP are on their way! Mary posted a video of the SUVs driving through town!

NEEKO: How many?

ERIC: She wasn't sure, it was about six trucks that drove through all headed this way. Do you think they know about Jim's passing?

NEEKO: Of course, they know. That's probably why they are coming now.

ERIC: Assholes.

NEEKO: Yah.

ERIC: What should we do?

NEEKO: Go back to Camp. Get all the young ones out the back road. Don't let the Elders come to the bridge, we don't want anyone else getting hurt. But the settlers who have come here to help now have a job to do.

ERIC: I'll run back and get them. Neeko, we need you here, you can't get arrested.

NEEKO: Hurry, Eric! Run back and get the others, we don't have time to stand around lips flappin'.

> *ERIC runs off back to the camp. As he exits, one RCMP SUV pulls up on the opposite side of the bridge. NEEKO looks over the barricade and sees an officer get out. She starts to sing her Nookomis' song more loudly. The officer walks slowly over the bridge toward the barricade but is only being lit from his headlights shinning from behind. NEEKO gets to the end of her song.*

KENNY: Neeko, is that you?

> *NEEKO recognizes her friend KENNY's voice. They knew each other a few months ago, had a couple drinks and hit it off. He's an RCMP.*

NEEKO: Get out of here, Kenny. There are more RCMPs on the way, and I know you don't wanna be around when they get here.

KENNY: That's why I came. I'm not supposed to be here but I wanted to warn you what was gonna happen.

NEEKO: It was posted all over our Facebook. We have people in town, so thanks but unless you can turn those colonizers around, you won't be able to help us.

KENNY: I'm not trying to help you, just wanted to give you a heads up.

NEEKO: Save it. Don't need it.

KENNY: You only know what you've seen – but there's more on the way. Fuck it, I don't even know why I'm here, you don't want to hear it.

NEEKO: Tell your buddies they are not welcome on our territory, stand up for us. That's one way of helping.

KENNY: You know I can't do that. I'd lose my job. I've already made the case to them not to come out here, but now I'm stuck doing the shit jobs no one else wants to do.

NEEKO: Are you really complaining to me about your shit job? We have been out here for months. RCMP coming onto our territory asking us to move for them. No, not for them, for a fucking corporation! Apparently that's more valuable than our treaties, our lives, our *nibi*.[23] Did you know that Elder Jim died on Friday?

KENNY: I heard about that.

NEEKO: So did they. And that's why they chose tonight to come. An Elder dies in our community and we are grieving so that is the perfect time to make arrests and end this. That is what your uniform represents.

She spits.

Fucking disgusting.

KENNY: We're just doing our job.

ERIC comes running back in.

ERIC: Kenny, what the fuck – get out of here, man. We have enough to deal with out here without your bringing your shit into it.

KENNY: I'm not bringing my shit.

NEEKO: He came to warn us.

KENNY: Just a heads up. I was nearby so I thought I should.

ERIC: Well it won't do any good. So will you just sneak off before they arrive, pretend you were never here?

---

[23] *Nibi* means water in *Anishinaabemowin*, or the Ojibwe language.

NEEKO: What a hero.

KENNY turns and starts walking back toward his SUV. NEEKO yells after him.

A hero would stand with us. Would stand for what's right.

Pause.

Is your paycheck worth more than our clean drinking water?

KENNY stops.

We're doing this for all of us.

KENNY turns to face them.

KENNY: I know. That's why I came.

KENNY turns around and gets into his truck and drives off. A group of water protectors arrive at the barricade blocking it in as a dozen RCMP trucks with flashing lights and sirens speed down the snowy dirt road toward the bridge. NEEKO sings again and the water protectors join her as the RCMP walk toward the barricade.

COREY PAYETTE is proud of his Oji-Cree heritage from Northern Ontario. He has worked as a playwright, actor, composer, and director across Canada. He is the Artistic Director of Urban Ink (Vancouver), past Artist-in-Residence with National Arts Centre (NAC) English Theatre, and founder of Raven Theatre. *Children of God* (Urban Ink, NAC, The Cultch, Citadel Theatre, Western Canada Theatre, Segal Centre), *Moonlodge* (Urban Ink/NAC), *Les Filles du Roi* (Urban Ink, Fugue, Raven), *Sedna* (Urban Ink, Caravan Farm). Winner of John Hirsch Prize (Canada Council for the Arts).

THE EARTH'S BLUE HEART

Katie Pearl

This play was inspired by the transcription of a conversation between the Indigenous activist Frank Ettiwageshek and the violinist and ethnographer Tanya Kalmanovitch. Frank was explaining early treaty rights to Tanya, treaties giving Indigenous communities rights to fish in certain waters. I loved the perception shift his explanation sparked in me – that the rights were actually to the *relationship* with the fish, rather than to the fish themselves. In this play, the idea of relationship is extended to immersion: to be in the ocean is to be in relationship to it, to aspects of it.

~~~~~~~~~~~~

Two humans stand together on the stage.

They hold their hands up to their eyes as though holding binoculars. They peer in front of them, over the heads of the audience.

It is as though they are traveling by staying in one place: time and space are shuttling past them at high speed. They see what might be road signs flash by. They try to read them before they're gone.

Anticipation grows:

1: The sign says: …
   "Competent Swimmers Welcome"!

2: …Okay…!

1: The sign says: …
   "Changed Priorities ahead"!

2: …Good good. Good!

1: The signs says: ...
   "Living Laboratory – Please Be Aware"!!

2: ...Oh my god great yes!

1: The sign says:

2: ...yes?

1: The sign says...

2: Can you read it?!

1: The sign says...

2: What??!

1: The sign says...
   "You Have Now Entered Earth's Blue Heart."

> *A sudden enormous inhale.*
> *A slow exhale. Binoculars down.*
> *Their arms might float away from their bodies.*
>
> *They might drift slightly apart.*
>
> *They might be in the ocean.*
> *They might be in the sky.*
>
> *They remain there, drifting.*
>
> *Meanwhile.*
>
> *Three others have stepped forward as though to microphones.*
> *A very public discourse. Imagine cameras flashing.*

3: What we are asking for here is to have a relationship
   is the *right* to have a

4: (is that the right word?)

3: Yes. A relationship
   the right to
   to be in relationship

4: with the fish.

5: And then of course we will *have* the fish we will have all the fish

3: No not have

5: and we can take
   the fish we need

3: No. Not *have*.
   Not *have*. I said *be*. I said *be in relationship with the fish*
   That's what we want. That's what we want to reserve.

> *The floaters are still drifting.*

2: I am so happy.

1: I am so happy. Look where we are.
   Are you happy?

2: I am so happy.

1: Look at where we are.

2: I am so happy.

> *Back at the microphones.*

5: But those are our fish. That's our water. We *fish*!

4: We do!

5: We won that right!

3: What we have *won*
the right we have *won* is
the right NOT to say "those are *our* fish!"
We never have to say that again!

4: But the right *to* fish

5: I am saying that we reserve the right *to* the fish!

3: We reserve the right to pray for the fish.
We reserve the right to dance for the fish, to sing for the fish, to catch and eat the fish.
To live with the fish; to have a relationship with the fish.[24]
That's what we're reserving.

> *Still floating:*

2: I feel... free.

3: Isn't that a relief?

1: I feel... like I'm being held.

3: Doesn't that feel better?

5, *an admission*: It does take a weight off.

2: Being held. That's hopeful.

> *A brief pause.*

> *Perhaps the people at the microphones begin to float, just slightly. Imperceptibly.*

---

[24] Spoken by Frank Ettawageshik, 2019 President of the Association of American Indian Affairs, in a 2017-05-16 conversation with violist Tanya Kalmanovitch, author of *Tar Sands Songbook*.

4: Did you know the Antarctic Blackfin Icefish have blood that is clear? It's like they have evolved to have useful anemia.

3: We can be in relationship with the Antarctic Blackfin Icefish.

4: And a heart three times bigger than it should be.

3: Four.

4: Four times bigger.

3: A heart 60 times bigger than it should be!
The heart of the Antarctic Blackfin Icefish is actually on the outside of the body. It's like a heart with a fish swimming inside of it.

5: That's not true.

Still floating:

1: Hope is not something you feel, it's something you do.

5: Is that true?

4: The Stoplight Loosejaw Dragon Fish has red lights under its eyes that other fish can't see. So it can see them but they can't see it.

3: We can be in relationship with the Stoplight Loosejaw Dragon Fish.

1: It's so possible. Isn't it so possible to adapt?

4: The octopus has a brain contained in its entire body.

3: We can be in relationship with the octopus.
With the elephant.

5: With the elephant?

3: With the elephant.

With the ocean.
With all of it.

Still floating:

2: I'm so happy.

1: Are you happy?

2: I'm so happy.

All five people take another big inhale and exhale together, feeling the relationship to all of it.

KATIE PEARL is an American playwright, director, and interdisciplinary theater artist. As Co-Artistic Director of the Obie-winning PearlDamour, she regularly pushes the boundaries of contemporary theater with projects such as the eight-hour performed installation *HOW TO BUILD A FOREST* and the five-city / five-year *MILTON*. Pearl was the 2018 Quinn Martin Guest Chair of Directing at UCSD and the 2017 Anschutz Distinguished Fellow at Princeton. She is currently an Assistant Professor of Directing at Wesleyan University.

TRÉS MARIAS: CATEGORIES AND LUZ

Shy Richardson and Karina Yager

This piece is an excerpt from the larger *Trés Marias*, a theatre and spoken word piece exploring communities affected by climate change, and specifically Hurricane Maria. *Categories* and *Luz* are an ode to the human cost of climate change, and the light and resilience of the communities that emerge from the wreckage. This collaborative piece was supported by the Superhero Clubhouse Climate Fellowship for Environmental Justice.

CATEGORIES

SCIENTIST: I'm starting support meetings for other data addicts like me. Together, we can talk about the planetary boundaries, the correlations of temperature rise and greenhouse gas emissions, slowdowns of thermohaline circulation... how it was like in the last interglacial, you know, the Eemian analogue, 125,000 years ago when it was 2°C warmer and sea level rise up to nine meters higher. Should we call it the Anthropocene, the Capitalocene?

We could talk about wind categories together, debate whether they were sufficient in grasping the force of a hurricane. We'd muse about the current allocated gradients from "*some damage*" to "*extensive*" to "*devastating*" to "*catastrophic*" to "*more catastrophic.*" Is that Saffir-Simpson Index really saying anything?

Category One: Seventy-seven miles an hour, that's 33 meters per second. Your mobile home will topple if it's not anchored, weak trees will snap, a few shingles will blow off, the lights may go out for a few days.

HUMAN: Did somebody say... HURRICANE PARTY?! Little bit of rain ain't gon' stop this train! You need a ride to the supermarket – gotta stock up on the essentials: beer, chips, snacks, and maybe probably grab some batteries or something just in case. The news is always hyping it up, but besides a few storm drain overflows, you aren't worried.

WATER: When the sea meets the air, the eye is born. The heat gives strength to this nation of rain drops, turning vapor to gasoline, propelled by the steam beneath the surface.

SCIENTIST: Category Two: Your roof may be damaged, probably your windows and doors too. Trees will be uprooted. Total power outage likely.

HUMAN: The news cycle is non-stop. The supermarket shelves have emptied. The streets are bare, aware of what looms. You hope that the news speaks too soon. You know that hurricanes only prey on those islands God forgot to bless and favor. The power of your prayers never waver.

WATER: Like a cloud descending from the heavens, when the heat rises, born in the middle of an ocean of nowhere. Every drop a cog, every gust like a footstep, somewhere.

SCIENTIST: Category Three: Many homes will be damaged, flooding for days expected, many more trees lost, sewage leaks likely, power out for weeks.

HUMAN: When a hurricane comes, it isn't the wind or the rain that will kill you. It is the pieces of the places you used to know, flying through the air at breakneck... break-skull... break-heart velocity. It is the pieces of your neighborhood shaken loose and weaponized, projectile mangos and lawn chairs. The playgrounds you, and then your children, used to climb on, leveled. Your memories, twisted amongst the rubble.

WATER: I'm letting off some steam... I've been holding on to your heat for too long.

SCIENTIST: Category Four: Irreparable damage to homes and gas stations. Beaches eroded. Reefs damaged. Trees cleared. Flooding, flooding, more flooding. Months of power outages and no clean water.

HUMAN: You wish for the arms of Atlas, for the ability to hoist your world between the blades of your shoulders, for the strength to not have to leave it behind. Though there is strength in the leaving, strength in the living. But how do you evacuate your own life? What makes the cut of carrying – perhaps it is the photographs of your dead grandmother, or the birth certificates of your children, or the couch your mother gave you. Maybe you will keep it because if the sea comes knocking on your front door, you can hope to float.

WATER: Letting it all go. Giving it all back.

SCIENTIST: Category Five: Total destruction prevalent. No building, garage, school, home, or hotel spared. All flooded. Trees debarked. Who knows when the power will be back.

HUMAN: God can't hear your prayers over the roar of wind. Before the water comes, your kneecaps are aching altar, your spine tight with the tension of tomorrow. Your home is an island, sinking into itself. You stand on the bed to see out of the window without approaching it, as it shakes against the pane. There is violence in the rage of the wind. When was your favor ripped from beneath you? You have lived a life of rosary beads and altar knees. The phone calls stop as the lights flicker. Telephone poles are down, the sky is dark and the streets are electric. All there is, is rain. All there is, is prayer. All there is, is quiet dark.

WATER: Shhhhhhh…

Lights fade to black.

LUZ

CHORUS OF VOICES: *Se fue la luz!*

And what's a people to do?
When the sky caves in
And you are reminded of what you have always been:
Another motherflower
At the mercy of the Sun

At the root you remember
It could always be worse
At the root, that's who you are
Ain't gotta look far to find a blessing to count

So when the sun sets out to sleep
Behind the mountainside
Or its orange gold melts behind the skyline
And the darkness sets in
It begins

Sing a song to the moon
When she pops out
And plants a kiss of glow
On foreheads and techos in every pueblo

What is darkness
When you are a lightbulb
Powered by stars?

What is fear
When you are shield and lightsaber
In the face of danger
Mighty matriarch made of moonrock and motherhood

What is a hurricane
When you've raised a nation?
What is a hurricane
But a deep exhale
Yemaya tryna find the strength
You keep buried in your lungs

When the power is down
We can depend on you to turn up
You who keeps the axis
Tilted between your shoulder blades

In the dark
They say we become people again
Word to Juan Luis Gonzales
And you'll hear it when you turn your ears to the street
In the morning

When the sun comes back
Sprawls and stretches
Across the horizon
Lets the moon kick her feet up
And pull the darkness up by her ear for a nap
You'll hear it

    Sound of balls bouncing.

The calming of calamity
Sounds like kids just coming back
Outside to play

It smells like
Food cooked over open fire
Breaking bread
Because death is a kind of
Eternal famine
So you find flame and you feast
Because you are alive

KARINA YAGER specializes in interdisciplinary research aimed at monitoring the impacts of climate change in mountain regions, while also understanding the human dimensions of unprecedented socio-ecological change on Earth. Yager's research combines remote sensing analysis with alpine vegetation studies and ethnographic fieldwork with Indigenous Andean pastoralists. She is currently an Assistant Professor in the School of Marine and Atmospheric Sciences at Stony Brook University in New York.

SHY RICHARDSON is a writer, performer, youth advocate, and hip hop head from New York City (before it turned into a bike lane). She believes wholeheartedly in the transformative nature of the arts, and hopes to create work that explores Black and Brown folks and the spaces we inhabit, create, and break free of.

KUMU KUKUI

Kiki Rivera

This piece is inspired by countless conversations with Indigenous people from Oceania and Turtle Island regarding climate change and land acknowledgement. It is written against the backdrop of Thirty Meter Telescope protests on Mauna a Wākea, gunshots, and traditional percussions.

NOTE:
This play is intended for a child of any age or gender and three adults (gender and age open).

~~~~~~~~~~~~~

> *Darkness. The sounds of traditional Philippine drums and gongs play, fading into Polynesian pate drums. Under the drum beats are sounds of gunshots. Lights come up on a modern dressed CHILD, who sits in the center of a sandbox. CHILD is surrounded by THREE BEINGS dressed all in white, building a house of sand for the child. The sandbox sits under a kukui nut tree; the kukui nuts were used as lamps in ancient times.*

1: Do you remember?

2: Do you remember?

3: Do you remember?

1: A time where the people navigated by stars...

2: Sailed the seas...

3: Read the waters...

1: Read the wind...

2: Read the birds?

3: You were brought here by navigators...

1: By storytellers...

2: By weavers of pond fronds...

3: And beaters of bark.

1: You don't remember.

2: You don't remember?

3: You need reminding.

1: Your people came by wind and by water.

2: Your people are wind and water...

3: And fire and earth.

1: Your ancestors settled on the land of Kānaka Oiwi.

2: They settled on the land of the Tongva.

3: And the land of Muwekma Ohlone.

1: Your grandmother is buried there.

2: Her bones are cared for by the spirits of that land.

3: As we build this house for you...

1: You must not forget.

2: To acknowledge the first caretakers of the land...

3: On which you build your house.

1: You must not forget…

2: To thank them…

3: To fight alongside them as they protect sacred lands…

1: Waters…

2: And mountains.

> *The sounds of the drums and gunshots get louder. Voices join the soundscape of drums and gunshots, chanting, "Kū kia'i mauna!"*

3: Fight

1: Fight

2: Fight

3: With prayer

1: With song

2: With dance

3: Fight using your voice.

1: Here. Take this. You'll need it.

> *1 hands CHILD a pen.*

> *2 hands CHILD a journal.*

2: Its pages are empty. Fill them with your voice.

3: Speak truth!

1: The house is built!

2: The house is built!

3: The house is built!

> *The THREE BEINGS lift CHILD to their feet, dust CHILD off, then disappear into the kukui nut tree. All sounds fade away. CHILD is unsure of what to do next. The sound of a chainsaw is heard, then a masked man carrying a chainsaw enters. The man checks out the tree and finds a spot to cut into. CHILD panics.*

CHILD: Stop!

> *The masked man ignores CHILD and goes to cut. CHILD starts writing the word "STOP!!!" in the journal and puts it in the MASKED MAN's face while shouting "Stop!" MASKED MAN stops and puts his chainsaw down, picks up CHILD and moves CHILD away from the tree. CHILD is kicking and screaming.*

CHILD: Stop! Help! Stop!

> *CHILD is put down and CHILD begins to dance. MASKED MAN watches CHILD for a moment, laughs, and walks back to his chainsaw. CHILD gets ahead of MASKED MAN and dances between the chainsaw and MASKED MAN.*

> *CHILD points directly to an audience member.*

CHILD: Help!

> *CHILD continues pointing and begging for help until the audience member joins. Once audience member joins.*

CHILD: Dance!

Audience member dances, distracting MASKED MAN while CHILD grabs another member of the audience.

CHILD repeats "Help!" to each audience member CHILD takes. CHILD does this to gather enough participants to form a circle around the tree. CHILD makes participants hold hands with their backs toward the tree. MASKED MAN picks up his chainsaw and revs it to scare the people. CHILD encourages participants to chant:

CHILD: Stop!

The intention is to get louder, scaring MASKED MAN away. MASKED MAN leaves defeated.

Music starts to play. CHILD encourages all to dance.

CHILD: Thank you. Thank you. Thank you.

Lights and sound stay up. CHILD exits.

KIKI RIVERA (she, he, they) is an educated gender-queer person of color (Samoan-Filipinx, born and raised in Hawaii) and recognizes her privilege and responsibility to those marginalized communities. Her work focuses on cultural and sexual identity and the effects of colonization. Her play *Puzzy* is published in *Samoan Queer Lives*. Kiki believes in self-reflective storytelling from a contemporary Indigenous perspective and in creating space for marginalized theatre artists of color.

BLOOD ON THE LEAVES

Madeline Sayet

This short play is based on the traditional story of the Hunter and the Bear passed down by Gladys Tantaquidgeon to remind us that humans were always meant to make sacrifices so that nature can do what it needs, not the other way around.

~~~~~~~~~~~~~~~~~~~

A and B can be anyone. We are outside in New England, present.

A runs out through the audience, A is looking to the sky – trying to see the stars clearly.

B follows begrudgingly.

A: The stars – we need to check the stars. It's too cloudy. Can you see? What are they doing?

B: Who?

A: The Hunter and the Bear? Can you see them?

B: Why? My show is about to come on – it's cold – what are we doing out here?

A: It's very important. We need to figure out what they are doing.

B: It's too dark. They are just stars. Why does it matter?

A: Ha. Just stars? Those lights matter more than you can possibly imagine.

B: You're acting crazy.

A: I swear I saw him he was – when was the last time you saw blood on the leaves?

B: Okay, now I know you're crazy. I'm going back inside.

A: Blood on the leaves! When was the last time you saw it?

B: ....

A: What color is this leaf?

B: Brown

A: Exactly. Something is very, very, very wrong.

B: Oh my god – you New Englanders and your leaves – you are so weird. I'm going back inside.

A: It is not about the leaf – it is bigger than the leaf. A leaf is not just a leaf. Look at the leaf and look at the stars and tell me what you see.

B: I don't see anything.

A: Exactly. That is exactly the problem.

>   *A tries to see something in the sky.*

And you don't know where to begin looking.

>   *Looks up at the sky.*

What is he doing?

B: Who? I don't see – actually, I do see something – I see a crazy person running around talking about blood on the leaves.

A: I'm not crazy, I'm upset. We need to find the hunter. He's stopped doing what he is supposed to do.

B: Right…. Are you going to tell me what's going on?

A: He hasn't killed him. He's forgotten his sacrifice. How important it is.

B: Yes – I have just followed a sociopath outside, it is now confirmed.

A: Many things have happened – since the beginning of time – to maintain balance in the world. Some of them happen down here – but many happen up there – on the celestial level. A long, long time ago, the hunter and the bear were friends. Great friends.

B: Sorry, you are telling me two constellations are friends?

A: Laugh if you like – but the relationship between the hunter and the bear is extremely important. It's –

B: Okay – humor me – why does it matter that they are friends? Is their relationship in retrograde?

A: Things don't just happen. You think that the moon and the stars and the seasons just go – but that's not how it works – nature – it doesn't do things for us. There are sacrifices we must make for nature to do what it must. That is how the world works. How it's always worked.

B: So, you are mad at the sky now? Because?

A: I'm not mad at the sky – I'm mad at – Long, long ago the great spirit told the hunter he had to kill the bear.

B: Whatttttt – I thought you said they were friends.

A: They are, that's the point. He didn't want to do it. He never wants to do it. But he has to do it for the leaves.
Every year, at the end of summer – the hunter will not want to kill the bear – but he must do it. The bear will not want to die – but die he must. It's their duty to the earth. When the hunter kills the bear – the bear's blood and fat drips down onto the leaves, as he roasts the meat, and the dripping fat and blood is what causes the leaves to change colors.

B: Ew.

A: Not helping.

B: Okay but the leaves aren't changing colors – they are just brown. So why are we crazy chasing the sky.

A: People forget why they have to do things. The leaves don't change color for us. We have to make sacrifices for them.

B: And this is a big deal why?

A: Our entire world operates this way. He is supposed to be our reminder that we must sacrifice for each other. And every time this is forgotten we take one step closer to –

B: You're paranoid.

A: You are holding a brown leaf in autumn. And I don't see him.

B: Well, star beings can't just leave the sky... can they?

A: I don't know, this has never happened before.

>   *They search and search.*

B: Maybe it's a good thing. Maybe the bear will get to stay alive. Go bear! Go!

A: And who dies instead? There are sacrifices we must make for the world to go on as it should.

>   *They look, they search the sky, they look.*

A: What would you do if you were the hunter?

B: Go inside and watch my show. Maybe make some popcorn. Order a pizza...

A: Why did I even ask. New England – people come for the foliage – they admire it – judge whether it was as good as the year before. But most people don't know where it came from. They don't know the stories that come from the ground we stand on – the sky above us – those stories remind us that balance is required. And without it, everything stops working.

B: So let's say this year the hunter doesn't want to kill the bear...

A: And the bear says – please do not betray us...

B: And the leaves stop turning.

A: And the hunter buys a suit, and builds a skyscraper, and the leaves, they stop turning.

B: And he drops down to the world, and gets a television and a microwave

A: And the bear says please remember me, I am waiting. And the leaves, they are waiting too. For they know their part in the relationship. They all know what they are supposed to do.

B: But the hunter stopped doing what must be done.

A: So if the hunter stops

B: The bear stops

A: The leaves stop

B: And the great spirit?

> *They look up once more.*

A: I don't see the hunter.

B: I found the bear!

A: There he is... waiting... for...

B: I'm tired of this, I've got to go inside, I want to watch my show.

A: You don't care?

B: It's just a leaf. It's just a story. I'm sure the constellation will show back up later when it's less cloudy. Let it go.

> *B hands A the leaf. B exits.*

> *A sits down on the ground.*

> *A stares at the leaf and stares at the sky.*

A: Please come back. We need you to light the way.

MADELINE SAYET is a member of the Mohegan Tribe and the Executive Director of the Yale Indigenous Performing Arts Program. She is an award-winning theater maker who believes the stories we pass down inform our collective possible futures. For her work, she has been honored as a 2019 Drama League Director-in-Residence, a 2018 Forbes 30 Under 30 in Hollywood & Entertainment, TED Fellow, MIT Media Lab Director's Fellow, National Directing Fellow, and a recipient of The White House Champion of Change Award from President Obama.

THE REASON

Stephen Sewell

I teach young writers – wonderfully creative young people at the beginning of their lives and careers – and it has been heartbreaking to hear them say on numerous occasions that they don't want to have children because of the terrible prospects ahead for the world. We are in the midst of a catastrophic collapse of belief in the future, provoked in part by the refusal of people in positions of authority and power to take not only the science, but also our communal experience of disastrous climate change and habitat collapse seriously. This short play tries to convey my horror and sadness.

~~~~~~~~~~~~~~~~~

An interior somewhere. Night. Two people face one another...

DANZ: So here's the thing – this is what you're saying –

GRESH: I know what I'm saying –

DANZ: You love me –

GRESH: Of course I love you –

DANZ: And I love you –

GRESH: I love you, alright?

DANZ: And we want to live together and get married –

GRESH: Yes.

DANZ: That's what you said –

GRESH: Yes, I said –

DANZ: Live together and get married –

GRESH: Yes.

DANZ: Share our lives –

GRESH: Oh, shut up, will you?

DANZ: Do all the things married people do –

GRESH: Why are you doing this?

DANZ: But not have children.

GRESH: No – no children – I don't want to have children –

DANZ: Even though we can – even though we could – there's nothing wrong with us –

GRESH: I don't want children.

DANZ: And even if there was, we could do IVF –

GRESH: I don't want children.

DANZ: Surrogacy – we could do surrogacy.

GRESH: I don't want children.

DANZ: We could just have fucking kids, couldn't we –

GRESH: I don't want children.

DANZ: But you don't want children.

GRESH: I don't want children.

DANZ: Why?

GRESH: LOOK AT THE WORLD! LOOK AT THE WORLD!

DANZ: Jeezus...

GRESH: Look at the world – the disaster of the world – global warming, environmental collapse, the animals dying –

DANZ: Animals dying?

GRESH: Yes! Animals dying! LOOK AT THE WORLD!

DANZ: Alright – let's just say you're right –

GRESH: I am right – fuck – all you have to do is turn on the TV –

DANZ: But that's not –

GRESH: What?

DANZ: They just put that stuff on –

GRESH: What?

DANZ: They make it up –

GRESH: Who?

DANZ: The TV stations – the media –

GRESH: What?

DANZ: To sell stuff.

GRESH: Sell stuff?

DANZ: Yes – sell stuff – they make stuff up –

GRESH: Who?

DANZ: The media – fake news –

GRESH: Oh, the ice caps melting is fake news, is it?

DANZ: Well how do you know?

GRESH: The hottest year ever recorded – the Middle East dying of drought –

DANZ: All I'm saying –

GRESH: Millions of refugees trying to escape.

DANZ: All I'm saying is I LOVE YOU!

GRESH: AND I LOVE YOU BUT I DON'T WANT TO BRING A CHILD INTO A WORLD LIKE THIS!

DANZ: We can change it – we can do things to make it better.

GRESH: By not bringing one more mouth to feed into the world –

DANZ: No.

GRESH: What do you want a kid for? It's just narcissism and bullshit –

DANZ: It's love, for fuck's sake – it's what love is – two people don't get married to do the gardening together!

GRESH: Why not? Why not do the gardening together, and cook, and share a life –

DANZ: Until we both die shriveled up and cooked in the global disaster you mean?

GRESH: Well how much worse would it be holding your kids in your arms as you did it??

DANZ: No, no – that's not our future – we'll find a way – people will find a way.

GRESH: No, we won't. Don't you get it. It's over. The world is finished. And you know why the world is finished? It's because of people like you.

DANZ: Like me?

GRESH: Yes, people like you who won't look it in the face and call it what it is: there is no hope, and as long as people think there is, we won't do a fucking thing except dream of falling in love and having children.

DANZ, *slight pause*: So you don't love me at all?

GRESH, *slight pause*: I don't know what love is anymore.

DANZ: I love you.

GRESH: Why do you keep saying that?

DANZ: Because I don't want to die.

GRESH: You will.

DANZ: Well I don't want to die like this.

GRESH: Like what?

DANZ: Angry. Bitter. Hopeless.

GRESH: That's the world.

DANZ: No, it's not, it's you.

GRESH: Then why do you love me?

DANZ: Because I know you're none of those things.

GRESH: I love you.

DANZ: I know.

GRESH: And I don't know what to do.

STEPHEN SEWELL is an Australian writer and teacher who heads the Writing Department at the National Institute of Dramatic Art in Sydney, Australia. A prize-winning playwright and screenwriter, he is a well-known and public advocate of progressive issues, ranging from the environment to Indigenous and workers' rights. As a writer, he believes in a future that is creative, free, and respectful, not only of human rights but also of our fellow creatures on this beautiful, fragile planet.

THREE CONVERSATIONS

Lena Šimić with Neal Anderson and Sid Anderson

These conversations are both a memory of our family protests and a present enactment of thinking with children about climate change. The three of us promise to spill this writing into action.

CHARACTERS:
MOTHER, 44
SON 1, 18
SON 2, 16
SON 3, 11

~~~~~~~~~~~~~~~~~

Conversation 1: MOTHER and SON 1

SON 1 is looking at an old photograph of his mother at the age of 35. She is now 44.

SON 1: You were full of energy back then, now you are just spent.

MOTHER: I was 35 then and we went to Copenhagen for COP15; it all seemed possible. You were nine and you said, a bit underwhelmed by the number of demonstrators at the Reclaim the Power march on a cold December day, "Mum, is this all we came here for?" I remember that. Then I started to age. But you are 18 now, it's your turn to care, to begin anew, to save the world.

SON 1: Yeah, yeah, I'm off to the School Strike. I already told you.

He exits.

Conversation 2: MOTHER and SON 2

MOTHER: I had a dream that I was in Vrboska on the island of Hvar, where my grandfather is from – your great grandfather – and the land beneath my feet started to sink, one street in particular. I could feel it through each paving stone I placed my foot on. It was like I was too heavy, I was breaking the land, slab by slab, stone by stone. Am I too heavy for this land? A group of older men were sitting nearby chatting. It was summer and it was very hot, a typical Dalmatian scene, with all those older men sitting around on the street corners, hanging out in their white vests and shorts in hot weather. I was so worried they would see me destroying the land, their land, all these sinking stones.

SON 2: That's funny, and those old men are scary. I remember Hvar.

You know, I never went to that first School Strike in the end. There were too many self-righteous sixth-formers there, so eager, so shameful. They're all over on Instagram.

I remember us in Paris for COP21, all in a massive line holding up the red banner – the banner about red lines we can't cross because of climate change – and I remember the street angels as well.

MOTHER: Do you remember the arrival of the inflatables in silver and red, massive, coming towards us from the Arch of Triumph? Playful and inviting, but too heavy for the little kids. Large and beautiful, charging towards us, bouncing over the heads of the people marching... This was some kind of adult fun, triumphant teenage joy, with strong arms and open smiles. Wild and powerful, these stunningly demanding silver and red massive inflatables. They were mighty paving stones.

SON 2: Beneath the paving stones, the beach. *Sous les pavés, la plage!*
You were explaining to me the Situationists and their street interventions and their slogans like "Beneath the paving stones, the beach." You said that was from May 1968. You said that was the revolutionary year, the workers and the students united, all under one banner, against the system, all wanting something else. Be realistic, demand the impossible. *Soyez réalistes, demandez l'impossible.*

MOTHER: You remember well.

Conversation 3: MOTHER and SON 3

MOTHER: For my 42nd birthday I was performing a Nina Zaryechnaia monologue from *The Seagull* at Crosby Beach, among the iron statues, for my family, friends, and pets. You held my cues.

Donald Trump had just been elected president of the United States. Soon after, he withdrew the country from the Paris Agreement. All that hard work undone.

I shouted: "The men, the lions, the eagles, the partridges, the antlered deer, the geese, the spiders, the silent fishes of the deep, starfishes and creatures unseen to the eye – in short, all living things, all living things, having completed their mournful cycles, have been snuffed out."[25]

SON 3: Oh yes, you were sinking in the muddy sand. It was really funny.
There was lots of plastic and rubbish on the beach.
There were jellyfish everywhere.
There were all those rusty statues underwater.
They are something that will probably be there for a couple of generations.
And then they will just go and stay underwater.

MOTHER: Do you know that some of the statues have gone bendy already?

SON 3: They've gone past their elastic limit, like with an elastic band when you stretch it and it breaks... it's gone past its limit.

MOTHER: Where did you learn that?

SON 3: In science. Nothing's ever certain. Nothing lasts forever.
Happiness can go for a long time.

Pause.

---

[25] Nina Zaryechnaia monologue from Anton Chekhov's *The Seagull*, translated by Elisaveta Fen.

MOTHER: Do you remember going to Copenhagen for a protest against climate change? You were only two. You were looking at the train and saying "train choo choo."

SON 3: No, but I remember us being in some protest where police were guarding Maccies.

MOTHER: London, Time to Act on Climate Change, 2015, in the lead up to COP21 in Paris. We seemed especially bothered about climate in the years 2009 and 2015.

SON 2 enters and overhears the conversation.

SON 2: Sounds like 1968.

SON 3: You weren't even born then. We could riot, or protest now.

SON 2: Well, I'm going to the School Strike on Friday dressed as a polar bear, with a sign that says: "Be realistic, demand the impossible. Save us through system change."

MOTHER: Neal is going as well. Take Sid with you. I'm all spent.

NEAL ANDERSON, born in 2000 in Liverpool, has been a part of the anti-globalization social movement since 2001. Since 2009, Neal has attended climate change protests, starting with COP15, through Climate Camps and Occupy Movement, to Time to Act and COP21. His most recent engagement is with Climate Change School Strikes. He is a student at the Blue Coat School in Liverpool doing A level in History, English Literature, and Mathematics. He enjoys hip hop and walking his dog Tesla.

SID ANDERSON, born in 2007, started protesting in 2009 against the G20 Summit and the financial crisis. Sid has attended Climate Camps and slow-travelled across Europe for artist residencies, part of the Institute for the Art and Practice of Dissent at Home. Sid is a member of Family Activist Network and has attended both COP15 and COP21 summit protests against climate change. Sid is a dancer and an actor, currently rehearsing *Little Shop of Horrors*.

LENA ŠIMIĆ, born in 1974, is a mother of four boys and a transnational citizen, born a Yugoslav, now both Croatian and British. Lena identifies as an artist/activist, part of the Institute for the Art and Practice of Dissent at Home, Family Activist Network, and Artists4Corbyn collectives. Her current research interests include maternal performance, environmental theatre, and active engagement in mainstream politics in the UK. Lena is a Reader in Drama at Edge Hill University.

A LETTER FROM THE OCEAN

Caridad Svich

This piece is inspired by the book *Ecoacoustics*, edited by Almo Faina & Stuart H. Gage, Hoboken, NJ: Wiley, 2017.

What you have to remember is that there was nothing then
In the sense that there were no real amenities
Everything had to be done by hand
And the few machines that had been invented were rudimentary at best

All you had were your wits and what you had read, if you had read anything
It took a lot of doing, someone said, to make anything happen

And sometimes the doing had to be done by candlelight
And at other times by the glow of a small lantern

There was cooking involved, too
Before you say anything – know this:
Cooking is an ancient art. It holds some secrets

The hut was more than a hut then
It was what some called a cabin
And even though it was in the middle of the woods
It had something of a reputation

Meetings were held in this hut
Most of them had to do with civil liberties and progress
Even though, yes, poetry was discussed too

There's this myth that nothing much got done back then
And that a hut like this was merely an excuse
For some people to gather together
And amuse themselves by telling each other stories

But what you have to remember is this:
The stories happened at the end of the day
After the work got done
After everything

The real work in the hut happened before the stories were told
There was cooking and tending to the small garden out back
Searching through the woods for new ingredients and new species
And yes, there were long walks
Where a great deal of reflection occurred
About how one should live an honest life

Often there were encounters
Except then, then, the encounters were perhaps less plain
Because most people coming through these woods
Were running away from the worst conditions imaginable
And had heard that the poet and the people that lived in this hut
Would provide food, shelter, and safe passage
And they were right

The poet and their people did offer these things
In exchange for nothing

In exchange for nothing

Except maybe a little song
Or a story
Or maybe a new recipe

If you walk into this hut
You won't see it now
But over there, there used to be a shelf
Where all the little stories and songs and recipes were held
In small makeshift books written by hand
And if you were to run your hands along the shelf
You could hear all their voices –

...

Shall we talk to each other for a while?
Shall we listen to our stories?
In exchange for nothing
Except to be here, just be here, with each other?

...

...

I'd been thinking about what the world would be like now
After I'd been in the hut
I'd been thinking about how it was that we were able to recall the songs
Of those who had passed, but couldn't make our own songs last

A letter came from the ocean
It was addressed to "the person who went away to the hut in the woods"

The letter was enclosed in a small envelope that smelled of lilac

I opened the seal carefully
It's not every day, after all, that the ocean writes you a letter

The paper was gossamer thin
The letter began

Dear person that went away to the hut in the woods while the world was
    on fire,

I don't imagine that you know what you sound like.
But from where I live, it sounds as if every word is dandelion.

I hadn't heard that word in a long time.
Just like I hadn't heard the words "nectar," "willow,"
Since you were seven years of age.

I missed those words. I like them better than "blog" and "cut and paste."
But then again, you know that, because you are here. In the woods.
In the hut where a poet once lived and others too.

And soon, you will go back to your city and try to live your life again.
And perhaps let go of some of your rage,
And perhaps start to look at others with kindness.

It's not easy. I know.
I am used to my rage, too.
It can be useful. It is a part of us, after all.

Sometimes I rage so much that my waves destroy everything.
And I think, they will learn now.
These humans will learn, because they have brains.
They have logic and reason. And they have this thing too called imagination,
And with it, they can do so much, so much good, and so much beauty,
And so much music.

And sometimes when I hear their songs, I can't help but get emotional.

I'm a softie that way. I hope you can forgive me.
I know being soft is not in fashion these days.
But sometimes I can't help myself.

Because sometimes – on certain days, when the light hits the sky a certain
    way,
Or I see someone walking along the beach, their eyes full of possibility,
Or some child is rescued in a peacekeeper's arms
While bombs carry their city away,
I think: I'm in love.

I really am.
I love you all so much.

CARIDAD SVICH is a playwright. She received the 2012 OBIE for Lifetime Achievement. Her play *RED BIKE* is currently sustaining an NNPN Rolling World Premiere. She is editor of *Stages of Resistance: Theatre and Politics in the Capitalocene* (NoPassport Press, 2018) .

LIN AND ASH

Elspeth Tilley

Sometimes my students tell me climate change seems too big, too global, too monolithic to do anything about. I wanted *Lin and Ash* to give them a place to start, grounded in ideas of the power of allyship – or what something akin to allyship might mean in the climate action context. I also think what Rob Greenfield did was pretty cool, so I'm hoping to get a whole bunch of us wearing our trash (or going zero waste so that we don't have to wear our trash!) during (and beyond) CCTA 2019.

SETTING:
Ideally this would be staged outdoors, in a busy public place, as street theatre, with no barrier between actors and audience, and you could make your chorus of litterers seem like real passers-by, and have them act very startled to be accosted (play for laughs), but it could also be staged in a more traditional theatre space.

CHARACTERS:
LIN, ASH, and TAYLOR, three college students
CAMPUS SECURITY GUARD
PERSONS A, B, C, and D, passers-by, could be played by one actor

~~~~~~~~~~~~~~~~~~~~~~

LIN, a college student, sits on a park bench, studying intently. A second student, ASH, wearing multi-pocket pants with slightly bulging pockets, approaches, sits down.

LIN, *still focused on studying*: Hey.

ASH: Hey.

LIN *sniffs air slightly, looks up from books, hesitates*: Um, I don't wanna seem rude, but you know, friends tell friends. So. Um. You kinda smell a bit off, or something. Did your housemates use all the hot water? You can totally come by my place if you need to shower, you know.

ASH: It's cool, I've showered. It's my waste.

LIN: Your what?

ASH: My rubbish. Plastics, packaging, stuff. Anything that would go to landfill. It's in my pockets. I'm doing Rob Greenfield's Trash Me challenge.

LIN: That guy? The guy who looked like the Michelin Man, he had so much garbage strapped on him? Why would you wanna look like that guy?

ASH: I dunno. I just wanted to try it.

LIN: He couldn't even get through doorways by the end of the month. That's insane. Please tell me you're not doing it for a month?

ASH: I thought I'd try. I just want to see what it looks like. My trash footprint. I want to face it.

LIN: Couldn't you just put it all in a corner? You'd still see what it looks like. Why do you have to carry it around? This is going to seriously tank your dating game.

ASH: I want other people to see it too. And I have no dating game anyways.

LIN, *teasing*: Yah, coz you smell scuzzy.

ASH: Wanna do it with me?

LIN: Nope. No way. Nothin' doin. Nada. Nichts. Niente.

ASH: Okay my multilingual friend, well, I'm outies.

Starts to leave.

LIN: You're supposed to rinse the trash before you wear it.

ASH: No shit, Sherlock. But it still stinks anyway. Ingrained grease.

LIN: Ugh. You've really outdone yourself this time.

> *ASH leaves. PERSON A walks past LIN's bench, eating some packaged food, drops their packaging, keeps walking. LIN gestures pointedly at the packaging, then at the departing person, who scurries off. LIN shakes head, resumes studying. ASH returns, with visible bags of packaging pinned to the outside of their clothing.*

LIN: Whoa. You've got a growth. Does it hurt?

ASH: There was this tin can jabbing me right in the ribs. But I've done a bit of rearranging, put the soft plastics on the inside. Much better.

LIN: So, had any dates?

ASH: Still no, miraculously. They don't know what they're missing out on.

LIN: Yeah, trash talk, garbage conversation, and completely rubbish sex.

ASH: Ha ha.

> *PERSON B passes and drops a wrapper, keeps walking. ASH picks it up absentmindedly and puts it into their worn trash stash. TAYLOR arrives, with CAMPUS SECURITY OFFICER.*

TAYLOR: This is what I was talking about. It's going to incite campus unrest. It's a deliberate act of provocation.

ASH: Pardon?

TAYLOR: It's a health and safety issue. I had to sit next to *this* in my philosophy lecture this morning and it was disrupting my ability to learn. I couldn't hear the lecture, I was so distracted. There were *flies*. And they were *buzzing*.

ASH: Free speech. That's what the lecture was about.

LIN: Apt.

TAYLOR: App? There's an app for that?

LIN: No, apt. It means... oh never mind.

TAYLOR: Officer, please. There's a campus bylaw. No visible litter. This is super-visible. It's damaging our tone. What will prospective students think?

ASH: That we encourage critical thinking and creative activism? Like, what the hey, that we're a university?

SECURITY OFFICER: Everybody relax, no need to get heated. We can resolve this in the Provost's office. Come on.

> *All exit, other than LIN, who remains, studying intently. PERSON C goes past, drops litter.*

LIN: Oi! You can't...

> *PERSON C startles, bolts out of earshot. LIN returns to studying. ASH enters, carrying, not wearing, the trash packs.*

LIN: What happened?

ASH: Provost special ruling: If the majority of people on campus would be offended by me wearing my trash for a month, then majority rules, and I'm not allowed to do it. So I quit.

> *Throws rubbish packs on ground and kicks them.*

I give up. I only got to day six. I stink at this.

LIN: Literally.

ASH. Meh. Your jokes stink worse.

LIN: Majority rules, huh?

Picks up one of the trash bags and pins it on themselves.

ASH: Now what are you doing?

PERSON D goes past, drops litter. LIN jumps up and grabs their litter and some wearable litter bags and runs after them.

LIN: Hey you, yes you, stop right there, have I got a deal for you! Did you know there's a campus bylaw against littering? So you and I could go see the Provost right now for your disciplinary hearing, or you could join me and my friend here and wear your litter loud and proud on the outside.

Pins a bag onto PERSON D, who looks bewildered but doesn't remove it and exits wearing it, with a congratulatory slap on the back from LIN as they go. PERSON A enters.

LIN: Ooh, and we have another contender. Here you go.

LIN pins a trash package onto PERSON A.

LIN: Join our creative protest – it's the latest thing. It'll get you lots of hot dates, I promise. Just ask my friend Ash here.

Litterer exits, still wearing the trash bag. LIN picks up remaining bags and pins them back onto ASH.

LIN: C'mon then, let's get you suited up. Majority rules, aye? That's four so far out of 6,350 students on campus. Only 6,346 to go.

ASH: Actually, even just one makes a massive difference.

LIN and ASH do a sort of sumo wrestling run at each other, and bounce off, laughing, protected by their puffy trash packs. They then either hug or high-five or whatever works in the moment, to show their solidarity. They exit.

ELSPETH TILLEY, of Aotearoa-New Zealand, is a three-time winner of the British Theatre Challenge and three-time CCTA playwright. She teaches creative activism at Te Kunenga ki Pūrehuroa (Massey University) and writes political plays exploring issues ranging from feminism, climate change, colonialism, and homelessness to animal rights. Her short plays have been published in the U.S., the UK, Canada, and New Zealand, and performed worldwide. Elspeth received the Playwrights' Association of New Zealand Outstanding Achievement Award in 2018.

BIGGER LOVE

Peterson Toscano

Climate change is a threat multiplier. This not only extends to weather patterns and events, but also to existing social conditions. If on a pleasant sunny day someone experiences challenges in regards to housing, policing, healthcare, and mobility, what happens when an extreme weather event hits? While every resident is affected, some are affected more and for a longer period after a weather event. While we are all in the same boat together, we are not all on the same deck. Some inspiration for this play came while I did research for the article "We're All in the Same Boat Together? Reflections on Hurricanes, Undocumented Residents, and LGBTQ People," published by HuffPost.[26] I was also inspired by the following queries: *What is a queer response to climate change? Who are the climate action figures of the future? As impacts magnify, how will our empathy and creative caring for each other also increase?*

SETTING:
A New York City apartment. A door opens to a long hall leading to a cross-section of a bedroom space

CHARACTERS:
KYLE, 27 year-old, white cisgender gay man originally from rural Missouri. Studied art history. Works at gift shop in Metropolitan Museum of Art.
JOEY, 29 year-old cisgender bisexual Italian/Puerto Rican native New Yorker. Graduated with a degree in Political Science, works at a coffee shop and volunteers at various nonprofits around the city.

Apartment door unlocks, opens. KYLE enters. Puts backpack on the floor, removes his shoes, and adds them to the large diverse pile of shoes at the entrance.

---

26 Toscano, Peterson. "We're All in the Same Boat Together? Reflections on Hurricanes, Undocumented Residents, and LGBTQ People." *HuffPost*. September 6, 2017. https://www.huffpost.com/entry/were-all-in-the-same-boat-together-reflections-on_b_59afd535e4b0bef3378cdc80?guccounter=1

KYLE: Hey, I'm home.

JOEY, *from bedroom*: I'm in the bedroom

KYLE walks to bedroom.

KYLE: Gosh, it's crazy out there still.

JOEY: There's food in the kitchen that Sammy made.

KYLE: Uh, no, (*laughs*) I'm good.

JOEY: What?! He's a good cook.

KYLE: I don't like all that "free food." You know: free of meat and dairy and gluten and flavor. I get it, he's a vegan, we know.

Laughs. Kisses JOEY.

KYLE, *affectionately*: Hey you.

Have you noticed Sammy looks great, but he has really bad breath?

JOEY: Yeah, I know, and he hovers too.

KYLE: Well, they all hover.

Laughs. KYLE settles on bed next to JOEY.

JOEY: So, how did the art move go?

KYLE: We barely got a dent in it. The Met had over a million pieces in that underground tunnel. It's a miracle almost none of it got damaged. Some guy from the Mayor's Office said almost every basement in the city got flooded out this time.

JOEY: Still flooded in some places I heard.

Quick pause.

So where they moving it to?

KYLE: An "undisclosed location."

JOEY: Some place Upstate, I bet.

KYLE: Or Svalbard, where they store the strategic art reserves. Oh! I actually got to pack up a Marsden Hartley! Who would have thought a farm boy from Missouri would be handling priceless pieces of art?

JOEY: Big deal. I get to handle priceless art every day.

JOEY slaps KYLE on the butt. They giggle and cuddle.

KYLE: Where is everyone?

JOEY: Well, let's see. Sammy is out foraging...

KYLE: Dumpster diving.

JOEY: Sure. Um, Jenna actually has an audition for a drag revue. She's like really into being trans and doing drag at the same time.
Nino is, who knows? *(doubtful)* He said he was going to see if his work is open again. He's gotten no response there. And I think Louis is looking for some place to do laundry.
Oh, and by the way, he wants to know if you have any extra meds he can borrow. He's not been able to get in touch with his doctor.

KYLE, *thinking*: Uh, yeah, I think so. What's up with his doctor?

JOEY: Well, she's out on Long Island.

KYLE: What the hell is he going to a doctor on Long Island for?

JOEY: It's complicated. But he said she's the only trans male-friendly doctor in all New York.

KYLE: What? Jesus! It's 2028!

JOEY: Yeah well, I was just reading this terrible story, this trans woman who after the storm, she cut her leg on some debris or something and went to one of the emergency clinics, and they treated her like shit.

KYLE, *disgusted*: It just sucks.

> *Heavy sigh, pause. Thinking about roommates.*

They're like all gone? You know this is the first time we've been alone in the apartment since the refugee crisis. (*laughing*)

JOEY: Yeah, I think you're right.

> *Snuggling pause.*

KYLE: So do you think we should move?

JOEY: Ay! Not that again!

KYLE: I mean a lot of people are.

JOEY, *snaps*: You know a lot of people can't!

> *Pause. Softens tone.*

I'm just glad we have this place and can take in some people. Maybe we can see about getting a bigger apartment or something.

KYLE, *giggles*: A hostel for the weary, storm-driven queers of New York City.

JOEY: It's something. It's community. We can do more to help.

KYLE: Oh my God, you totally sound like Mayor Morales, "Bigger Storms need Bigger Love!"

JOEY, *laughs*: Well it's true. (*suggestively*) And what's wrong with Bigger Love?

KYLE: Oh, now we're alone you're thinking about big love hey?

JOEY: Well I miss you.

KYLE: I miss you too.

Pause.

JOEY: And I'm feeling the atmospheric pressure has dramatically changed.

KYLE: Oh, has it?

JOEY: Yeah, yeah there's brewing a storm, a big nasty storm.

KYLE: Oh is that right, city boy? What, you do weather reports now?

JOEY: Uh-huh... the swirling masses of pressure and heat are building up and the storm surge...

KYLE, *laughs*: The storm surge...

Sound of locks on the apartment door.

KYLE: Oh shit someone's back.

They laugh. KYLE quickly gets up and slams the bedroom door. Blackout.

Music.

PETERSON TOSCANO, a quirky queer Quaker living in Amish Country in the U.S., uses comic storytelling to explore LGBTQ issues, religion, justice, privilege, and climate in theatre, film, and radio/podcasts. His plays

328 | LIGHTING THE WAY

include *Doin' Time in the Homo No Mo Halfway House, Does This Apocalypse Make Me Look Fat?*, and *A Queer Response to Climate Change – What Would Walt Whitman Do?* He produced the film *Transfigurations – Transgressing Gender in the Bible*, and hosts Citizens Climate Radio.

HASHTAG YOU TOO (OR #YOUTOO)

Mike van Graan

The play genuflects to the book *Wild Law: A Manifesto for Earth Justice*, written by Cormac Cullinan, a personal friend. "Wild Laws" are designed to balance the rights and responsibilities of humans against those of other members of the community of beings within the natural environment that constitutes Earth (i.e., plants, animals, rivers, ecosystems, etc.) in order to safeguard the rights of all the members of the Earth community. The purpose of the play is to catalyze discussion and debate around the rights of the Earth and its constituent parts in contemporary society.

SETTING:
The play takes place in a courtroom.

STYLE:
The play should be produced with an emphasis on portability, without sacrificing spectacle, so that it can be performed in as many different locations as possible.

CHARACTERS:
The principal characters are the JUDGE (a woman) and a LAWYER (any gender).
The play can be done with just two actors, or with as many as the director/producer would like to include.

~~~~~~~~~~~~~~~~~~~~

VOICE/ORDERLY: All rise in court! The Honorable Judge Wendy Empathy presiding.

> *JUDGE enters and takes her seat. She puts on a pair of glasses and looks through her papers.*

JUDGE: In the case of #metoo 11.59, who is for the plaintiff?

> *LAWYER stands up.*

LAWYER: I am, Your Honor.

JUDGE: Your client is seeking damages...

LAWYER: With respect, Your Honor, my client is seeking reparations. For the damage done to her. And we are applying for an urgent interdict against further assaults.

JUDGE: I would have you know that I am deeply sympathetic to your cause. It is long past 11.59; now is the time to put a stop to the hurricane of violence, the plague of abuse, this tidal wave of destructiveness. And we will use the full might of the law to do so.

LAWYER: I thank you, Your Honor...

JUDGE: So... let's get down to jury selection. First up is Mr. Generous Giver, a most upstanding member of our society, a businessman with a conscience who regularly donates to Rape Crisis, People Against Abuse of Women, and Project Alert on Violence Against Women. I'm sure that you would have no objection to Mr. Generous.

LAWYER: Well, actually, Your Honor, we do have objections. Mr. Generous Giver has shares in a coltan mine in the Democratic Republic of Congo. He supports the campaigns of politicians who advocate for fossil fuels...

JUDGE: But he gives generously to many good social causes. Surely it's not how he makes his money, but the good that he does with it.

LAWYER: How he makes his money is exactly what does violence to my client, the daily assaults on her wellbeing, the abuse that she suffers...

JUDGE: Is your client in the courtroom?

LAWYER: I'm afraid not, Your Honor. She is on life support.

JUDGE: I'm sorry to hear that. Best we get on with our jury selection so that we may hear your client's case.

LAWYER: Thank you, your honor.

JUDGE: The next candidate for consideration is Ms. Hoppa Plane, a social justice activist who has attended numerous conferences and seminars, delivered award-winning papers, appeared on television, TEDx, and has her own YouTube channel to talk about addressing inequality.

> *Beat, smiles.*

If you don't have any objections, we'll move on to...

LAWYER: Your Honor, we would like to object to Ms. Hoppa Plane as much as we did to Mr. Generous Giver.

JUDGE, *irritated*: And why is that?

LAWYER: We appreciate her social activism and her commitment to improving the lives of the poor...

JUDGE: But...

LAWYER: But she has no sympathy for my client; in fact, she believes that in order to improve the lives of the poor, my client should be abused even more. She has an excessive carbon footprint, travelling by plane from conference to conference around the world...

JUDGE, *sarcastically*: You don't expect her to swim, do you?

LAWYER: With the dire pollution of our oceans, I wouldn't wish that upon even my worst enemies.

JUDGE: You will surely have no objection to our next candidate... Ms. Pollyanna, who describes herself as "just an ordinary housewife."

LAWYER: Your Honor, if there is one thing that is the biggest threat to my client, it is the lack of care by "ordinary people," the vast majority of particularly middle-class people who are quite happy to live their lives without reflecting on what their carefree lives actually cost my client...

Beat.

JUDGE: Counsellor... who exactly is your client, and why is she so special?

LAWYER: Your Honor, I am here to promote the rights of Mother Earth, she upon whom all life is dependent.

JUDGE, *angrily*: You should have said so in the first place!

LAWYER: Would it have made a difference?

JUDGE: I would have told you that Mother Earth, Mother Nature, the Mother Goddess, or whatever you tree-huggers would like to call her, has no rights here. We are a civilized country, not some backward, plant-worshipping pagan society! You are subverting the noble cause of the fight against violence against women to sneak your environmental nonsense through the backdoor!

> *From this point on, the JUDGE gets more and more agitated, foaming at the mouth, while the LAWYER remains calm.*

LAWYER: With respect, Your Honor, my client is raped... daily!

JUDGE: Objection!

LAWYER: Violated by conscienceless men and women for short-term pleasure.

JUDGE: You are in contempt of this court!

LAWYER: Even as she screams "No!" she is desecrated.

JUDGE: I will have you struck from the roll!

> *LAWYER takes off their legal gown.*

LAWYER: No need for that, Your Honor. For the law is an ass. If it were not, I would have brought as our witnesses the forests before they are turned into deserts, the rivers before they choke on waste, the butterflies before their colors go extinct.

I lay down my robe, to fight another way, to fight another day. In fighting for my client, Your Honor, I fight for all of us. For #youtoo.

MIKE VAN GRAAN serves on the Steering Committee of the African Cultural Policy Network and is an award-winning playwright with 34 plays under his belt. Based in Cape Town, South Africa, his creative work generally explores the post-apartheid condition as well as international themes like migration and refugees. His brief at the University of Pretoria where he was an artist-in-residence in 2019 was to write a play on the Sustainable Development Goals, which has now been prescribed by some schools for study in 2021.

BY THE RIVER

Meaza Worku

In Addis Ababa, there is a city riverside development project announced, discussed, and financially backed by the government of Ethiopia. As an Addis Ababian, what flows in my mind is what is written in this short play.

~~~~~~~~~~~~~~

The stage is split, divided by a wall into two sections. In one section, there is a man, THE SPEAKER, delivering a speech to an audience which is invisible to us. EWNETU and LIYA, in the other section of the stage, watch THE SPEAKER from the back.

At lights up, EWNETU fixes his voice recorder in front of the speaker, gets back to where LIYA stands. She smiles as he approaches, but he is distraught.

LIYA: Relax! Everything will turn out just fine.

EWNETU: Pardon?

LIYA: The city riverside project – it will work. I hope.

EWNETU: As if hope has no expiration…. Are you not supposed to be taking his picture?

LIYA: Yes, I took some, but not enough memory space on my camera. Full.

EWNETU: Full with his pictures? Making speeches? Meetings? Visits? And having yet another speech?

LIYA: That's what I am hired to do. I am not hating it, though. He is photogenic. And he knows how to dress well. No doubt about it.

EWNET: Lucky you! At least you capture a different suit every day, but with words? You can neither dress them up to look different nor make them sound serious. You can only change the dates, the verb, and echo it. I am tired of it. Journalism sucks!

LIYA, *as she hears THE SPEAKER clear his throat*: There he starts! *(shouts louder)* Keep shining, man! Keep walking, we are keen to follow!

THE SPEAKER: My people –

Interrupted by an ovation from his audience.

This is the day when I am going to hand over to you... the city of your dreams. A dream you deserve to reside in.

LIYA, *louder*: Bravo!!

EWNETU: Bravado!

THE SPEAKER: As a result of fast population growth, uncontrolled urbanization, and the industrialization of our city... this project will elevate the city to a tourism site, enhancing the wellbeing of its inhabitants and nurturing riverside economies.

LIYA: He's done a remarkable job. This county is back on its feet again. Thanks to him, change is at the door.

THE SPEAKER: Our city is home to more than 2,000 industries, which represent 65 percent of all the industries in the country. Ninety percent of them do not have any kind of treatment plant and discharge their solid, liquid, and gaseous waste untreated into the environment. Let me promise you one thing...

EWNETU, *to himself*: Please shut them all down? Then I will see you eaten alive by your own people.

LIYA: That is so unfair. Just be optimistic for a change. This country has been in a daze. There wasn't any hope for the future because there was no one in charge to inspire it. People have found someone to love, to listen to, to watch, and to touch... Oh! How we adore him. He is going to make this country great and the planet protected. No doubt about it.

EWNETU: Seriously, Liya?

LIYA: I don't care whether you agree with my point of view or not. I say what I say because I believe it is true. After all, what do I know? I am a photographer. I can only judge by the look. And when I look at Addis Ababa's rivers... nothing attractive about them.

EWNET: Do you believe him?

LIYA: I believe in God.

EWNETU: I mean, do you believe in any of his words? Do you believe in the very idea that the face of this city can ever change?

LIYA: No doubt about it!

THE SPEAKER: Imagine, out of an estimated population of eight million, 25 percent of city residents have no toilets. As a result, people use the river as a toilet. Houses that are built on the banks of rivers flush their toilets directly into them. Look at the rivers of Addis! Don't they have a greenish dark color and a bad odor? No one has to live with that anymore.

Applause and cheering.

No more! We clean our mess and make the city a holy place.

EWNETU: Holy shit!

LIYA: Let us give him the benefit of the doubt.

EWNETU: Too many promises, too many lies, too many problems, too many projects, speeches, no commitments. It's all a manipulation of words for emotional effects to achieve political purposes.

LIYA: It would be a hell of a city if everyone felt the way you did.

EWNETU: I know. No one does. No one ever has and probably ever will. And it's still a hell of a city in spite of that.

THE SPEAKER: There will be no illegal settlements. No factory, urban waste water, hospital discharges.

EWNETU: We are in deep shit!

LIYA: We are sure we are going to make it!!!

THE SPEAKER: We are in a desperate situation here.

LIYA: Have I ever told you my earliest and fondest memory of my childhood?

EWNETU: Not sure.

LIYA: I began to swim in the river of Kebena, which was strictly forbidden by my parents. We couldn't even stand near it.

EWNETU: Like many other kids in Addis, in those good old days.

LIYA: Once I was caught by my mother – swimming naked in broad daylight. It was a little late to be thinking about clothes. I think that was just maybe the stupidest moment of my life. I tried to hide in the water but the water was so clear, it couldn't even hide the stones at the bottom.

EWNETU: Now, in contrast, the water hides itself in the dirt.

LIYA: I was a free spirit. I went home naked. After my mother took my dry clothes home.

EWNETU: How I will always miss those days.

THE SPEAKER: I promise, we can change our city into an ideal place to live in. Let's make Addis Ababa live up to its name, *New Flower*.

Applause.

Let us make this city a city of beauty and purity.

Ovation.

Yeees!

EWNETU: Such rhetoric!

LIYA: Let's hope the future is bright!

EWNETU: I guess I lost faith in politicians.

LIYA: I guess he is done with his speech.

EWNETU: My voice recorder!!

> *EWNETU hurriedly goes to the section where THE SPEAKER is standing and applauds with the crowd.*

MEAZA WORKU is an Ethiopian dramatist best known for her radio, stage, television, and comic book writing. She studied Theatre Arts at the University of Addis Ababa, and has written numerous short radio plays, radio serials, and the economic and political satire radio sitcom *Wefe komech.* Her stage play *Desperate to Fight* was selected for development by the Sundance Institute East African Theatre program, and has been performed internationally. Meaza is now devoting herself to writing and directing the television serial *Derso Mels.*

DUST

Marcus Youssef

This play was inspired by reading Yuval Noah Harari's *21 Lessons for the 21ˢᵗ Century* and Shoshana Zuboff's *The Age of Surveillance Capitalism*, feeling convinced that the impact of digital and bio technologies is primarily defined by our species' (preternatural?) devotion to capitalism as an organizing principle, and remembering that its consequences are being visited on our planet by schmucks just like me (us?).

~~~~~~~~~~~~~~~~~~~~~~

Using technology, an ActuaPerson addresses a group in our present, across time and space.

ACTUAPERSON: Before I begin: housekeeping. I speak to you across a vast expanse of time as a representative of the ActuaLife Program, a division of EnerSense LLC.

Hello?

Squints.

Can you hear me? Apologies. It's always like this. The technology I'm employing to speak to you from a century into your theoretical future only works well in one direction. To me you're very fuzzy. I hear it's often the same for you, when you – what is it – Skype?

We know more about ourselves now than we are physically capable of comprehending. In 2119 the EnerSense ActuaLife OS automatically analyzes up to six billion neural signals per second through chemical micro changes perpetually monitored in every ActuaPerson's Digiskin.

I am scared. Today is a very big day.

*

The backstory:

When the seas rose, the climate didn't just change. It split. In two. Climate Polarization they called it.

ActuaLife tells me you also use the term "polarized." Which is interesting. Because your two words: "environment" and "internet?" In our collective future, they are one and the same.

It was in the Fields of Death that the discovery was made. This was where they piled the bodies, during the catastrophe. As high as skyscrapers. Those that weren't swept out to sea had to be dealt with. They burned them, damn the consequences to global warming. The mountains of flesh smoldered for months, like mountains of rubber.

Until key players in the Consolidated Funeral Industry began to meet secretly with Silicon Valley engineers – recently relocated to Idaho. They wondered: Could these megatons of incinerated human remains – euphemistically referred to as Dust – be used for good?

The introduction of proton-accelerated fiber optics provided the necessary disruption. When combined with Dust, the reaction produced harnessable energy yields comparable to low-grade nuclear fission. With no waste, no toxicity, and no seeming limit to the amount of energy that could be generated.

Except one: the availability of human bodies. It has to be humans. Though the remains of higher primates also produce energy, it is at a significantly less efficient rate. Lower mammals barely register.

No one could explain why. Until the founder of EnerSense proposed that what we had captured was the energy of the human soul. And that, in partnership with each other, we had begun to collectively embody a real, tangible, physical manifestation of our own God.

Once the surplus was gone, there was resistance to the farming of human beings, like chickens or pigs. They are bred in captivity, kept in small pens, with hands, teeth and feet removed, to reduce aggression and conflict. Through one market-led innovation, it is now possible to purchase Dust from ethical suppliers, where the HumAnimals are allowed outside and – in some cases – even to touch each other. But this is considerably more expensive and so remains a niche, popular only among the most urbane and liberal of intelligentsia ActuaPersons, or Those With Privilege.

Those With Privilege is an official designation. TWPs for short. Or TWERPs, if you're not one. Privilege is calculated across several major categories as defined by data gathered by ActuaLife. The Privilege Algorithm is neither moral nor aspirational. It simply reflects what is.

*

I am a TWP.

Hello?
Hello?

Sorry, I can't tell if you're still there.
Just give me a second...

*

It was me who suggested a pivotal alteration to the system (if I can toot my own horn). This has allowed it to thrive.

Once a generation, the families of Those With Privilege are required to sacrifice one of their own. It mollifies the HumAnimals, offers them a sense that their suffering is shared by all.

In a way, it does the same thing for us TWPs. We too pay a price for our comforts, our privilege. This makes it more possible for us to live with what we are doing to each other and the world.

As I said, today is a big day. For me.

Only those in a very specific situation are chosen to speak backwards. To our past, our together before. EnerSense has limited interested in history. We prefer to look forward.

Today I will return to what your primitive religion taught us is where we began. Become something fundamentally more useful: a provider.

I have been chosen. It is the gift we have all been given, to understand that we are dinosaurs. Literally. Our flesh organic. Our decomposed bodies a resource.

Today I return to dust.

You're scared too. Just looking at you, I can tell.

There's no need to worry. It's fine. No matter what happens. It's what we all become.

Every single one.

Are you there? Hello?

They walk off.

MARCUS YOUSSEF is based in Vancouver, Canada, on unceded Coast Salish territory. His fifteen or so plays, several co-written with longtime collaborators, have been produced in multiple languages across North America, Europe, and Asia, from Seattle to New York to Reykjavik, London, Hong Kong, and Berlin. He is the recipient of Canada's largest cultural prize, the Siminovitch Prize for Theatre, the Rio Tinto Alcan Performing Arts Award, the Vancouver Mayor's Arts Award, the Chalmers Canadian Play Award, the Seattle Times Footlight Award, the Vancouver Critics' Innovation Award (three times), the Canada Council Staunch Lynton Award and Berlin, Germany's Ikarus Prize.

MISS VIOLA EVIE ANDERSON'S DINING HALL FOR BEES

Nathan Yungerberg

I am continually disturbed and saddened by the number of us who have fallen asleep to the world around us because our noses are always buried in our phones. I like to fantasize about the possibility of hidden metaphysical benefits provided by the seemingly apparent actions of the plant and animal kingdom. Someone once told me that the frequency emitted by whales is a guidance system for our planet, so I figured the vibrational frequency of bees could contribute to waking human beings up.

CHARACTERS:
COLETTE ANGELICA JONES, 33, full-figured, Black, natural hair, sad
MISS VIOLA EVIE ANDERSON, 70s, slight, Black, bright eyes

A time-lapse projection of the daily working stiff procession to and from the subway in Bed-Stuy, Brooklyn, from fall to winter. (This could be animated, shadows, live footage, live actors, or stage directions could be read by a narrator). Beautiful, emotion-filled jazz, reminiscent of the soundtrack from If Beale Street Could Talk, plays until COLETTE enters the garden.

A diverse group of people in dark, dreary, monochromatic, business casual clothing walk past a tall wooden fence with a hand-painted sign that says "Miss Viola Evie Anderson's Dining Hall for Bees." But no one notices the sign. They are all sleepwalking zombies, unaware of anything other than their thoughts and their phones.

COLETTE walks back and forth in front of the projection in real time. She wears bright yellow, blue, and pink.

344 | LIGHTING THE WAY

Spring. The door of the fence with the dining hall sign is open. COLETTE glides past the open door, stops in her tracks and turns back. She inhales deeply like it was her last breath, or maybe her first, and reads the sign, smiling for the first time in months, perhaps even a year.

MISS VIOLA EVIE ANDERSON: Well I don't know what you're waitin' for.... Yes, girl, come on in! The day ain't gettin' any younger and neither are you!

The projection screen rises to reveal a spectacular flower garden. MISS VIOLA EVIE ANDERSON is assembling a bouquet of blue, pink, and yellow flowers which she hands to COLETTE.

MISS VIOLA EVIE ANDERSON: Your favorite colors!

COLETTE: Yeah... they are... how did you... do I know you?

MISS VIOLA EVIE ANDERSON: I live there across the street. I see the bright colors you be wearin'. You're different than the others. I sit in that big window most mornings and watch all y'all zombies going to and fro. Some days when I'm comin' from the bodega, I smile atcha'll and say mornin', but y'all walk right through me, as if I was a ghost.

COLETTE: I don't recall –

MISS VIOLA EVIE ANDERSON: Cause ya nose is always buried in that damn cellular phone. Surprised ya ain't ever fell into a hole. That could happen you know! At least you'd be awake then, if the fall didn't kill ya that is! But then I guess you'd be wide awake at the table of the Lord!

COLETTE: I need to get to –

MISS VIOLA EVIE ANDERSON: Nonsense, sit, I made some tea, chamomile, right?

COLETTE: How did you –

MISS VIOLA EVIE ANDERSON: You stop at that coffee shop 'round the corner every morning at 7:16 and you order a blueberry scone and chamomile tea with some room at the top for –

COLETTE: Honey.

MISS VIOLA EVIE ANDERSON: I'm Viola Evie Anderson.

COLETTE: I'm –

MISS VIOLA EVIE ANDERSON: Colette Angelica Jones!

COLETTE: This is getting a little –

MISS VIOLA EVIE ANDERSON: Relax! I ain't no night stalker! You're always makin' business calls in this professional voice and talkin' all loud while ya walkin' towards the train in the mornin'. (*mocking*) This Colette Angelica Jones! I can hear ya from my window, girl! The whole damn neighborhood probably knows ya name by now and all ya bizness!

COLETTE: I really need to –

MISS VIOLA EVIE ANDERSON: Take a tour of my dining hall for bees! Free of charge today!

COLETTE: Um... what is a... dining hall... for bees?

MISS VIOLA EVIE ANDERSON: Bees eat pollen and nectar, and pollen and nectar come from flowers, hello!

COLETTE gets lost in a thought.

COLETTE: My mom, grandma, and great granny all had flower gardens, back in –

MISS VIOLA EVIE ANDERSON: Bloomington, Indiana? ...Don't give me that look! You're the one who broadcasts all ya bizness to the whole wide world on that cellular phone!

COLETTE walks through the garden.

COLETTE: I'll try to... lower... my voice.

MISS VIOLA EVIE ANDERSON: And it's time to get over that man you used to be with. What was his name, Charles?

COLETTE: Do you know my social security number too?

MISS VIOLA EVIE ANDERSON: He's hangin' all over you like a dark cloud or a bad stink, or maybe both.

> *COLETTE smells some flowers. The scent seems to alter her spirit positively.*

COLETTE: Jasmine, lilac, and...

MISS VIOLA EVIE ANDERSON: Peony!

> *COLETTE notices the many bees.*

MISS VIOLA EVIE ANDERSON: Don't be afraid. These are bumblebees, baby, they're way less defensive than –

COLETTE: I'm not afraid. I played a bumblebee in my first grade play!

> *COLETTE skips around the garden like a child.*

COLETTE, *singing: I'm bringing home a baby bumblebee. Won't my Mommy be so proud of me!*

MISS VIOLA EVIE ANDERSON: Well ain't that cute!

COLETTE: It smells soooooo good! Thank you for planting this flower garden!

MISS VIOLA EVIE ANDERSON: You're welcome, but I didn't plant it for you, or any other person for that matter.

COLETTE observes the bees again.

COLETTE: The bees... but why?

MISS VIOLA EVIE ANDERSON: The buzzin'! A bee's wings flap around 200 times a second, imagine if there are a hundred bees, a thousand bees, a million bees! Now that's a whole lotta buzzin' and buzzin' is vibration and everything in the universe vibrates including us! 'Cept most people these days vibrate at dangerously low frequencies and people do crazy, careless things when they're walkin' through their life half asleep! The bee's buzzin' raises frequencies, it wakes people up!

COLETTE: I've never... is there any scientific evidence to substantiate –

MISS VIOLA EVIE ANDERSON: What is science but the intellect's attempt at rationalizin' God! And if God can make dinosaurs and rainbows and unicorns, yes I believe in unicorns, I don't see any reason why God didn't make the buzzin' of the bees to raise the vibrational frequency of humankind!

COLETTE: People save the bees because they pollinate! Because they're crucial to a healthy eco –

MISS VIOLA EVIE ANDERSON: That's a given, but what good is a healthy ecosystem if the world is overrun by careless, sleep walkin' zombies who'll continue to find inventive ways to fuck this planet up? Bzzzzzzzzzzzzzzzzzzzzzzzzzzzzzzzzzzz.

> *COLETTE smells the peonies and almost becomes high, or maybe she does. She looks at MISS VIOLA curiously and then she looks up at the bees and then she starts dancing around the garden again. Jazz music comes in again.*

COLETTE, *singing:* I'm bringing home my baby bumblebee. Won't my Mommy be so proud of me. I'm bringing home my baby bumblebee...

NATHAN YUNGERBERG is a New York-based playwright. His work has been developed or featured by Cherry Lane (2017 Mentor Project with Stephen Adly Guirgis), Roundabout Theatre, The Playwrights' Center, Crowded Fire, The Lark, The Fire This Time Festival, The National Black Theatre, and The Bushwick Starr. Nathan is one of seven Black playwrights commissioned by The New Black Fest for *HANDS UP: 7 Playwrights, 7 Testaments*, which was published by Samuel French. Nathan was a 2019 Djerassi Artist.

ABOUT THE EDITORS

CHANTAL BILODEAU is a Montreal-born, New York-based playwright and translator. In her capacity as Artistic Director of The Arctic Cycle, she has been instrumental in getting the theatre and educational communities, as well as diverse audiences in the U.S. and abroad, to engage in climate action through programming that includes live events, talks, publications, workshops, national and international convenings, and a worldwide distributed theatre festival. She is writing a series of plays that look at the social and environmental changes taking place in the eight Arctic states and was recently named one of "8 Trailblazers Who Are Changing the Climate Conversation" by Audubon Magazine.

THOMAS PETERSON is an organizer, writer, and director whose work focuses on the climate crisis. He is an Artistic Associate with The Arctic Cycle, with whom he co-organizes Climate Change Theatre Action, and a field organizer with Green Corps. He graduated *summa cum laude* from Harvard College and was a Williams-Lodge Scholar in Paris. He has written about theatre and locality, climate propaganda, the aesthetic of the sublime in climate theatre, and about the cultural history of the infamous lawyer Roy Cohn. He is currently developing *The Woods Avenge Themselves*, an original adaptation of Ibsen's *The Wild Duck*.

CPSIA information can be obtained
at www.ICGtesting.com
Printed in the USA
LVHW080510120922
728111LV00006B/227